The New Muslim Guide

Simple Rules and Important Islamic Guidelines for New Muslims in all Aspects of Life

Fahd Salem Bahammam

AUTHOR	FAHD SALEM BAHAMMAM
TRANSLATOR	LARBI BENREZZOUK
PROJECT MANAGER	KHALED AHMED AL-AHMADI
FOLLOW-UP AND COORDINATION	AHMED KHALED ALKATHERI
DESIGN AND PRODUCTION	MUHAMMAD SAALIM AR-RADIY FAYIZ MUSLIM IBN MADI
AUDIO BOOK	MIKE COOPER
PHOTOGRAPHY	DPI STUDIO ET AL.

AUTHOR	FAHD SALEM BAHAMMAM
TRANSLATOR	LARBI BENREZZOUK
PROJECT MANAGER	KHALED AHMED AL-AHMADI
FOLLOW-UP AND COORDINATION	AHMED KHALED ALKATHERI
DESIGN AND PRODUCTION	MUHAMMAD SAALIM AR-RADIY FAYIZ MUSLIM IBN MADI
AUDIO BOOK	MIKE COOPER
PHOTOGRAPHY	DPI STUDIO ET AL.

Table of Contents

Preliminaries

Contents	Page
The Greatest Blessing Ever	24
How can we show gratefulness to Allah?	25
The Purpose of Human Existence	25
Islam Is a Universal Religion	26
The Entire Earth Is a Place of Worship	26
No Intermediaries between God and Man	27
Islam came to honour and dignify man	27
Islam has liberated the human mind	28
Islam Is a Religion of Life	29
Developing the Earth	29
Maintaining Social Relationships	29
Knowledge Acquisition	29
Learning Islamic Rulings	30
The Five Islamic Rulings	31

Contents	Page
Waajib (Obligatory), *Haraam* (Prohibited), *Mustahabb* (also called *Sunnah*, Recommended), *Makrooh* (Disliked), *Mubaah* (Permissible)	31
The Five Pillars of Islam	31
How to Find out about the Rulings of Islam	33
Trusted Internet Websites	33
Islam is a Moderate Religion	34
Islam Covers All Aspects of Life	35
Islam is a comprehensive way of life	35
Islam Must Be Judged by its Sublime Principles and not by the Bad Conduct of Some Muslims	36
The Five Necessities	37
Religion	37
Life	38
The Mind	38
Progeny	38
Property	39

1. Your Faith

Contents	Page
Testimony of Faith: Meaning and Requirements	42
I bear witness that there is no god worthy of worship except Allah	42
Why the Statement "*Laa ilaaha illallaah*"?	42
The Meaning of *Laa ilaaha illallaah*	42
The Two Main Parts of *Laa ilaaha illallaah*	43
The Testimony that Muhammad is Allah's Messenger	44
Who is Allah's Messenger?	44
His Birth	44
His Life and Upbringing	44
His Mission	45
The Beginning of His Mission	45
His Migration	46
His Efforts to Spread Islam	46
His Death	46
The Meaning of the Testimony that Muhammad is Allah's Messenger	48
To believe all the statements he made about everything	48
To do the acts he enjoined and avoid the acts he prohibited	48
To worship Allah in accordance with the Prophet's instructions	50
Innovations in religious matters are strictly forbidden	51
The Six Pillars of Faith (*Eemaan*)	51
The Meaning of Belief in Allah	51
Belief in the Existence of Allah	51
The Innate Disposition to Believe in Allah (*Fitrah*)	51
Proofs for Allah's Existence are Clear and Countless	51
Belief in Allah's Lordship	52
The Arab Polytheists at the Time of the Prophet Believed in Allah's Lordship	54
Belief in Allah's Lordship Sets the Heart at Rest	54
The Belief that only Allah is Worthy of Worship	55
Importance of the Belief that Allah is the Only God Worthy of Worship	56
The Meaning of Worship (*'Ibaadah*)	57
Worship Encompasses all Aspects of Life	57
The Reason behind the Creation of the Jinn and Mankind	57
Pillars of Worship	58
Conditions of Worship	59
Sincerity: It has to be directed sincerely to Allah alone	59
Following the guidance of Allah's Messenger	59
Associating Partners with Allah in Worship (*Shirk*)	60
Major *Shirk*	60
Minor *Shirk*	60
Does Asking People Amount to Committing *Shirk*?	61
Belief in Allah's Names and Attributes	63
The Meaning of Belief in Allah's Names and Attributes	63

Contents	Page
Some of Allah's Most Beautiful Names	63
Benefits of Belief in Allah's Names and Attributes	64
The Highest Level of *Eeman* (Faith)	64
Some Benefits of Belief in Allah ﷻ	65
Belief in the Angels	66
The Meaning of Belief in Allah's Angels	66
What Does Belief in the Angels Include?	66
Benefits of Belief in the Angels	67
Belief in the Divine Books	68
The Meaning of Belief in the Divine Books	68
What Does Belief in the Divine Books Include?	68
The Unique and Distinctive Characteristics of the Qur'an	69
What Is Our Duty Towards the Qur'an?	70
What Is Our Stance Regarding the Contents of the Previous Revealed Books?	71
Benefits of Belief in the Divine Books	72
Belief in the Messengers	73
People's Need for a Divine Message	73
It Is One of the Pillars of Faith	74
The Meaning of Belief in the Messengers	74
What Does Belief in the Messengers Include?	74
To believe that their message was truly from Allah ﷻ	74

Contents	Page
To believe in all the prophets and messengers	74
To believe the authentic reports and accounts of the prophets	74
To act according to the dictates of the law revealed to Prophet Muḥammad	74
Some Characteristics of the Messengers	75
The Messengers' Signs and Miracles	76
A Muslim's Beliefs regarding Jesus ﷺ	76
He was one of the greatest of Allah's messengers	76
He was a mere human being with no divine attributes whatsoever	76
He was the son of Mary	76
There was no prophet between him and Muḥammad ﷺ	76
We believe in the miracles he performed by Allah's permission	76
A person will not be considered a true believer unless he believes that Jesus ﷺ was Allah's servant and messenger	76
He was neither killed, nor crucified	77
Characteristics of Prophet Muḥammad's Message	79
It was the final divine message	79
It abrogated all previous messages and laws	79
It is addressed to both the jinn and mankind	79
Benefits of Belief in Allah's Messengers	80
Belief in the Last Day	81
Meaning of Belief in the Last Day	81
Why Does the Qur'an Emphasise Belief in the Last Day?	81
What Does Belief in the Last Day Include?	82

Contents	Page	Contents	Page
Belief in the Ultimate Resurrection and Gathering	82	What Does Belief in the Divine Decree Include?	86
Belief in the Judgement and the Balance of Deeds	83	Man Has Free Will, Free Choice and the Ability to Do as He Pleases	87
Paradise and Hellfire	83	Using Divine Decree as an Excuse to Commit Sins	88
Punishment and Bliss in the Grave	84		
Benefits of Belief in the Last Day	85	Benefits of Belief in the Divine Decree	89
Belief in the Divine Decree	86		
What Does Belief in the Divine Decree Mean?	86		

2 Your Purification

Contents	Page	Contents	Page
Meaning of Purification	92	Manner of Performing the Partial Ablution (*Wudoo'*)	96
What is the Required Purification for Performing the Prayer?	92		
Purification from Physical Impurity	93	The Major Ritual Impurity and the Full Ablution (*Ghusl*/Bath)	98
The general rule in Islamic law (*Sharee'ah*) is that all things are considered pure	93	Things which Require a Person to Perform Full Ablution	98
		How to Remove the Major Ritual Impurity?	99
Removing Physical Impurity	93	What to Do in Case One Is Unable to Use Water	99
Toilet Etiquette	94		
Ritual Impurity (*Hadath*)	95	Wiping over the Socks	99
The Minor Ritual Impurity and *Wudoo'*	95		

3 Your Prayer

Contents	Page
The Prayer	102
Position and Virtues of *Salaat* in Islam	102
It Has Numerous Virtues	103
For Whom Is It Obligatory?	104
What Are the Conditions that Must Be Met before Engaging in Prayer?	105
Removing physical impurity and ritual impurity	105
Covering the intimate parts of the body	105
'Awrah for an adult woman, for a small child and for a man	105
Facing the *Qiblah*	106
When its appointed time becomes due	106
The Five Obligatory Prayers and Their Times	107
The Place of Prayer	108
Performing the Prayer	111
The Intention	111
Reciting the *takbeer* and standing	111
The opening supplication	111
Reciting *Soorat Al-Faatihah*	111
What Should a Person Who Does not Know *Soorat Al-Faatihah* and the Post-Obligatory Prayer Supplications by Heart Do?	112
Soorat Al-Faatihah Explained	113
Bowing and resuming the standing position	114
Reciting the *tashahhud* and concluding the prayer	117

Contents	Page
Recommended supplications after the prayer	117
How to Pray	118
The Pillars and the Obligatory Acts of the Prayer	122
The pillars and the obligatory acts of the prayer	122
The recommended acts of the prayer	122
Acts which Invalidate the Prayer	124
Acts which Are Disliked During the Prayer	124
The Recommended Voluntary Prayers	125
Times During Which It Is Not Permissible to Offer the Supererogatory Prayers	126
The Congregational Prayer	127
Following the *Imaam* in Prayer	127
Who Should Lead the Prayer?	127
Where Does the *Imaam* and Those He Leads in Prayer Stand?	127
How to Make up for Missed Prayer Units?	128
How to Determine that a Complete *Rak'ah* Is Offered?	128
The Call to Prayer	129
The Manner of reciting the *Adhaan* and the *Iqaamah*	129
Responding to the *Adhaan*	130
Humility and Attentiveness in Prayer	131
Virtues of Observing *Khushoo'*	131

Contents	Page	Contents	Page
Means of Observing *Khushoo'* in Prayer	131	Those who Are Exempt from Attending the Friday Prayer	134
The Friday Prayer (*Salaat-ul-Jumu'ah*)	133	When Can a Career Be Considered a Valid Excuse to Miss the Friday Prayer?	136
Virtues of Friday	133	The Prayer of the Sick	136
Who Must Perform the Friday Prayer?	133	The Traveller's Prayer	137
The Friday Prayer: Manner and Rulings	134		

4 Your Fast

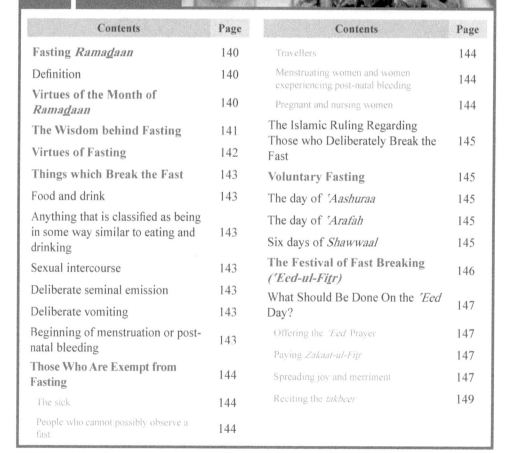

Contents	Page	Contents	Page
Fasting *Ramadaan*	140	Travellers	144
Definition	140	Menstruating women and women experiencing post-natal bleeding	144
Virtues of the Month of *Ramadaan*	140	Pregnant and nursing women	144
The Wisdom behind Fasting	141	**The Islamic Ruling Regarding Those who Deliberately Break the Fast**	145
Virtues of Fasting	142		
Things which Break the Fast	143	**Voluntary Fasting**	145
Food and drink	143	The day of *'Aashuraa*	145
Anything that is classified as being in some way similar to eating and drinking	143	The day of *'Arafah*	145
		Six days of *Shawwaal*	145
Sexual intercourse	143	**The Festival of Fast Breaking (*'Eed-ul-Fitr*)**	146
Deliberate seminal emission	143		
Deliberate vomiting	143	What Should Be Done On the *'Eed* Day?	147
Beginning of menstruation or post-natal bleeding	143	Offering the *'Eed* Prayer	147
Those Who Are Exempt from Fasting	144	Paying *Zakaat-ul-Fitr*	147
		Spreading joy and merriment	147
The sick	144	Reciting the *takbeer*	149
People who cannot possibly observe a fast	144		

5 | Your ZAKAAT

Contents	Page	Contents	Page
The Ultimate Objectives of Zakaat	152	Commercial commodities	154
		Farm produce	154
Types of Wealth upon which Zakaat Is Due	153	Livestock	154
Gold and silver	153	Recipients of Zakaat	155
All types of currency (banknotes and coins)	153	Those who qualify to receive zakaat funds	155

6 | Your Pilgrimage

Contents	Page	Contents	Page
Special Importance and Virtues of Makkah and the Sacred Mosque:	158	The Festival of Sacrifice ('Eed-ul-Adhaa)	166
The Meaning of Hajj	160	What Should Be Done On the 'Eed Day?	166
Time of Performing Hajj	160	Ud-hiyah, or sacrificial animal	166
Who must perform it?	160	The Conditions that the Sacrificial Animal Must Satisfy	167
The Ability to Perform Hajj: Different Circumstances	161	What Should Be Done with the Sacrificial Animal?	167
A Woman Needs a Mahram as a Companion to Perform Hajj	162	Visiting Madeenah	168
Virtues of Hajj	162	Madeenah	168
The Ultimate Goals of Hajj	163	Places in Madeenah that Are Worth Visiting	168
'Umrah	165		

7 Your Financial Transactions

Contents	Page
Allah ﷻ commands and encourages Muslims to earn their livelihoods	172
All Types of Transactions Are Generally Allowed in Islam	172
Things That Are prohibited Due to Their Innate Impurity	172
Examples of things which Islam has prohibited due to their innate impurity	172
Things That Are prohibited Due to the Manner They Are Acquired	173
Usury (*Ribaa*)	173
Ribaa on Debts	173
Ribaa on Loans	173
The Islamic Ruling on *Ribaa*	174
Punishment for *Ribaa*	174
Detrimental Effects of *Ribaa* on the Individual and Society	175
It causes a severe disorder in the distribution of wealth	175
It encourages wasteful extravagance	175
It dissuades investors from investing in domestic beneficial projects	175
It deprives wealth of all blessing and leads to economic crises	175
What is the ruling regarding a person who embraces Islam while he is a party to a usurious contract?	176
Deception through Ignorance and Uncertainty (*Gharar*)	177
Examples of sale contracts that involve deception through ignorance	177

Contents	Page
Circumstances under which *gharar* may affect the contract	177
Injustice and Wrongfully Taking Other People's Property	178
Coercion	178
Dishonesty	178
Manipulating the Law	178
Bribery	179
What is the Islamic ruling regarding a person who has taken people's property before embracing Islam?	179
Gambling	180
What is Gambling?	180
The Islamic Ruling on Gambling	180
Detrimental Effects of Gambling on the Individual and Society	180
It precipitates enmity and hatred among gamblers	180
It destroys wealth	181
The thrill of gambling and the possibility of winning becomes addictive	181
Types of Gambling	181
Examples of Business Ethics which Islam Has Stressed	182
Honesty	182
Truthfulness	183
Proficiency	183

8. Your Food and Drink

Contents	Page	Contents	Page
The General Rule Regarding Food and Drink	186	Forbidden animals for human consumption	189
Plants and Fruits	186	Islamic Slaughter	190
Intoxicants and Alcoholic Beverages	187	Types of Meat Served in Restaurants and Shops	190
Preservation of the Mind	187	Hunting according to Islamic Law	191
The Islamic Ruling on Alcoholic Drinks	187	Conditions that must be met for hunting wild animals	191
Drugs	188	Etiquette of Eating and Drinking	192
Seafood	188		
Land Animals	189		
What are the lawful animals?	189		

9. Your Dress Code

Contents	Page	Contents	Page
Clothing from an Islamic Perspective	196	Clothing that involves dressing like or imitating the opposite sex	197
Clothing Serves a Number of Purposes	196	Clothing that involves imitation of the dress traditionally worn by non-Muslims	198
The General Rule Regarding Clothing	197	Clothing that is worn with pride and conceit	198
Forbidden Types of Clothing	197	Silk clothing or clothing adorned with gold or silk for men	199
Clothing that reveals the private parts	197	Extravagant clothing	199

10 Your Family

Contents	Page
The Position of the Family in Islam	202
Islam stresses the importance of marriage to form a family	202
It has shown respect to every member of the family	202
It encourages children to recognise and honour parents	203
It commands parents to safeguard their children's rights	203
It directs its adherents to maintain the ties of kinship	203
The Position of Women in Islam	203
Examples of forms of respect Islam shows to women	203
Women Islam Enjoins Muslims to Look after	204
The Mother	204
The Daughter	204
The Wife	204
No Place for a Struggle between the Sexes	205
Categories of Women in Relation to a Man	205
She could be his wife	205
She could be a relative whom he is never permitted to marry at any time in his life whatsoever (*mahram*)	206
She could be one he is allowed to marry (*ajnabiyah*, literally, foreigner, not related to him)	208

Contents	Page
Rules Governing the Relationship between a Man and Women He Is Allowed to Marry	208
Lowering the Gaze	208
Observing Modesty in Speech	209
Avoiding Private Seclusion with Non-*Mahram* Women Altogether (*Khalwah*)	209
Wearing the *Hijaab* (the Modest Muslim Style of Dress)	209
What Must the *Hijaab* Cover?	210
Criteria of Proper *Hijaab*	210
Marriage in Islam	211
The Conditions Islam Stipulates Regarding the Wife	211
The Conditions Islam Stipulates Regarding the Husband	212
The Spouses' Rights and Obligations	213
The Wife's Rights	213
Maintenance and Residence	213
Living with Her in Kindness	214
Patience and Tolerance	214
Spending the Night with the Wife	215
Defending Her, Representing His Honour	215
Not Revealing Bedroom Secrets	215
Not Engaging in Aggressive or Hostile Action against Her	215
Teaching and Advising Her	215
Honouring the Conditions Stipulated by the Wife	216

Contents	Page	Contents	Page
The Husband's Rights	217	Seriousness of disobedience to parents	220
Obedience in Kindness	217		
Attentiveness to His Sexual Needs	217	Dutifulness to parents but without Disobeying Allah	220
Not Allowing Anyone He Does not Like in His House	217	Showing kindness to them in their old age	220
Not Leaving the House without His Permission	217	Non-Muslim parents	220
Service	217	Children's Rights	221
Islam urges that the marriage contract be permanent	218	Marrying a good devout woman	221
		Giving children good names	221
Islam allows marriage dissolution through divorce as a last resort	218	Teaching them the principles of Islam	221
Some rules and criteria concerning divorce	218	Maintenance	221
		Justice	221
Parents' Rights	219		
Showing kindness to parents is one of the most meritorious acts in the sight of Allah	219		

11 Your Moral Character

Contents	Page	Contents	Page
The Position of Good Character in Islam	224	Preservation of the environment	227
Perfection of noble character was one of the most important objectives of the Prophet's mission	224	Noble character in all aspects of life	228
		The Family	228
		Trade	228
Noble character is part and parcel of faith and belief	224	Industry	229
Noble character permeates all acts of worship	224	Noble character under all circumstances	229
		Some War Ethics in Islam	229
The immense rewards Allah has in store for those who observe good character	225	Some Aspects of the Prophet's Life and High Moral Standards	230
Distinguishing Features of Noble Character in Islam	226	Humility	230
		Mercy	230
Noble character is not confined to a particular type of people	226	Mercy towards children	231
		Mercy towards Women	231
How to Treat Non-Muslims	226	Mercy to the weak members of society	232
Noble character is not confined only to human beings	227	Justice	233
		Benevolence and Generosity	234
Good treatment of animals	227		

12 Your New Life

Contents	Page	Contents	Page
How to Convert to Islam	238	To give up the sin immediately	239
Pronouncing the testimony of faith (*shahaadah*)	238	To feel deep sorrow and regret for having committed it	239
Taking a Bath	238	To sincerely resolve not to commit it again	239
Sincere Repentance	239	Steps towards Acquiring Determination	239
Meaning of Repentance (*Tawbah*)	239		
Conditions of Sincere Repentance	239	What after Repentance?	240

Contents	Page
The Husband's Rights	217
Obedience in Kindness	217
Attentiveness to His Sexual Needs	217
Not Allowing Anyone He Does not Like in His House	217
Not Leaving the House without His Permission	217
Service	217
Islam urges that the marriage contract be permanent	218
Islam allows marriage dissolution through divorce as a last resort	218
Some rules and criteria concerning divorce	218
Parents' Rights	219
Showing kindness to parents is one of the most meritorious acts in the sight of Allah	219
Seriousness of disobedience to parents	220
Dutifulness to parents but without Disobeying Allah	220
Showing kindness to them in their old age	220
Non-Muslim parents	220
Children's Rights	221
Marrying a good devout woman	221
Giving children good names	221
Teaching them the principles of Islam	221
Maintenance	221
Justice	221

11 Your Moral Character

Contents	Page	Contents	Page
The Position of Good Character in Islam	224	Preservation of the environment	227
Perfection of noble character was one of the most important objectives of the Prophet's mission	224	Noble character in all aspects of life	228
		The Family	228
		Trade	228
Noble character is part and parcel of faith and belief	224	Industry	229
Noble character permeates all acts of worship	224	Noble character under all circumstances	229
		Some War Ethics in Islam	229
The immense rewards Allah ﷻ has in store for those who observe good character	225	Some Aspects of the Prophet's Life and High Moral Standards	230
Distinguishing Features of Noble Character in Islam	226	Humility	230
		Mercy	230
Noble character is not confined to a particular type of people	226	Mercy towards children	231
		Mercy towards Women	231
How to Treat Non-Muslims	226	Mercy to the weak members of society	232
Noble character is not confined only to human beings	227	Justice	233
		Benevolence and Generosity	234
Good treatment of animals	227		

12 Your New Life

Contents	Page	Contents	Page
How to Convert to Islam	238	To give up the sin immediately	239
Pronouncing the testimony of faith (*shahaadah*)	238	To feel deep sorrow and regret for having committed it	239
Taking a Bath	238	To sincerely resolve not to commit it again	239
Sincere Repentance	239		
Meaning of Repentance (*Tawbah*)	239	Steps towards Acquiring Determination	239
Conditions of Sincere Repentance	239	What after Repentance?	240

Contents	Page
Sweetness of Faith	240
Showing Gratefulness to Allah for His Guidance	241
Holding Fast to Islam and Patiently Enduring Hardships that Come One's Way	241
Doing One's Best to Call to Islam with Wisdom and Fair Admonition	241
Calling Others to Islam (Da'wah)	242
Virtues of Calling Others to Islam	242
Da'wah is the means to success in this life and in the hereafter	242
No one has a better speech than that of those who engage in da'wah	242
Engaging in da'wah work testifies to one's compliance with Allah's command	242
Engaging in da'wah work was the very task carried out by all of Allah's messengers without exception	242
Inviting people to Islam is the source of unlimited goodness	242
The reward Allah has for those who invite others to Islam is far better than all the enjoyments of the present world	243
Requirements of the Correct Manner of Inviting Others to Islam	243

Contents	Page
Insight and Knowledge	243
Wisdom	244
Inviting Family Members and Relatives to Islam	244
Children's Religion	246
All human beings without exception are born Muslim	246
When can we consider non-Muslim parents' children Muslim in this life?	246
Is it recommended to change one's name after embracing Islam?	248
Cases in which a name may be changed	248
Sunan Al-Fitrah (Practices dictated by Man's Pure Nature)	250
Circumcision	250
Removing the coarse hair that grows in the pubic area	250
Trimming the moustache	251
Letting the beard grow	251
Clipping the nails	251
Plucking underarm hair	251

Appendix	Page
TRANSLITERATION SYSTEM USED IN THE BOOK	252
CONSONANTS	252

Appendix	Page
VOWELS	256
Symbols Used in the Book and their Meanings	257

Introduction

Congratulations on embracing this great religion of Islam, choosing true guidance and stepping out of the darkness of ignorance into the light of faith!

Congratulations on your boldness and objectivity in your search for the truth before taking the most important decision in your life by embracing this great religion!

A person who purchases a new device or joins a club, a team or an institute spares no effort to learn and read about his rights and obligations and to deal with the new circumstances.

Similarly, a person whom Allah has guided to Islam and brought out of the darkness of ignorance into the light of faith must leave no stone unturned in learning about the rulings of Islam in all aspects of life in order to worship Allah on the basis of sound knowledge and deal with the new conditions around him in accordance with the teachings of Islam.

The good news you must surely relish while acquiring Islamic knowledge is that all the religious information that you acquire constitutes in its totality the prophets' inheritance, for Allah's prophets bequeath neither dinar nor dirham; rather, they, as Prophet Muhammad states, "bequeath knowledge. Whoever acquires this knowledge has in fact acquired an abundant portion". (*Sunan Abu Daawood* 88)

This exquisitely illustrated guide presents you with the first step and the foundation stage in learning about this great religion, which is undoubtedly the best blessing Allah has bestowed upon man. It provides you with guidelines in most aspects of life you encounter, responds to your urgent queries and gives you ample support to deal with people around you and successfully deal with the various situations in which you are most likely to find yourself. Presented in a straightforward style, this guide also provides you with documented information from the Qur'an and the *Sunnah* of the Prophet.

In addition to being a delightful, detailed book, it is a reference guide which you can consult whenever you encounter a situation or need to find out about the Islamic ruling on a given issue.

We pray to Almighty Allah to grant you abundant prosperity and more guidance, make your heart adhere firmly to His religion, make you blessed wherever you may be and admit all of us into Paradise, among those upon whom Allah has bestowed grace and favour, the prophets and the truthful.

The author

Preliminaries

Contents

The Greatest Blessing Ever

The Purpose of Human Existence

Islam is a Universal Religion

No Intermediaries between God and Man

Islam is a Religion of Life

Learning Islamic Rulings

The Five Islamic Rulings

How to Find out about the Rulings of Islam

Islam is a Moderate Religion

Islam Covers All Aspects of Life

Islam Must Be Judged by its Sublime Principles and not by the Bad Conduct of Some Muslims

The Five Necessities

> The Greatest Blessing Ever

Allah has bestowed countless blessings upon us. He has endowed us with the gifts of sight and hearing, the intellect, health, wealth and family. He has even subjected everything in the universe for us: the sun, the moon, the heavens and the earth, and many countless things, as the Qur'an states, "If you tried to number Allah's blessings, you could never count them." (*Soorat Al-Maa'idah*, 16:18)

However, all these blessings will cease to exist when our short worldly life comes to an end. The only blessing that is bound to bring about happiness and tranquillity in this life and eternal bliss in the hereafter is the blessing of being a Muslim, which is undeniably the greatest blessing Allah has ever bestowed upon us.

It is for this reason that Allah attributes this blessing to Him, giving it great honour over other blessings, as the Qur'an states, "Today I have perfected your religion for you, completed My blessing upon you, and have chosen for you Islam as your religion." (*Soorat Al-Maa'idah*, 5:3)

How great Allah's blessings upon us are! He has taken us out of the darkness of ignorance into the light of faith and guided us to the true religion which He has chosen for us in order to realise the objective behind our existence, namely, to worship Him and thus lead a happy life in this world and obtain an excellent reward in the hereafter.

How great Allah's favours upon us are! He has chosen us and made us the best community that has ever been brought forth for the good of mankind, bearing the testimony of faith, *Laa ilaaha illallaah* (There is no god worthy of worship except Allah), with which He has sent all His prophets.

> Islam is the Greatest Blessing Ever

When some ignorant people mistakenly thought that they had done the Prophet ﷺ a favour by embracing Islam, Allah reminded them that it was indeed Allah who had favoured them by guiding them to Islam in the first place, as the Qur'an states, "They think they have done you a favour by becoming Muslims! Say: "Do not consider your Islam a favour to me. No indeed! It is Allah who has favoured you by guiding you to the faith if you are telling the truth." (*Soorat Al-Hujuraat*, 49:17)

It is true that Allah's blessings are numerous, but the only blessing, as the verse makes it clear, regarding which Allah declares He has bestowed a favour upon us is that of guiding us to Islam and to worshipping Him alone without associating any partners with Him whatsoever.

Therefore, in order to continue benefiting from such immense blessing, we need to express gratefulness to Allah for bestowing such a favour upon us, as the Qur'an states, "If you are grateful, I will certainly give you increase." (*Soorat Ibraaheem*, 14:7)

How can we then possibly show gratefulness to Allah for such a blessing?

This can be done by doing the following two things:

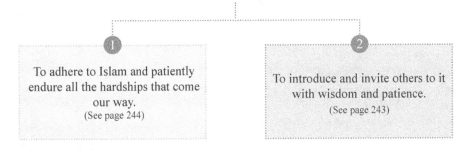

1. To adhere to Islam and patiently endure all the hardships that come our way. (See page 244)

2. To introduce and invite others to it with wisdom and patience. (See page 243)

> The Purpose of Human Existence

Many philosophers and lay people alike find it awfully puzzling to answer the most important question in our life:

Why are we here?

What is the real purpose of human existence?

The Qur'an has clearly and accurately stated the purpose of human existence thus: "I have only created the jinn and man to worship Me." (*Soorat Adh-Dhaariyaat*, 51:56) It is clear, therefore, that we are here to worship Allah the Almighty.

It is worth noting here, however, that worship, or *'ibaadah*, in Islam does not imply abandonment of the life of the world and its pleasures. It is a comprehensive term which includes, in addition to such acts of worship as prayer, fasting and the obligatory charity (*zakaat*), all human acts as long as they are done for the sake of Allah, as the Prophet ﷺ once observed, "You will be rewarded even when you engage in sexual intercourse with your wives."

In this way, worship, despite being the main purpose behind human existence, becomes the essence of life, affording a Muslim the opportunity to turn all daily lawful practices into great acts of worship. The Qur'an says, "Say: 'My prayer and my sacrifice, my living and my dying, are for Allah alone, the Lord of all the worlds.'" (*Soorat Al-An'aam*, 6:162)

> Islam is a Universal Religion

Islam is a universal religion in that its Prophet was sent to all peoples of the world, regardless of their race, colour, culture, traditions and geographical location, as the Qur'an states, "We have only sent you (O Muḥammad) as a mercy to all the worlds." (*Soorat Al-Anbiyaa'*, 21:107)

That is why Islam respects all the various human traditions and does not require new Muslims to change their own traditions unless they contravene some of the Islamic teachings. Thus, any traditions that go against Islamic teachings must be changed and replaced with a better alternative, for it is after all Allah, the All-Knowing, the All-Aware, who commands and forbids whatever He wills, and our faith in Him requires us to act in accordance with His laws.

Islam also teaches that Muslims' traditions that are not related to Islam and its teachings must not be considered 'Islamic', and that a new Muslim does not have to honour or observe them, for they merely constitute a set of permissible customs of a certain group of people.

The Entire Earth Is a Place of Worship

Islam considers any place in the world to be appropriate for worshipping Allah, and that there is no particular place or country that Muslims must migrate to and settle in, for the criterion here is the possibility to worship Allah in peace.

Nor does it oblige them to emigrate to another country unless they are prevented from worshipping Allah, in which case they may go to another country where they can worship Allah in total peace, as the Qur'an states, "My servants, you who have believed, My earth is wide, so worship Me alone!" (*Soorat Al-'Ankaboot*, 29:56)

> No Intermediaries between God and Man

Many religions have given certain religious privileges to some individuals and made people's worship and faith dependent upon such individuals' approval. In other words, they constitute intermediaries between God and them and falsely claim they can pardon their sins and even have knowledge of the unseen!

Thus, Islam came to honour and dignify man and refute the false idea that man's worship, repentance or salvation is dependent upon certain individuals' sanction no matter how devout and virtuous they may be.

In Islam, a Muslim worships Allah directly, without any intermediaries whatsoever between him and his Lord; for Allah is close to His servants; He can hear their prayer and respond to them and see their worship and reward them for performing it. No one in Islam claims to forgive sins and offer 'indulgences'. If a person commits a sin and sincerely seeks Allah's forgiveness, Allah certainly pardons his sin. No one possesses supernatural powers or can influence the universe in any way, for the power of decision rests with Allah alone.

> No Intermediaries between God and Man.

Islam has also liberated the human mind and encourages Muslims, when differences arise, to refer to the Qur'an and the authentic sayings and actions (*Sunnah*) of the Prophet ﷺ; for no human being has the prerogative to decide on religious matters after Allah ﷻ except Allah's Messenger ﷺ, the recipient of Allah's revelations who does not speak out of his own desire, as the Qur'an states, "He does not speak from his own desire. It is nothing but revelation revealed." (*Soorat An-Najm*, 53:3-4)

How great this religion is! It is in utter harmony with the pure natural disposition upon which Allah originated man, making him his own master and enabling him to exchange the servitude to false gods for the perfect freedom of worshipping Allah alone.

> Islam Is a Religion of Life

Islam is a religion which balances the worldly life and the life to come. According to Islam, the worldly life is like a farm in which a Muslim sows the seeds of good deeds in all aspects of life in order to reap the rewards of his hard work both in this life and the hereafter. This endeavour requires an optimistic attitude, dedication, seriousness and determination, which is obvious in the following points:

Developing the Earth

The Qur'an says, "He brought you into being from the earth and made you its inhabitants." (*Soorat Hood,* 11:61) Allah created us and placed us on this earth, commanding us to develop it and establish a civilisation to benefit humanity in a way that does not contradict Islamic teachings. Indeed, He considers doing so an act of worship for which its doer will be rewarded, even if it is done in times of great turmoil and under terrifying circumstances, such as the Day of Judgement. The Prophet once said, "If the Day of Judgement takes place [and you recognize the Event], while a man is holding a palm-tree seedling [to plant in the soil], let him, if he can, plant it." (*Musnad Ahmad:* 2712)

Maintaining Social Relationships

Islam calls its adherents to cooperate with people around them, regardless of their culture and religion, in order to establish a civilisation and build a healthy society. It urges them to associate with them and build relationships of the highest order, governed by the sublime moral standards Islam teaches. It also warns them against isolation and withdrawal from society, considering such a course to go against the right method naturally adopted by those dedicated to preaching Islam and calling to its sublime principles. Indeed, the Prophet once observed that a believer who mixes with people and endures their harm is far better than one who does not associate with them altogether. (*Sunan Ibn Maajah:* 4032)

Knowledge Acquisition

It was not a coincidence that the first word revealed to the Prophet was 'Read'. In fact, Islam stresses the importance of acquiring beneficial knowledge in all fields of human interest and considers the path that a Muslim follows to seek knowledge a path that actually leads to Paradise. As the Prophet said, "Whoever treads a path in search of knowledge, Allah will ease the way to Paradise for him." (*Saheeh Ibn Hibbaan:* 84)

In fact, Islam has never witnessed a conflict between religion and science, as is the case in other religions. On the contrary, it has always supported it and called its adherents to acquire it and teach it to others as long as it is bound to benefit mankind.

> Islam has never witnessed a conflict between religion and science, as is the case in other religions.

Islam even honours those who teach people and impart knowledge to them, holding them in high esteem and promising them abundant rewards. The Prophet ﷺ informs us in one of his traditions that all Allah's creation prays for those who impart beneficial knowledge to people. (*Sunan At-Tirmidhee:* 2685)

> Learning Islamic Rulings

A Muslim is required to learn about the Islamic rulings in all aspects of life—acts of worship, social relationships, among other things—in order to carry out his duties with accurate knowledge and immense certainty, as the Prophet ﷺ said, "Whomever Allah wishes to show goodness, He gives him understanding of the religion." (*Saheeh Al-Bukhaaree:* 71; *Saheeh Muslim:* 1037)

Therefore, he must learn all about the religious duties he is required to undertake, such as purification, the manner of performing the prayer (*salaat*) and the lawful and unlawful foods and drinks in Islam. He is also urged to learn about acts which are recommended but not obligatory.

> The Five Islamic Rulings

All human actions fall into five categories:

Waajib (Obligatory)	This denotes those acts which Allah commands Muslims to do. Those who do them will be rewarded, but those who neglect them will be subject to punishment. Examples of such acts include the five obligatory daily prayers and fasting during the lunar month of *Ramadaan*.
Haraam (Prohibited)	This denotes those acts which Allah has prohibited. Those who leave them will be rewarded, but those who engage in them will be punished. Examples of such acts include drinking alcohol and committing illicit sexual intercourse.
Mustahabb (also called *Sunnah*. Recommended)	This is used to describe acts which are rewarded but not punishable for their omission, such as smiling at people, initiating the greeting of Islam (by saying *Assalaamu 'Alaykum*) when meeting them and removing dirt or harmful objects from the road.
Makrooh (Disliked)	This denotes those acts which Islam urges its adherents to avoid. Those who avoid them will be rewarded, and those who do them will not be subject to punishment. They include such acts as fiddling with one's fingers during the prayer.
Mubaah (Permissible)	This denotes those acts that are neither forbidden nor recommended. They are rather neutral and thus subject neither to reward nor to punishment. They include eating, drinking and talking.

> The Five Pillars of Islam

The Prophet ﷺ said, "Islam has been built on five [pillars]: Testifying that there is no god but Allah and that Muhammad is the messenger of Allah, performing the prayers, paying *zakaat*, making the pilgrimage to the House, and fasting in *Ramadaan*." (*Saheeh Al-Bukhaaree:* 8; *Saheeh Muslim:* 16)

These five pillars constitute the very foundation of Islam. We will examine them and discuss their rulings in the following chapters.

The first of these is faith and the affirmation of Allah's unity, or *tawheed*. This is discussed in the next chapter titled 'Your Faith'.

After this comes the prayer (*salaat*), which is the greatest and the most exalted of all acts of worship. The Prophet ﷺ once described it as "the pillar of religion." (*Sunan At-Tirmidhee:* 2749). This means it is the pillar upon which Islam is firmly established. A pillar is a post that is used to support a building, without which the building will collapse.

However, for the prayer to be valid, a Muslim must offer it after purifying himself. Hence, the chapter 'Your Faith' is logically followed by 'Your Purification' and then 'Your Prayer'.

Testifying that there is no god but Allah and that Muḥammad is the Messenger of Allah

Performing the prayers

Paying *zakaat*

Fasting during the month of Ramaḍaan

Making the pilgrimage to the Ka'bah and Holy Mosque in Makkah

	The Five Pillars of Islam
1	Testifying that there is no god but Allah and that Muḥammad is the Messenger of Allah
2	Performing the prayers
3	Paying *zakaat*
4	Fasting during the month of Ramaḍaan
5	Making the pilgrimage to the Ka'bah and Holy Mosque in Makkah

> How to Find out about the Rulings of Islam

If a person contracts an illness and wants to get medical treatment, he will definitely look for the most proficient doctors he could possibly find to obtain the most effective treatment possible for his illness. He will certainly not take a prescription from any doctor because his life is dear to him.

Religion is undoubtedly the most important thing in our life, and we must therefore do our best to find out about its rulings and teachings and seek answers to questions about matters we do not know from trustworthy, knowledgeable scholars.

Reading the present book, which teaches you matters relating to your religion in their true light, is a step in the right direction. Searching for the right information requires you to ask scholars' opinions. The present book serves you well because it contains scholars' statements and answers to your queries. As the Qur'an states, "If you do not know, then ask the people of expert knowledge." (*Soorat An-Nahl*, 16:43) You must also take further steps if you are in doubt as to any of Islamic rulings on any given issue. You can do this by contacting Islamic centres and mosques near you, ensuring that they are from amongst those adhering to the Qur'an and authentic *Sunnah*. You can find out about their locations and contact details by visiting the following website:

www.islamicfinder.org

You must also refer to trusted Internet websites which will clarify the facts of Islam for you, such as

www.newmuslimguide.com

www.guide-muslim.com

> A new Muslim ought to visit and keep in touch with the nearby Islamic centres and to consult reliable books and trusted Internet websites.

> Islam is a Moderate Religion

Islam is a moderate religion which follows a middle course between exaggeration and negligence, extremism and total rejection of religion. This moderation pervades all acts of worship and rituals.

It is for this reason that Allah ﷻ commands the Prophet ﷺ, his companions and the believers at large to observe moderation, which can be realised by doing two things:

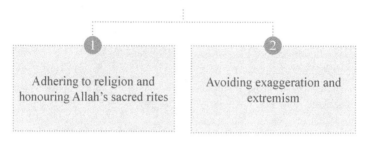

1. Adhering to religion and honouring Allah's sacred rites

2. Avoiding exaggeration and extremism

The Qur'an says, "Keep to the right course as you have been commanded, and also those who turn with you to Allah, and do not exceed the bounds. He sees what you do." (*Soorat Hood*, 11:112)

This means: Be steadfast in following the truth, to the best of your ability, without overstepping the limits through exaggeration and extremism.

Once, while teaching his companions one of the rites of pilgrimage, the Prophet ﷺ warned them against going to extremes, pointing out that doing so was the reason behind the destruction of past nations: "Beware of extremism in religion, for the only thing that destroyed those before you was extremism in religion." (*Sunan Ibn Maajah:* 3029)

That is why he also noted, "Take upon yourself only those actions for which you have the strength to carry out consistently." (*Saheeh Al-Bukhaaree:* 1100)

On another occasion, he revealed the spirit of the message with which he was sent, namely, not to burden people beyond their capacity but to teach them with wisdom and make things easy for them: "Allah did not send me to be harsh or cause harm, but He sent me to teach [people] and make things easy [for them]." (*Saheeh Muslim:* 1478)

> Islam Covers All Aspects of Life

Islam is not only a spiritual need fulfilled by Muslims in mosques through prayers and supplications.

Nor is it a mere set of views and beliefs espoused by its adherents;

Nor is it merely a comprehensive economic system;

Nor is it simply a set of rules and principles for building society and a system;

Nor is it only a set of moral values and manners for dealing with others;

Rather, it is a comprehensive way of life which covers all aspects of life without exception.

Indeed, Almighty Allah has completed His favour upon Muslims by choosing Islam for them as their religion and a complete way of life, as the Qur'an states, "This day have I perfected your religion for you, completed My favour upon you, and have chosen for you Islam as your religion." (*Soorat Al-Maa'idah,* 5:3)

Once, when one of the polytheists sarcastically said to Salman Al-Faarisee ☙, one of the Prophet's companions, "Your Prophet has taught you everything, even the proper manner of defecating," "Yes, indeed," Salman proudly replied, and he went about showing him the etiquette of using the toilet.

> Islam encompasses all aspects of life.

> Islam Must Be Judged by its Sublime Principles and not by the Bad Conduct of Some Muslims

If you find a doctor who adopts harmful medical procedures or a teacher with bad moral character, you will certainly disapprove of their wrong practices, which are obviously at odds with their social position and the type of knowledge they have acquired. This, however, will not make you change your mind about the great benefits medical science has afforded mankind or the great position education and learning occupies in society and civilisation.

You will undoubtedly reach the conclusion that such a doctor or teacher actually misrepresents his professional qualifications and affiliations.

By the same token, if you find some Muslims who follow some bad practices, you may mistakenly assume that such practices reflect the spirit of Islam, which is obviously not true. Just because the wrong practices of that doctor or teacher cannot be possibly attributed to the medical or educational profession, such Muslims' bad practices cannot, with an even stronger reason, be attributed to Islam; they merely constitute an aspect of human weakness and could therefore be attributed to wrong cultural practices which have nothing to do with Islam.

> The Five Necessities

> Allah commands us to preserve human life even if doing so involves the commission of a sin.

These are the ultimate benefits which man must enjoy in order to lead an honourable life. Indeed, all divine laws have commanded their preservation and prohibited anything that contradicts them.

Islam urges its adherents to protect such necessities so that they may serve them well in the worldly life and the life to come and thus live in total peace and security.

Muslims in all parts of the world form one single community (*ummah*) whose members support one another as if they were a solid cemented structure, each part strengthening and giving support to the others. They are, as the Prophet ﷺ once described them, like one body—when any part of it aches, the whole body aches because of sleeplessness and fever. These five necessities can be preserved by:

1. recognising and appreciating them
2. protecting them against any violations

Religion

This is the main reason why Allah ﷻ created people and sent messengers to convey it to them and to preserve it, as the Qur'an states, "We sent a messenger among every people saying: 'Worship Allah and keep clear of all false gods.'" (*Soorat An-Nahl*, 16:36)

Indeed, Islam insists on preserving religion and protecting it against anything which is bound to mar its purity, such as worshipping false gods besides Allah or instead of Him (*shirk*) and engaging in superstitions and committing forbidden acts.

② Life

Allah ﷻ commands us to preserve human life even if this involves the commission of a sin, especially if one is driven by necessity to do so, as the Qur'an states, "But whoever is forced [by necessity], neither desiring [it] nor transgressing [its limit], there is no sin upon him. Indeed, Allah is Forgiving and Merciful." (*Soorat Al-Baqarah*, 2:173)

He has forbidden suicide or any act against human life in general: "Do not cast yourselves into destruction." (*Soorat Al-Baqarah*, 2:195)

He has also legislated punishments which serve to deter people from unjustly harming others, no matter what their religion may be: "O you who believe, fair retribution is prescribed for you in cases of murder." (*Soorat Al-Baqarah*, 2:178)

③ The Mind

Islam prohibits anything that is bound to have a negative effect on the mind and impair discernment. Indeed, the intellect is one of the greatest blessings Allah has bestowed upon us; it is the very faculty by which Allah has honoured man and favoured him over other creatures; it is also the reason that makes him subject to accountability in this life and in the hereafter.

It is for this reason that Allah ﷻ has forbidden all types of intoxicants and drugs, which He describes as an abomination of Satan's handiwork: "O you who believe, intoxicants, gambling, stone altars and divining arrows are abominations devised by Satan. Avoid them so that you may be successful." (*Soorat Al-Maa'idah*, 5:90)

④ Progeny

Islam stresses the importance of preserving progeny and starting a family in which the new generation acquire good manners and learn lofty principles. This is clear in a number of rulings which include the following:

* It encourages marriage and prompts its adherents to make it easy for the unmarried people with the least expenses: "Marry off those among you who are unmarried." (*Soorat An-Noor*, 24:32)

* It prohibits all sinful, illicit relationships and has blocked all the ways leading to them: "Do not go near to fornication. It is an indecent act and an evil way." (*Soorat Al-Israa'*, 17:32)

> Islam prohibits anything that is harmful to health and the mind.

- It forbids slandering or defaming people's lineage and considers this act a major sin for which the perpetrator is subject to a specified punishment in this life in addition to severe chastisement in the hereafter.

- It commands its adherents to preserve people's honour and considers a person who is killed defending his honour or that of his family, a martyr. (See page 203)

5 Property

Islam urges its followers to protect their property and preserve their wealth and commands them to earn a living, making all commercial transactions lawful.

In order to protect wealth, it considers usury, deception and misappropriation of people's wealth by using wrongful means, strictly forbidden. The Qur'an warns perpetrators of such acts, of severe punishments. (See page 172)

> Preservation of one's honour and lineage is one of the loftiest objectives of Islamic law (*Sharee'ah*).

Your Faith

1

All divine messages, which the prophets brought to their people, called to the worship of Allah alone without associating anyone in worship with Him and to reject all false deities. In fact, this is the exact meaning of the testimony of faith through which one enters the fold of Islam by pronouncing it.

Contents

Testimony of Faith: Meaning and Requirements
- Why the Statement "*Laa ilaaha illallaah*"?
- The Meaning of *Laa ilaaha illallaah*
- The Two Main Parts of *Laa ilaaha illallaah*

The Testimony that Muḥammad is Allah's Messenger
- Who is Allah's Messenger?
- The Meaning of the Testimony that Muḥammad is Allah's Messenger

The Six Pillars of Faith (*Eemaan*)

The Meaning of Worship (*'Ibaadah*)

Associating Partners with Allah in Worship (*Shirk*)

Belief in Allah's Names and Attributes

Belief in the Angels

Belief in the Divine Books

Belief in the Messengers

Belief in the Last Day

Belief in the Divine Decree

> Testimony of Faith: Meaning and Requirements

Ash hadu an laa ilaaha illallaah, wa ash hadu anna Muhammadan rasool-ullaah (I bear witness that there is no god worthy of worship except Allah and that Muhammad is the Messenger of Allah)

Why the Statement "*Laa ilaaha illallaah*"?

- Because it is the first duty of a Muslim. Therefore, whoever intends to accept Islam must make such a declaration of faith and believe in it.

- Because whoever says it, sincerely believing in it and seeking thereby Allah's pleasure, will be saved from Hellfire, as the Prophet ﷺ said, "Allah has forbidden for the Hellfire anyone who says, 'There is no one worthy of worship except Allah,' seeking thereby Allah's pleasure." (*Saheeh Al-Bukhaaree:* 415)

- Because whoever dies while believing in it will be admitted into Paradise, as the Prophet ﷺ said, "Whoever dies knowing full well that there is no god but Allah will enter Paradise." (*Musnad Ahmad:*464)

- Because knowledge of its meaning and dictates is unquestionably the greatest and most important duty of a Muslim.

The Meaning of *Laa ilaaha illallaah*

This means no one is worthy of worship except Allah. In fact, this statement negates the existence of any other deity besides Allah ﷻ and confirms that Allah is the only True God worthy of being worshipped.

The Arabic word *ilaah* (god) refers to any being that is worshipped. Thus, whoever worships something has in fact taken it as a god besides or instead of Allah. All such deities are indeed false except for one God—Allah, the true Lord and Creator.

Therefore, Allah ﷻ alone deserves to be worshipped. It is He alone whom human hearts must worship with utmost love, glorification, humility and fear, and He alone should be relied upon and invoked. No one should be called upon, sought for help or relied upon except Allah. Prayers and sacrifices must be offered to Him alone, and He ought to be worshipped in all sincerity, as the Qur'an states, "They were only ordered to worship Allah, keeping religion pure for Him." (*Soorat Al-Bayyinah,* 98:5)

Those who sincerely worship Allah, following the dictates of the testimony of faith, will certainly lead a happy life, for it is only by worshipping Allah alone that hearts find peace and real satisfaction, as the Qur'an states, "Whoever does good, whether male or female, and he is a believer., We will most certainly make him live a happy life." (*Soorat An-Nahl,* 16:97)

The Two main Parts of *Laa ilaaha illallaah*

This great statement comprises two parts which must be known in order to understand its meaning and requirements:

> **The First Part:** *Laa ilaaha* (There is no god), negates the existence of any other deity besides Allah ﷻ, rejects association of partners with Allah in worship (*shirk*), and requires disbelief in any being or thing that is worshipped besides Allah, be it a human being, an animal, an idol, a star or anything else.

> **The Second Part:** *illallaah* (except Allah), confirms that Allah is the only True God worthy of being worshipped and thus all acts of worship, such as the prayer, invocation and reliance, must be directed to Him alone.

All acts of worship must be directed to Allah alone; whoever directs any act of worship to other than Allah is, strictly speaking, an unbeliever.

The Qur'an states, "Whoever calls on another god together with Allah has no proof for doing so at all, and his reckoning is with his Lord. Truly the unbelievers have no success." (*Soorat Al-Mu'minoon,* 23:117)

The significance of *Laa ilaaha illallaah* along with its two main parts are mentioned in the following verse: "Whoever rejects false gods and believes in Allah has grasped the firmest handhold, which will never give way." (*Soorat Al-Baqarah,* 2:256)

The words "whoever rejects false gods" provides the meaning of the first part of the testimony of faith, namely, *Laa ilaaha;* while the words "and believes in Allah" provides the meaning of its second part, namely, *illallaah.*

> The Testimony that Muhammad is Allah's Messenger

Who is Allah's Messenger?

1. His Birth

Prophet Muhammad ﷺ was born in Makkah in 570 CE. His father died before his birth, and his mother also died when he was very young. Thus, he was placed under the care of his paternal grandfather, 'Abdul-Muttalib, and, after his grandfather's death, he was placed under the care of Abu Taalib, one of his paternal uncles.

2. His Life and Upbringing

Muhammad ﷺ spent forty years before he received revelation in the Makkan tribe of Quraysh into which he was born, and during this period (570-610 CE) he came to be known amongst his people as *as-saadiq al-ameen* (the truthful and trustworthy) because of his uprightness and excellent manners. He worked as a shepherd and later as a merchant.

Before the advent of Islam, he maintained the pure monotheistic beliefs of Prophet Abraham ﷺ, a *haneef*, worshipping Allah alone without ascribing any partners to Him and rejecting idol worship and pagan practices.

Our Prophet's Name

Muhammad ﷺ was the son of 'Abdullaah, son of 'Abd Al-Muttalib of the Banu Haashim clan of the Quraysh. He was indisputably the noblest of all Arabs.

A Messenger to All Mankind

Allah ﷻ sent Muhammad ﷺ as a messenger to people of all races, classes and colours, and He made it everybody's duty to obey him, as the Qur'an states, "Say: 'O Mankind! I am the Messenger of Allah to you all.'" (*Soorat Al-A'raaf,* 7:158)

③ His Mission

When Allah's Messenger ﷺ turned forty, he would regularly retreat to the Cave of Hiraa', on the peak of Mount Noor on the outskirts of Makkah, in present-day Saudi Arabia, meditating and worshiping Allah. It was then that he started receiving revelation from Allah. The first verses he received there were: "Read in the name of your Lord who created. He created man from a clot of blood. Read, and your Lord is the Most Generous; He who taught by the pen; taught man that which he knew not." (*Soorat Al-'Alaq*, 96:1-5) These verses ushered in a new era of knowledge, reading, light and guidance. The Qur'anic revelations continued until his death twenty-three years later.

④ The Beginning of His Mission

After three years of preaching secretly, Allah's Messenger ﷺ spent another ten years preaching Islam openly. During this period, he and his Companions were subjected to all forms of injustice and persecution at the hands of the Quraysh pagans. Not losing heart, he began presenting himself during the pilgrimage season to the pilgrims who came from various tribes, calling them to the new faith. Pilgrims from Madeenah accepted Islam and, soon afterwards, Muslims started migrating to their city in successive groups.

The Qur'an was Revealed to Him

Allah ﷻ sent down to him the greatest of His divine scriptures, the Holy Qur'an, which falsehood can reach neither from before it nor from behind it. (*Soorat Fussilat*, 41:42)

He was the Seal of the Prophets and Messengers

Muhammad ﷺ was the final prophet sent by Almighty Allah; therefore, there will be no prophet after him, as evidenced by the verse: "Muhammad is not the father of any of your men, but the Messenger of Allah and the Final Seal of the Prophets." (*Soorat Al-Ahzaab*, 33:40)

5. His Migration

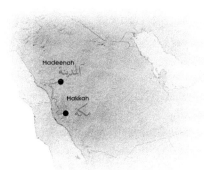

At the age of fifty-three, Allah's Messenger ﷺ migrated to Madeenah, which was then called Yathrib, in 622 CE, after the Quraysh notables who had opposed his mission plotted to kill him. He spent ten years there, inviting people to Islam, and enjoined the prayer, *zakaat* and the other Islamic rituals on the Muslims.

6. His Efforts to Spread Islam

Following his migration to Madeenah (622-623 CE), Allah's Messenger ﷺ laid the foundation for Islamic civilisation and determined the aspects of the Muslim society. He eradicated tribal fanaticism, spread knowledge, established the principles of justice, righteousness, fraternity, cooperation and organisation. Some tribes attempted to put an end to Islam once and for all, leading to a number of skirmishes and wars, but Allah ﷻ supported His Messenger and made Islam reign supreme. Then, people in Makkah and in most cities and tribes in the Arabian Peninsula willingly began entering this great religion in crowds, fully convinced that it is the true religion.

7 His Death

In the lunar month of *Safar*, 11 AH (June 632 CE), after Allah's Messenger ﷺ disseminated the message of Islam and Allah had completed His favour upon the Muslims by perfecting His religion for them, the Messenger ﷺ had a sudden onset of fever which led to his death on Monday *Rabee' Al-Awwal* 11 AH (8 June 632 CE) at the age of 63. He was buried where he died, in the apartment of his wife 'Aa'ishah, which is now housed within the Prophet's Mosque in Madeenah.

The Meaning of the Testimony that Muhammad is Allah's Messenger

This means to believe his statements, do the acts he commanded, avoid the acts he prohibited and worship Allah according to the manner he prescribed and taught us.

What Does Belief that Muhammad is Allah's Messenger Entail?

 To believe all the statements he made about everything. This includes the following:

- Matters relating to the unseen world, such as the Last Day, the eternal bliss in Paradise and the everlasting punishment in Hellfire

- The events that will take place on the Day of Judgement, the signs of this day and the major incidents preceding the end of the world

- Stories of past nations and what happened between the prophets and their people

To do the acts he enjoined and avoid the acts he prohibited. This includes the following:

- To comply with his orders, fully convinced that he did not speak of his own desire and that what he came with was nothing but a revelation revealed to him, as the Qur'an states, "Whoever obeys the Messenger has obeyed Allah." (*Soorat An-Nisaa'*, 4:80)

- To avoid the acts he prohibited, such as erroneous practices and bad manners, fully convinced that he only prohibited us from doing so due to some divine wisdom and for our own benefit even if we may not be sometimes aware of such benefit.

- To be certain beyond any doubt that doing the acts he enjoined and avoiding the acts he prohibited will benefit us tremendously and bring us happiness in this life and in the hereafter, as the Qur'an states, "Obey Allah and the Messenger, that you may find mercy." (*Soorat Aal 'Imraan*, 3:132)

> A Muslim must believe all the statements authentically attributed to Allah's Messenger.

- To firmly believe that those who disobey Allah's Messenger ﷺ will suffer a grievous punishment, as the Qur'an states, "Those who oppose his command should beware of a testing trial coming to them or a painful punishment striking them." (*Soorat An-Noor*, 24:63)

3. To worship Allah ﷻ in accordance with the Prophet's instructions. This implies the following:

- **To follow his example:** We ought to follow the Prophet's *Sunnah*, or practice, including his words, deeds and tacit approval, in all aspects of our lives. Indeed, the more one follows the Prophet's example, the more one gets closer to Allah ﷻ and the higher the grades of honour one will have with one's Lord, as the Qur'an states, "Say, 'If you love Allah, then follow me, Allah will love you and forgive you your sins. Allah is Ever-Forgiving, Most Merciful.'" (*Soorat Aal 'Imraan*, 3:31)

- **Islam is complete:** Allah's Messenger ﷺ conveyed Islam and all its laws in full; thus, no one is allowed to introduce any practice in Islam which the Prophet ﷺ did not approve.

> Peace and tranquillity can only be attained by worshipping Allah alone without associating any partners with Him in worship.

- **Islam is relevant to all times and places:** Islamic rulings mentioned in the Qur'an and the Prophet's *Sunnah* are relevant to all times and places, for no one knows for certain what is best for people except Allah who created them in the first place.

- **To follow the Prophet's *Sunnah*:** For one's goods deeds and devotional acts to be accepted by Allah ﷻ, they have to be done in accordance with the manner prescribed by the Prophet ﷺ, as the Qur'an states, "So let him who hopes to meet his Lord do righteous work and not associate anyone in the worship of his Lord." (*Soorat Al-Kahf*, 18:110) The phrase 'righteous work' here denotes good deeds which are done in accordance with the Prophet's *Sunnah*.

- **Innovations in religious matters are strictly forbidden:** Those who introduce an innovation in religion (an act of worship which contradicts the Prophet's *Sunnah*), such as offering a prayer not sanctioned by the Prophet ﷺ blatantly go against his command and will have the innovation they have introduced rejected, as the Qur'an states, "Those who oppose his command should beware of a testing trial coming to them or a painful punishment striking them." (*Soorat An-Noor*, 24:63) The Prophet ﷺ also said in this connection, "He who innovates something in this religion of ours that is not of it will have it rejected." (*Saheeh Al-Bukhaaree*:2550; *Saheeh Muslim*:1718)

By strictly forbidding innovations in religion and adding or changing acts of worship, Islam intends to protect divine law against distortion and alterations and safeguard it against being subjected to people's whims and desires. Apart from this, Islam does, however, encourage the human mind to engage in innovative thinking and to explore the secrets of the universe in all aspects of life with a view to serving humanity and helping develop its present and future status.

> The Six Pillars of Faith (Eemaan)

The Meaning of Belief in Allah

This means firm belief that Allah exists, resolutely affirming His Lordship, Godship and Names and Attributes.

We will now discuss these four issues at length as follows:

Belief in the Existence of Allah

The Innate Disposition to Believe in Allah (*Fitrah*)

Affirming the existence of Allah is something that is innate in human beings and does not require anything to prove it. Indeed, it is for this reason that most people acknowledge God's existence despite their different religious beliefs.

We know in our heart of hearts that Allah exists because we always seek His assistance and support in times of hardship or when a calamity strikes because of the innate inclination to believe in Him and worship Him (*fitrah*) which He has instilled into us even though some people attempt to obliterate it or ignore it.

The numerous incidents we have heard or seen about people having their prayers answered, their wishes granted and their distress relieved proves beyond any shadow of doubt that Allah does exist.

Proofs for Allah's Existence are Clear and Countless

- Everybody inherently acknowledges the laws of causality, that is, everything has a determinate cause. The numerous creatures we see around us must have a causative agent, that is undoubtedly Allah, for it is impossible for anything to be created without a creator, just as it is impossible for it to create itself, as the verse states, "Or were they created out of nothing, or are

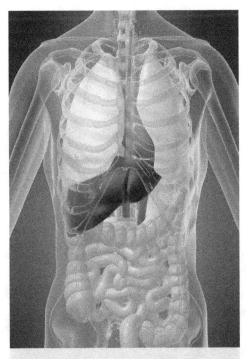

Man himself is one of the major signs which testify to Allah's existence. We only need to reflect on the blessings of reason, the senses and the well-proportioned and perfectly designed bodies with which Allah has endowed us, as the Qur'an states, "There are certainly signs [of Allah's existence] in yourselves as well. Do you not then see?" (*Soorat Adh-Dhaariyaat*, 51:21)

they the creators?"(*Soorat At-Toor*, 52:35) This verse simply means that people were not created without a Creator, nor could they have created themselves, which obviously means that it was Allah ﷻ who created them.

- The superbly flawless plan in the universe, including its most subtle elements, its heaven, earth, constellations and trees, among numerous other great marvels and impressive wonders, prove without a doubt that it has one Creator who is Allah, as the verse states, "This is the handiwork of Allah who has perfected all things." (*Soorat An-Naml*, 27:88)

All the stars and planets, for instance, consistently orbit around their respective common centre of mass.

As the Qur'an states, "The sun cannot overtake the moon, nor can the night outrun the day: each floats in its own orbit." (Soorat Yaa Seen, 36:40)

2 Belief in Allah's Lordship

The Meaning of Belief in Allah's Lordship

This means to firmly believe that Allah ﷻ is the Lord, the creator, the sustainer and the provider of everything; that He is the one who gives life and causes death; that He is the only one who can do harm and good; that all power of decision rests with Him; that in His hand is all good; that He has power over everything; and that He has no partner whatsoever in doing all this.

Belief in Allah's Lordship therefore requires a Muslim to believe that:

Allah is the only creator of everything in the universe, as the Qur'an states, "Allah is the Creator of everything." (*Soorat Az-Zumar*, 39:62)

Man's creativity merely involves such processes as transforming something from one state into another, assembling and building; it does not involve originating creation, creating something out of nothing or bringing it to life after death.

He is the only One who provides sustenance to His creation and no one else can do so, as the Qur'an states, "There is no creature on the earth which is not dependent upon Allah for its provision." (*Soorat Hood*, 11:6)

He is the master and owner of everything "The kingdom of the heavens and the earth and everything in them belongs to Allah." (*Soorat Al-Maa'idah*, 5:120)

He is the sole ruler who regulates all affairs of the universe: "He directs the whole affair from heaven to earth." (*Soorat As-Sajdah*, 32:5)

Man's management of his worldly affairs is rather limited and depends on whatever material is at his disposal. Besides, in so doing, he can either meet with success or experience failure. However, Allah's regulation of the affairs of the universe is comprehensive and is bound to be effectual, for there is nothing that would otherwise thwart it in any way, as the Qur'an states, "Both creation and command belong to Him. Blessed be Allah, the Lord of all the worlds." (*Soorat Al-A'raaf*, 7:54)

"There is no creature on the earth which is not dependent upon Allah for its provision." (*Soorat Hood*, 11:6)

The Arab Polytheists at the Time of the Prophet ﷺ Believed in Allah's Lordship

The Arab polytheists at the time of the Prophet ﷺ affirmed Allah's Lordship; they believed that He is the Creator, the Master and Disposer of all affairs, but such affirmation alone was not sufficient for them to be admitted into the fold of Islam. As the Qur'an states, "If you asked them, 'Who created the heavens and the earth?' they would say, 'Allah!' Say: 'Praise be to Allah!' But most of them do not know." (*Soorat Luqmaan*, 31:25)

Indeed, affirmation that Allah is the Lord of all the worlds, that He is the master and sustainer entails that all acts of worship must be directed to Him alone, without taking any partners whatsoever with Him in worship.

It would be ludicrous to affirm that Allah is the creator of everything, the disposal of all affairs and the one who gives life and causes death and then we direct an act of worship to other than Him. Indeed, doing so is a tremendous wrong and the worst of all sins, as the Qur'an states, "When Luqmaan said to his son, counselling him, 'My son, do not associate anything with Allah. Associating others with Him is a terrible wrong.'" (*Soorat Luqmaan*, 31:13)

When the Prophet ﷺ was asked about the greatest sin in the sight of Allah, he replied, "To set up a rival to Allah in worship though He alone created you." (*Saheeh Al-Bukhaaree:* 4207; *Saheeh Al-Bukhaaree:* 86)

Belief in Allah's Lordship Sets the Heart at Rest

When one firmly acknowledges that none of Allah's creation can challenge His decree, being the creator and king of all mankind who decrees whatever He deems wise for them, who is their only creator, sustainer and disposer of all affairs, whom nothing as small as an atom moves or settles except with His decree, one's heart becomes attached to Almighty Allah, asking none but Him, relying on Him in all worldly matters and dealing with all the ups and downs of life calmly and confidently, with determination and perseverance. For once we have done what we can possibly do to achieve a worldly goal and

> Belief in Allah's Lordship sets the heart at rest

have prayed to Allah for assistance, we have actually done our duty. In this way, we become contented, as we do not covet what others may have, fully aware that all power of decision rests with Allah who creates whatever He wills and chooses for mankind whatever is best for them.

3 The Belief that only Allah is Worthy of Worship

What Does this Mean?

This means firm belief that Allah is the only true god who deserves to be worshipped. This entails that all the apparent and hidden acts of worship, such as invocation, fear, reliance, the prayer, the obligatory charity (*zakaat*), fasting and seeking assistance, must be directed to Him alone, as the Qur'an states, "Your God is One God. There is no god but Him, the Most Beneficent the Most Merciful." (*Soorat Al-Baqarah*, 2:163)

This verse makes it abundantly clear that Allah is only one God, which means that He alone deserves to be worshipped and that no one else must be worshipped besides or instead of Him.

> Declaring Allah's oneness and directing all acts of worship to Him alone is the actual realisation of the meaning of the statement *Laa ilaaha illallaah*.

Importance of the Belief that Allah is the Only God Worthy of Worship

The importance of the belief that Allah is the only God who deserves to be worshipped is apparent in a number of aspects:

- Worshipping Allah is the ultimate purpose of human and jinn existence, as the Qur'an states, "I have only created the jinn and man to worship Me." (*Soorat Adh-Dhaariyaat*, 51:56)

- Worshipping Allah is also the reason behind Allah's sending messengers and revealing divine books to affirm that Allah is the only God worthy of worship and to reject false deities worshipped besides or along with Him, as the Qur'an states, "We sent a messenger among every people saying: 'Worship Allah and keep clear of all false gods.'" (*Soorat An-Nahl*, 16:36)

- Worshipping Allah is the first duty of man towards his creator. Giving instructions and orders to Mu'aadh ibn Jabal ﷺ upon sending him to Yemen, the Prophet ﷺ said to him, "You are going to a people from among the People of the Book. Let the first thing you call them to be to testify that there is no god worthy of worship except Allah." (*Saheeh Al-Bukhaaree:* 1389; *Saheeh Muslim.* 19)

That is, let them direct all acts of worship to Him alone.

- The belief that Allah is the only God worthy of worship is the actual realisation of the meaning of the statement *Laa ilaaha illallaah*. The Arabic word *ilaah* (generally translated 'God') refers to any being that is worshipped. Therefore, there is no God who truly deserves to be worshipped except Allah, and thus no act of worship must be dedicated except to Him alone.

- The belief that Allah is the only God worthy of worship is the logical outcome of the belief that He is the Creator, the Master and the Disposer of all affairs.

> The Meaning of Worship ('Ibaadah)

The Arabic term *'ibaadah* comprises all the words and deeds which Allah loves and approves of and which He has commanded or recommended, whether such words and deeds are apparent, such as the prayer, *zakaat* or pilgrimage; or hidden, such as love for Allah and His Messenger, fear of Allah, reliance upon Him and seeking His assistance.

Worship Encompasses all Aspects of Life

Worship (*'ibaadah*) embraces all the believer's acts if he intends to do them with the intention of getting closer to Allah. Therefore, the concept of worship in Islam is not confined to the common rituals, such as the prayer and fasting; rather, it includes all beneficial acts that are done with good intentions. In this way, all the good acts a Muslim does are considered acts of worship for which he will be rewarded in the hereafter. If he eats, drinks or sleeps, for instance, with the intention of getting strength to be able to obey Allah, he will be rewarded for this intention. A Muslim, therefore, lives all his life for Allah. His eating to get strength to obey Allah, his marriage to keep away from unlawful sexual acts, seeking knowledge, getting a university degree, making discoveries, and a woman's care for her husband, children and home are all acts of worship as long as they are coupled with a good intention.

The Reason behind the Creation of the Jinn and Mankind

Allah says, "I have only created the jinn and man to worship Me. I do not require any provision from them and I do not require them to nourish Me. Truly, Allah is the Provider, the Lord of Power, the Ever Mighty." (*Soorat Adh-Dhaariyaat*, 51:56-8)

Allah informs us in this verse that the reason behind creating the jinn and mankind is to worship Him. In fact, He is not in need of their worship; rather, it is they who need to worship Him because of their total dependence upon Him.

> All the good acts that are done with good intentions are considered acts of worship for which man will be rewarded.

If man neglects a duty towards his creator and gives free rein to the worldly pleasures without contemplating the divine reason behind his existence, he becomes just like any other creature without any privileges whatsoever over other creatures. Animals, too, eat and enjoy themselves but they will not be brought into account on the Day of Judgement, as man will be: "Those who reject Allah will enjoy this world and eat as cattle eat; and the Fire will be their abode." (*Soorat Muhammad*, 47:12) By neglecting their duty towards their Lord, they are just like animals, but contrary to animals, they will be punished for their disobedience because, unlike animals, they have been endowed with the faculty of reason.

Pillars of Worship

The kind of worship Allah has legislated is based on two important pillars:

The First Pillar: Total humility and fear

The Second Pillar: Complete love for Allah

Therefore, worship (*'ibaadah*), which Allah has commanded His slaves to observe must be accompanied with (1) total submission to, and humility before Allah while fearing Him, and (2) complete love for Him, asking, invoking and imploring none but Him.

Love that is not accompanied with fear and humility, such as love for food and wealth, cannot be considered worship. By the same token, fear that is not accompanied with love, such as fear of a ferocious beast or a tyrant ruler, cannot be considered worship. For worship to be realised when doing an act, both love and fear must be realised, and this can only be directed to Allah alone.

> For worship, or *'Ibaadah*, to be valid and accepted, it has to be directed sincerely to Allah alone and done in conformity with His Messenger's *Sunnah*.

Conditions of Worship

For worship, or *'ibaadah*, to be valid and accepted, two conditions must be met:

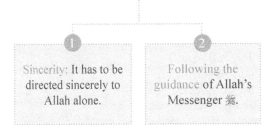

1. Sincerity: It has to be directed sincerely to Allah alone.

2. Following the guidance of Allah's Messenger ﷺ.

Highlighting this point, the Qur'an states, "Indeed, those who submit themselves to Allah and act righteously will be rewarded by their Lord: They will have no fear, nor will they grieve." (*Soorat Al-Baqarah*, 2:112)

The statement 'those who submit themselves to Allah' means that they realise the essence of monotheism by sincerely worshipping Allah alone.

The words 'act righteously' means that they follow Allah's law and the guidance (*Sunnah*) of Allah's Messenger ﷺ.

It is worth noting here, however, that following the Prophet's guidance relates only to pure acts of worship, such as the prayer, fasting and remembrance of Allah; it does not relate to those acts which fall under the general meaning of worship (*'ibaadah*), that is, those acts and practices which one does with a good intention in order to receive reward from Allah, such as exercising with the intention of getting strength to worship Allah better and engaging in trade to support one's family. Engaging in such activities only requires avoidance of acting against the Prophet's teachings or committing a forbidden act.

Associating Partners with Allah in Worship (Shirk)

- *Shirk* contradicts the belief that Allah alone is worthy of worship. While the belief that Allah alone deserves to be worshipped and that all acts of worship must be directed to Him constitutes the greatest and most important duty of a Muslim towards his Lord, *shirk* is considered to be the greatest sin in the sight of Allah and is the only sin which He never forgives without sincere repentance. The Qur'an says, "Allah does not forgive anything being associated with Him in worship, but He forgives whoever He wills for anything other than that." (*Soorat An-Nisaa', 4:48*) When the Prophet ﷺ was asked about the greatest sin in the sight of Allah, he replied, "To set up a rival to Allah in worship though He alone created you." (*Saheeh Al-Bukhaaree: 4207; Saheeh Muslim: 86*)

- Indeed, *shirk* renders acts of worship invalid and worthless, as the Qur'an states, "If they had associated others with Him, nothing they did would have been of any use." (*Soorat Al-An'aam, 6:88*)

Those who commit the unpardonable sin of *shirk* will be doomed to Hellfire for all eternity, as the Qur'an states, "Those who associate anything with Allah in worship, for them Allah has forbidden Paradise and their abode will be the Fire.'" (*Soorat Al-Maa'idah, 5:72*)

Shirk is of two Types: Major *Shirk* and Minor *Shirk*

Major *Shirk*: This involves directing any act of worship to other than Allah. Therefore, directing words or deeds that Allah loves to Him alone testifies to monotheism and true faith, while directing them to other than Allah constitutes an act of unbelief and *shirk*.

Examples of this type of shirk include asking someone other than Allah to cure one of an illness or to increase one's wealth, relying on other than Allah and prostrating to other than Him.

Allah says, "Your Lord says, 'Call on Me and I will answer you.'" (*Soorat Ghaafir, 40:60*)

"Put your trust in Allah if you are indeed believers." (*Soorat Al-Maa'idah, 5:23*)

"Prostrate before Allah and worship Him." (*Soorat An-Najm, 53:62*)

Therefore, whoever directs any act of worship to other than Allah is, strictly speaking, an unbeliever.

Minor *Shirk*: This involves those words or deeds which serve as a vehicle to commit the major shirk.

Examples of this type of *shirk* include making one's prayer sometimes a little longer or reciting the Qur'an a little louder for the sake of showing off. The Prophet ﷺ once observed, "The thing that I fear most for you is the minor *shirk*." His Companions asked, "What is the minor *shirk*, Messenger of Allah?" He replied, "Showing off." (*Musnad Ahmad: 23630*)

However, if a person performs acts of worship entirely for showing off, and were it not for the sake of people he would never offer the prayer or observe a fast, then he is definitely a hypocrite. Doing so is undoubtedly a major shirk which takes one out of the fold of Islam altogether.

Does Asking People Amount to Committing *Shirk*?

Islam aims to free the human mind from the shackles of superstitions and from submitting to none other than the One True God-Allah ﷻ.

Therefore, it is not permissible to ask the dead or inanimate beings for anything or humbly submit to them; doing so constitutes sheer superstition and is a blatant act of *shirk*.

It is permissible, however, to ask the living for whatever they can possibly do, such as saving us from drowning or asking them to pray to Allah for us.

> Asking the living for whatever they can possibly do for us is one of the forms of human relationships and one of the permissible daily dealings.

```
Are we allowed to ask for anything from a dead person or an inanimate being?
```

Yes →

This is a blatant act of *shirk* which contradicts Islam and faith (*eemaan*), for the dead and inanimate beings are not able to hear the prayer; even if they could hear it, they would not be able to respond to it. In fact, invocation is an act of worship, and thus directing it to other than Allah is an act of *shirk*. The Arab polytheists before the advent of Islam used to invoke the dead and inanimate beings.

No →

We can only ask the living who can hear our request. Are they, however, able to grant your request regarding matters which they can possibly do?

Yes →

This is permissible and is one of the forms of human relationships and one of people's daily dealings.

No →

Asking the living for something that they cannot possibly do is a major *shirk* which contradicts Islam, for it amounts to invoking other than Allah. A sterile person asking a person to grant him righteous children, for instance, is a case in point.

> Belief in Allah's Names and Attributes

This involves belief in the names and attributes which Allah has affirmed for Himself or which His Messenger ﷺ has affirmed for Him in a manner that suits His majesty.

Allah ﷻ has the most beautiful names and perfect attributes. All His names and attributes are unique, as the Qur'an states, "Nothing is like Him, and He is the All-Hearing, the All-Seeing." (*Soorat Ash-Shooraa,* 42:11) Therefore, none of whatever He has created has similar names or attributes in any way.

Some of Allah's Most Beautiful Names

"The Beneficent, the Merciful." (*Soorat Al-Faatihah,* 1:3)

"He is the All-Hearing, the All-Seeing." (*Soorat Ash-Shooraa,* 42:11)

"He is the Mighty, the Wise." (*Soorat Luqmaan,* 31:9)

"Allah, there is no god but Him, the Living, the Self-Sustaining." (*Soorat Al-Baqarah,* 2:255)

"All praise is due to Allah, Lord of all the worlds." (*Soorat Al-Faatihah,* 1:2)

Benefits of Belief in Allah's Names and Attributes

1. Getting to know Allah ﷻ better, for belief in Allah's names and attributes increases one's knowledge of Allah, which in turn increases one's faith in Him. Those who know and understand Allah's names and attributes are bound to have their hearts filled with awe of Him and love for Him and tend to submit to Him alone.

2. Praising Allah by using His most beautiful names, which is the best form of remembrance of Allah *(dhikr)*, as the Qur'an states, "O you who believe, remember Allah much." (*Soorat Al-Ahzaab*, 33:41)

3. Asking and invoking Allah by His names and attributes, as the Qur'an states, "To Allah belong the Most Beautiful Names, so call on Him by them." (*Soorat Al-A'raaf*, 7:180) An example of this is to say, *Yaa Tawwaab, tub 'alayya! Yaa Raheem, Irhamnee!* "O Most Forgiving, forgive me! O Most Merciful, have mercy on me!"

The Highest Level of *Eemaan* (Faith)

Faith, or *eemaan*, comprises different levels. The more a Muslim neglects his duty towards Allah and disobeys Him, the more his faith decreases. Conversely, the more he obeys Allah, worships Him and fears Him, the more his faith increases.

The highest level of faith is what Islam terms *ihsaan* (literally perfection, charity, performance of good deeds, etc.), which the Prophet ﷺ defined as follows: "It is to worship Allah as though you are seeing Him and while you see Him not, yet truly He sees you." (*Saheeh Al-Bukhaaree:* 50; *Saheeh Muslim:* 8)

Therefore, you must remember that Allah is watching you all the time, whether you are standing or sitting, being serious or joking, and thus you must not disobey Him while you know that He is always watching you. Do not let fear and despair get the better of you while you know that Allah is with you. You will by no means experience loneliness when you privately pray to Allah and invoke Him. How can you commit a sin while you firmly believe that Allah is fully aware of what you do secretly and publicly? If, however, you commit a sin, repent to Allah and seek His forgiveness, He will certainly forgive you and accept your repentance.

Some Benefits of Belief in Allah

1. Allah safeguards the believers against harm and adversity and protects them against their enemies' plots, as the Qur'an states, "Surely, Allah defends those who are true believers." (*Soorat Al-Hajj*, 22:38)

2. Belief in Allah brings happiness and is the source of a good life, as the Qur'an states, "To whoever does good deeds, man or woman, and is a believer, We will surely give a good life." (*Soorat An-Nahl*, 16:97)

3. Belief in Allah frees the human mind from superstitions. Those who believe in Allah completely rely on Him and are wholly devoted to Him, being the Lord of all the worlds and the only true God without any partners. As a result, they do not fear anyone and show their devotion to none but Allah. This frees them from all superstitions and misconceptions.

4. The best benefit of belief in Allah is attainment of Allah's good pleasure, admission into Paradise and enjoyment of everlasting bliss and Allah's boundless mercy.

Belief in the Angels

The Meaning of Belief in Allah's Angels

This means firm belief that they exist, that they belong to the unseen world, not our world, and that they are honoured and pious servants who worship Allah as He deserves to be worshipped, execute His commands and never disobey Him.

The Qur'an says about them, "They are honoured servants. They do not precede Him in speech and they act on His command." (*Soorat Al-Anbiyyaa'*, 21:26-7)

Belief in them is one of the six pillars of *eemaan* (faith), as the Qur'an states, "The Messenger believes in that which has been revealed to him from his Lord and so do the believers. Each one believes in Allah and His angels and His books and His messengers." (*Soorat Al-Baqarah*, 2:285)

When the Prophet ﷺ was asked about faith, he said, "It is to believe in Allah, His angels, His books, His messengers, the Last Day and to believe in the divine decree, the good and the bad of it." (*Saheeh Muslim:* 8)

What Does Belief in the Angels Include?

1. Belief in their existence: We believe that Allah made them from light and created them with a natural predisposition to worship and obey Him.

2. Belief in those angels whose names have been mentioned to us, such as Jibreel (Gabriel) ﷺ. We also generally believe in all those whose names have not been mentioned to us.

3. Belief in their attributes that have been mentioned to us. These include the following:

- They belong to the unseen world whom Almighty Allah created solely for His worship. They have no divine attributes whatsoever and are naturally disposed to show complete obedience to Allah, as the Qur'an states, "They do not disobey Allah in respect of any order He gives them and carry out what they are ordered to do." (*Soorat At-Tahreem*, 66:6)

- Allah created them from light, as evidenced by the *hadeeth*, "The angels were created from light." (*Saheeh Muslim:* 2996)

- They have wings, as the Qur'an states, "All praise is due to Allah, the Originator of the heavens and the earth, who made the angels messengers with two, three or four pairs of wings. He increases in creation what He pleases; surely, Allah has power over all things." (*Soorat Faatir*, 35:1)

4. Belief in the duties which have been mentioned to us and which they carry out with Allah's command. These include:

- The angel charged with the task of conveying Allah's revelation to His messengers, namely, Jibreel (Gabriel) ﷺ.

- The angel charged with the task of taking away the souls of those destined to die, namely the Angel of Death and his assistants.

- The angels charged with the task of recording all the good and bad deeds people do, known as the Noble Scribes (*al-kiraam al-kaatiboon*)

Benefits of Belief in the Angels

Belief in the angels has numerous benefits in the believer's life. These include the following:

1. **Being aware of Allah's absolute strength and power:** The magnificent and great creation of the angels clearly testify to the greatness of their Creator. The fact that Allah ﷻ created the mighty angels from light and with wings makes us appreciate His attributes with the importance and appreciation that He deserves and revere Him even more.

2. **Observing righteousness:** The firm belief that some angels record all our deeds prompts us to fear Allah ﷻ and to try not to disobey Him, whether we are alone or with others.

3. **Observing patience while carrying out our duties towards Allah**: When we become aware of the infinite number of angels in this vast universe who obey Allah and constantly worship Him, along with us, as He should be worshipped, we become prompted to endure all the adversities in carrying out our duties towards Allah. We also experience a great feeling of joy and reassurance.

4. **Showing gratitude to Allah:** The fact that Almighty Allah has created some angels whose task is to guard people against harm prompts us to thank Him for His divine care.

> The Prophet ﷺ informs us in a *hadeeth* that there is no space in the seven heavens a foot length or a hand-span or a palm's width which does not have an angel standing, bowing or prostrating.

> Belief in the Divine Books

The Meaning of Belief in the Divine Books

This means firm belief that Almighty Allah has sent down some divine books to some of His messengers, and that they contain the speech of Allah which must be thought of in a manner that suits His majesty. These books also contain the truth, light and guidance for people in both this world and in the hereafter.

Belief in the divine books is one of the six pillars of faith, as the Qur'an states, "O you who believe, believe in Allah and His Messenger and the Book which He has revealed to His Messenger and the Books which He revealed before." (*Soorat An-Nisaa'*, 4:136)

In this verse, Almighty Allah commands the believers to believe in Him and His Messenger and the book which He revealed to His Messenger ﷺ, namely, the Qur'an. He also commands them to believe in all the books He revealed before the Qur'an.

Defining faith *(eemaan)*, the Prophet ﷺ once said, "It is to believe in Allah, His angels, His books, His messengers, and the Last Day and to believe in the divine decree, both good and bad." (*Saheeh Muslim:* 8)

> The Holy Qur'an is written with great skill and precision, based on strict calligraphy rules.

What Does Belief in the Divine Books Include?

1. To believe that they were truly revealed by Allah.

2. To believe that they contain the speech of Allah ﷻ.

3. To believe in the divine books which Almighty Allah has named, such as the Qur'an, which He revealed to our Prophet Muhammad ﷺ, the Torah (*At-Tawraah*) which He revealed to Moses (Moosaa) ﷺ and the Gospel (*Al-Injeel*) which He revealed to Jesus ('Eesaa) ﷺ.

4. To believe the authentic stories mentioned in them.

The Unique and Distinctive Characteristics of the Qur'an

The Holy Qur'an is the Speech of Allah, which He revealed to our Prophet Muḥammad ﷺ. Therefore, we ought to venerate it, read it, ponder its verses and strive hard to abide by its instructions.

Suffice it to say that the Qur'an is our guide in this life and will be the cause of our salvation in the hereafter.

The Holy Qur'an has numerous unique features which distinguish it from the other revealed books. These include the following:

1. The Glorious Qur'an provides a summary of divine rulings. It also came to support and confirm the command to worship Allah alone contained in the previous divine books.

   The Qur'an says, "And We have revealed to you the Book with the truth, confirming the books before it and with final authority over them." (*Soorat Al-Maa'idah*, 5:48)

   This verse makes it clear that the Qur'an agrees with and confirms the truth, statements and beliefs, amongst other things, contained in the previous divine books and serves as a witness over them.

2. All people, regardless of their language or race, must adhere to the Qur'an and act according to its dictates, no matter how far removed they may be from the time the Qur'an was revealed, as opposed to the previous scriptures which were revealed for particular peoples at specific times. The Qur'an says, "This Qur'an has been revealed to me so that I may warn you by it, and anyone else it reaches." (*Soorat Al-An'aam*, 6:19)

3. While many additions and deletions have crept into the other divine books, the Qur'an has remained intact because Allah the Almighty has taken it upon Himself to protect it, as the Qur'an says, "We have sent down the Reminder, and We will surely guard it [from corruption]." (*Soorat al-Ḥijr*, 15:9)

What Is Our Duty Towards the Qur'an?

- We must love and venerate the Qur'an. We must also value its importance because it is the speech of Almighty Allah , which is unquestionably the best and most truthful speech.
- We must read it, recite it and ponder its verses. We must also reflect on its spiritual guidance, statements and stories and take it as a criterion in our lives whereby we distinguish between truth and falsehood.
- We must act on its dictates, obey its commands and make them our way of life.

When 'Aa'ishah , one of the Prophet's wives, was asked about the character of the Prophet , she replied, "His character was the Qur'an." (*Musnad A<u>h</u>mad:24601*; *Sa<u>h</u>eeh Muslim:* 746)

In other words, the Prophet was the practical embodiment of the Qur'anic injunctions in all his actions and worldly life. Indeed, he followed the guidance of the Qur'an in its entirety and provided an excellent example for us to follow, as the Qur'an states, "You have an excellent model in the Messenger of Allah, for all who hope for Allah and the Last Day and remember Allah much." (*Soorat Al-A<u>h</u>zaab,* 33:21)

What Is Our Stance regarding the Contents of the Previously Revealed Books?

A Muslim believes that the Torah, which was revealed to Moses ﷺ, and the Gospel, which was revealed to Jesus ﷺ, were the truth from Allah ﷻ. He also believes that they comprised rulings, guidance and lessons and news which had guidance and light for people in their worldly life and the life to come.

However, Almighty Allah informs us in the Holy Qur'an that the People of the Book, that is the Jews and the Christians, had distorted their divine books through alteration, omission or addition to the original text, and are thus not as authentic as Allah first revealed them.

The Torah, that is available today, is not the same Torah revealed to Moses ﷺ, because the Jews corrupted the original text by altering it and changing numerous rulings in it, as the Qur'an states, "Some of the Jews distort the true meaning of words." (*Soorat An-Nisaa'*, 4:46)

Similarly, the Gospel available to us today is not the same Gospel revealed to Jesus ﷺ, for the Christians distorted it and altered a large number of its rulings. Concerning this, the Qur'an says: "Among them is a group who distort the Book with their tongues so that you think it is from the Book when it is not from the Book. They say, 'It is from Allah,' but it is not from Allah. They tell a lie against Allah and they know it." (*Soorat Aal 'Imraan*, 3:78)

"We also made a covenant with those who say, 'We are Christians,' and they too forgot a good portion of what they were reminded of. So We stirred up enmity and hatred between them until the Day of Rising when Allah will inform them about what they did." (*Soorat Al-Maa'idah*, 5:14)

> A Muslim believes that the Torah and the Gospel were revealed by Allah ﷻ but that many additions and deletions have crept into them. Therefore, he believes only those statements in them which agree with what is mentioned in the Qur'an and the Prophet's traditions.

The Holy Bible available to the People of the Book today, which consists of the Old Testament and the New Testament, has numerous wrong beliefs, misleading misconceptions and false statements and stories. We believe those statements and reports which are shown by the Qur'an or the sound *Sunnah* to be true, and we disbelieve those ones which are shown by the Qur'an and *Sunnah* to be false. As for the rest of the statements and reports, we must neither believe nor disbelieve them, because they are not proven in the Qur'an or *Sunnah* to be either true or false.

Despite all this, a Muslim ought to respect these books and must not demean or desecrate them, for they may still contain some of Allah's speech which has not been distorted.

Benefits of Belief in the Divine Books

Belief in the divine books has a number of benefits, including the following:

1. Awareness of Allah's great care and immense mercy for His slaves for sending for every people a divine book to guide them, help them achieve happiness in this life and enjoy eternal bliss in the hereafter.

2. Awareness of Allah's absolute wisdom contained in His laws, for legislating for every people what perfectly suits their general circumstances and personalities, as the Qur'an states, "For each [community to which a Messenger was sent with a Book] have We appointed a law and a practice." (*Soorat Al-Maa'idah*, 5:48)

3. Showing gratefulness to Allah for sending down such books which contain light and guidance for us in this life and in the hereafter. Indeed, this is a great blessing for which we ought to offer thanks to Allah.

> Belief in the Messengers

People's Need for a Divine Message

People need a divine message to show them Allah's laws and guide them to the right path. Indeed, a divine message is the spirit, light and the very life of the world, without which the world would certainly be lifeless and man would be plunged into the darkness of ignorance and misguidance.

It is for this reason that Almighty Allah calls His message a spirit, for there is no life without a spirit, as the Qur'an says, "We have thus revealed a Spirit to you by Our command. You knew neither the Scripture nor the faith, but We made it a light, guiding with it whomever We will of Our servants. You are indeed guiding to the straight path." (*Soorat Ash-Shooraa,* 42:52)

Even though the intellect can generally distinguish between right and wrong, it cannot possibly comprehend the details of such a distinction, nor carry out acts of worship in the right manner without the dictates of revelation and the divine message.

Therefore, success and happiness can only be attained by following the guidance of Allah's messengers. Similarly, no accurate line of demarcation can be drawn between right and wrong without following in their footsteps. Thus, whoever rejects the divine message will definitely lead a miserable and wretched life depending on the extent of their rejection of it.

It Is One of the Pillars of Faith

Belief in Allah's messengers is one of the six pillars of *eemaan* (faith), as the Qur'an states, "The Messenger believes in that which has been revealed to him from his Lord and so do the believers. Each one believes in Allah and His angels and His books and His messengers." (*Soorat Al-Baqarah*, 2:285)

This verse makes it abundantly clear that we must believe in all of Allah's messengers without making a distinction between any of them. We must not, therefore, believe in some of them and reject some others, as did the Jews and the Christians.

Defining *eemaan* (faith), the Prophet ﷺ also said in this connection, "It is to believe in Allah, His angels, His books, His messengers and the Last Day, and to believe in the divine decree, both good and bad." (*Saheeh Muslim:* 8)

The Meaning of Belief in the Messengers

This means firm belief that Allah ﷻ sent a messenger to every nation and community, calling its members to worship Allah alone without any partners, that all Allah's messengers were truthful, virtuous, trustworthy and rightly-guided servants who strove hard to guide their people to the right path and conveyed Allah's message to them in full, without concealing, omitting or adding anything to it. The Qur'an says, "Therefore, the messengers' obligation is no more than to convey the message clearly." (*Soorat An-Nahl*, 16:35)

What Does Belief in the Messengers Include?

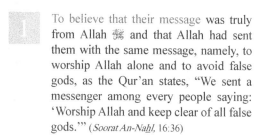

To believe that their message was truly from Allah ﷻ and that Allah had sent them with the same message, namely, to worship Allah alone and to avoid false gods, as the Qur'an states, "We sent a messenger among every people saying: 'Worship Allah and keep clear of all false gods.'" (*Soorat An-Nahl*, 16:36)

Laws may vary as to the do's and don'ts of the message with which prophets were sent to their people, depending on what laws suited their people best, as the Qur'an states, "For each [community to which a Messenger was sent with a Book] have We appointed a law and a practice." (*Soorat Al-Maa'idah*, 5:48)

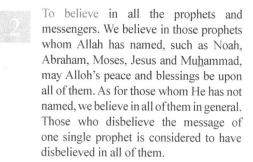

To believe in all the prophets and messengers. We believe in those prophets whom Allah has named, such as Noah, Abraham, Moses, Jesus and Muhammad, may Alloh's peace and blessings be upon all of them. As for those whom He has not named, we believe in all of them in general. Those who disbelieve the message of one single prophet is considered to have disbelieved in all of them.

To believe the authentic reports and accounts of the prophets and their miracles mentioned in the Qur'an and in the Prophet's traditions, such as the story of Allah's parting the Red Sea for Moses ﷺ.

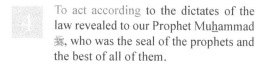

To act according to the dictates of the law revealed to our Prophet Muhammad ﷺ, who was the seal of the prophets and the best of all of them.

Some Characteristics of the Messengers

1. They are human, and the only difference between us and them is that Allah had chosen them to receive His revelation and convey His divine message, as the Qur'an says, "We have only ever sent before you men to whom We revealed the message." (*Soorat Al-Anbiyyaa'*, 21:7)

   Therefore, they have no divine attributes whatsoever. They are mere human beings who attained perfect physical appearance and enjoyed impeccable moral traits. They are also the most honourable of people in lineage and enjoyed sound judgement and clear, persuasive speech, which entitled them to assume the responsibility of conveying the divine message and bear the burden of prophethood.

   Almighty Allah has only chosen messengers from among people so that they can set a good example for them, and so that people can follow in their footsteps, which they can possibly do.

2. Allah has chosen them from among people so they can convey the divine message to people, as the Qur'an states, "Say: 'I am only a human being like you who has received revelation. Your god is One God. So let him who hopes to meet his Lord act rightly and not associate anyone in the worship of his Lord.'" (*Soorat Al-Kahf*, 18:110)

   It is clear, therefore, that prophethood cannot be attained as a result of spiritual purity, intelligence or mental logic, for the task of prophethood can only be determined by divine will, and Allah knows best whom to appoint as His messengers, as the Qur'an states, "Allah knows best upon whom to bestow His message." (*Soorat Al-An'aam*, 6:124)

3. They are infallible in the sense that they do not make mistakes when conveying Allah's message to the people and executing what Allah has revealed to them.

4. Truthfulness: They are truthful in their words and deeds, as the Qur'an states, "This is what the Most Merciful promised, and the messengers told the truth." (*Soorat Yaa Seen*, 36:52)

5. Patience and Perseverance: They called to Allah's religion, bringing good news and giving warning, and were subjected to various forms of harm and hardships, but they patiently bore all that for the sake of making the word of Allah reign supreme, as the Qur'an states, "So be steadfast as the Messengers with firm resolve were also steadfast." (*Soorat Al-Ahqaaf*, 46:35)

The Messengers' Signs and Miracles

Allah ﷻ supported His messengers with a number of signs and miracles to prove their truthfulness and prophethood.

A miracle, or *mu'jizah,* is an extraordinary event in the physical world that surpasses all known human or natural powers. It is performed by prophets, by Allah's command, for its credential value, to accredit them as Allah's true messengers.

Examples of miracles include:

- Moses's rod turning into a snake
- Jesus's informing his people of what they ate and stored in their houses
- The splitting of the moon for Prophet Muḥammad ﷺ

A Muslim's Beliefs regarding Jesus ﷺ

1. He was one of the greatest of Allah's messengers and one of those held in high esteem. Indeed, he is one of the messengers Allah describes in the Qur'an as having 'firm resolve', namely, Muḥammad Noah, Abraham, Moses, Jesus, may Allah's peace and blessings be upon all of them. About these prophets, the Qur'an states, "We made a covenant with all the Prophets – with you and with Noah and Abraham and Moses and Jesus son of Mary – We made a binding covenant with them." (*Soorat Al-Aḥzaab,* 33:7)

2. He was a mere human being with no divine attributes whatsoever, whom Almighty Allah sent to guide the Children of Israel and supported with a number of miracles, as the Qur'an states, "He is only a slave on whom We bestowed Our blessing and whom We made an example for the tribe of Israel." (*Soorat Az-Zukhruf,* 43:59) He never ordered his people to take him and his mother, Mary, as gods besides Allah; he only told them to do as Allah commanded him to tell them: "Worship Allah, my Lord and your Lord." (*Soorat Al-Maa'idah,* 5:117)

3. He was the son of Mary, a chaste, pious and truthful virgin who entirely devoted herself to the worship of Allah. She gave birth to Jesus after miraculously conceiving him without a human father, his likeness in this being as that of Adam, as the Qur'an states, "The likeness of Jesus in Allah's sight is the same as Adam. He created him from earth and then He said to him, 'Be!' and he was." (*Soorat Aal-'Imraan,* 3:59)

4. There was no prophet between him and Muḥammad ﷺ. In fact, Jesus ﷺ gave the good news of the advent of Prophet Muḥammad ﷺ, as the Qur'an states, "And when Jesus son of Mary said, 'O Children of Israel, I am the Messenger of Allah to you, confirming the Torah which came before me and giving you the good news of a Messenger to come after me whose name is Aḥmad.' When he brought them the Clear Signs, they said, 'This is downright magic.'" (*Soorat Aṣ-Ṣaff,* 61:6)

5. We believe in the miracles he performed by Allah's permission, such as his ability to heal the lepers, bringing dead people back to life and informing his people of what they ate and stored in their houses, all by Allah's permission. Allah gave him the ability to perform such miracles to prove he was a true prophet who came with a divine message from his Lord.

6. A person will not be considered a true believer unless he believes that Jesus ﷺ was Allah's servant and messenger and strongly rejects the false statements Jews make about him and which Allah dismisses as untrue. We must also strongly reject the Christian beliefs about Jesus, who have gone far astray for taking him and his mother as gods besides Allah, claiming that he was the son of God or adopting the doctrine of the Trinity, referring to Allah as "the third of three". Glorified is He and High Exalted above what they say!

7. He was neither killed, nor crucified; instead, he was raised up by Allah to heaven. In fact, Allah gave someone else Jesus' appearance, causing everyone to believe that Jesus was crucified. The Qur'an says about this, "And their saying, 'We killed the Messiah, Jesus, son of Mary, the Messenger of Allah.' They did not kill him and they did not crucify him but it was made to seem so to them. Those who argue about him are in doubt about it. They have no real knowledge of it, just conjecture. They did not really kill him. Allah raised him up to Himself. Allah is Almighty, All-Wise. There is not one of the People of the Book who will not believe in him before he dies; and on the Day of Rising he will be a witness against them." (*Soorat An-Nisaa'*, 4:157-59)

In this way, Allah ﷻ protected him and raised Him to heaven. He will eventually return to earth towards the end of the world, rule by Muḥammad's law; then he will die and be buried, and will eventually be resurrected, like all human beings, as the Qur'an states, "From it We created you, to it We will return you, and from it We will bring you forth a second time." (*Soorat Taa Haa*, 20:55)

> Muslims believe that Jesus ﷺ was one of the greatest of Allah's messengers, that he had no divine attributes whatsoever and that he was neither killed, nor crucified.

Belief in Muhammad ﷺ as a Prophet and Messenger

- We believe that Muhammad ﷺ was Allah's servant and messenger, that he is the best of all mankind without exception, the seal of the prophets and so there will be no prophet after him. He fully delivered the divine message assigned to him, discharged his prophetic duties, sincerely counselled the Muslim community, and strove hard for the cause of Allah to the best of his ability.

- We believe what he said, obey his commands and avoid the acts he prohibited and warned us against. We must worship Allah according to his guidance (*Sunnah*) and take none but him as our example. The Qur'an says, "You have an excellent model in the Messenger of Allah, for all who hope for Allah and the Last Day and remember Allah much." (*Soorat Al-Ahzaab*, 33:21)

- We must show more love for the Prophet ﷺ than for our own parents, children and indeed all humankind. "None of you will be a true believer," the Prophet ﷺ once observed, "until he loves me more than his parents, his children and all mankind." (*Saheeh Al-Bukhaaree*: 15 and *Saheeh Muslim*: 44). However, true love for the Prophet ﷺ can only be realised by following his *Sunnah*. Indeed, true happiness and complete guidance cannot be attained without obeying him, as the Qur'an states, "If you obey him, you will be guided.' The Messenger is only responsible for delivering the message clearly." (*Soorat An-Noor*, 24:54)

- We must accept everything he has brought to us from Almighty Allah, adhere to his *Sunnah*, holding his guidance in high esteem, as the Qur'an states, "By your Lord, they will not be true believers until they seek your arbitration in their disputes and find within themselves no doubt about what you decide and accept it wholeheartedly." (*Soorat An-Nisaa'*, 4:65)

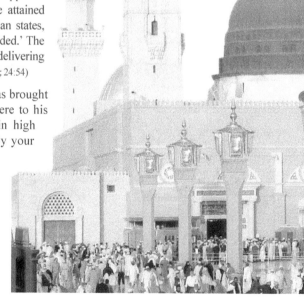

- We must avoid disobeying his orders, for doing so is bound to lead to trials, misguidance and a severe punishment in the hereafter, as the Qur'an states, "Those who oppose his command should beware of a testing trial coming to them or a painful punishment striking them." (*Soorat An-Noor*, 24:63)

Characteristics of Prophet Muhammad's Message

Prophet Muhammad's message has a number of characteristics which distinguish it from the previous divine messages. These include:

- It was the final divine message, as the Qur'an states, "Muhammad is not the father of any of your men, but the Messenger of Allah and the Final Seal of the Prophets." (*Soorat Al-Ahzaab*, 33:40)

- It abrogated all previous messages and laws, and thus no religion will be acceptable to Allah after Muhammad's mission except Islam. This can only be done by following Prophet Muhammad's guidance. Similarly, no one will be admitted into Paradise without following in his footsteps, for he is the most honourable of all Allah's messengers, his community (*ummah*) is the best community that has ever been brought forth for the good of mankind and his law is the most comprehensive of all divine laws. The Qur'an says, "If anyone desires anything other than Islam as a religion, it will not be accepted from him, and in the next world he will be among the losers." (*Soorat Aal-'Imraan*, 3:85) The Prophet ﷺ also said, «By Him in whose hand is the soul of Muhammad, any person of this Community, Jew or Christian, who hears of me and dies without believing in what I have been sent with will be among the inhabitants of Hell." (*Saheeh Muslim:* 153; *Musnad Ahmad:* 8609)

- It is addressed to both the jinn and mankind. Recounting the statements of some of the jinn who embraced Islam, the Qur'an states, "Our people, respond to Allah's caller and believe in Him." (*Soorat Al-Ahqaaf,* 46:31) Addressing Muhammad ﷺ, the Qur'an also says, "We only sent you for the whole of mankind, bringing good news and giving warning." (*Soorat Saba',* 34:28) In this connection, the Prophet ﷺ said, "I have been favoured over the other prophets in six ways: I have been given the gift of concise yet comprehensive speech; I have been supported with fear [which Allah cats into my enemies' hearts]; war booty has been made permissible for me; the entire earth has been made a means of purification and a place of worship for me; I have been sent to all of mankind; and the line of Prophets ends with me." (*Saheeh Al-Bukhaaree:* 2815; *Saheeh Muslim:* 523)

Benefits of Belief in Allah's Messengers

Belief in Allah's messengers has a number of benefits, including the following:

1. Awareness of Allah's care for His slaves for sending messengers to them to guide them to the right path and show them how to worship Allah. Indeed, the human mind cannot possibly do this. Addressing Prophet Muhammad ﷺ, Allah ﷻ says, "We have only sent you as a mercy to all the worlds." (*Soorat Al-Anbiyaa', 21:107*)

2. Showing gratefulness to Allah for this great blessing.

3. Showing love for Allah's messengers, holding them in high esteem and adequately praising them for delivering Allah's message to their people and giving them good counsel.

4. Following the guidance contained in the message which the messengers have brought from Allah, namely, to worship Allah alone without associating any partners with Him in worship and adhering to the dictates of this message. This will bring about happiness for the believers in both this life and in the life to come.

The Qur'an says, "Those who follow My guidance will not go astray and will not be wretched. But whoever turns away from My reminder, he will lead a miserable life." (*Soorat Taa Haa, 20:123-24*)

> Al-Aqsa Mosque, located in the old city of Jerusalem, is regarded by Muslims with great respect. It is the second mosque built upon the earth after the Sacred Mosque in Makkah. Indeed, Prophet Muhammad ﷺ, as well as all the other prophets, prayed in it.

> Belief in the Last Day

Meaning of Belief in the Last Day

Firm belief that Almighty Allah will raise people to life from their graves; He will then judge them according to their deeds. Those who deserve to go to Paradise will be sent to it, while those who deserve to go to Hellfire will be sent to it.

Belief in the last Day is one of the articles of faith, and faith will not be valid unless one believes in the Last Day, as the Qur'an states, "Truly pious are those who believe in Allah and the Last Day." (*Soorat Al-Baqarah*, 2:177)

Why Does the Qur'an Emphasise Belief in the Last Day?

The Qur'an emphasises belief in the last Day and draws attention to it on numerous occasions, employing different modes of expression in Arabic and linking belief in the Last Day with belief in Allah.

The reason for this is that belief in the Last Day is a necessary outcome of belief in Almighty Allah and His absolute justice. To illustrate:

Allah does not approve of injustice; He will not let the wrongdoers go unpunished, nor will He let the wronged down by not having them obtaining redress for the wrong done to them, nor will He disappoint the virtuous by not rewarding them for their righteousness. Many are those who spent all their lives oppressing others with impunity until they died; many are those who suffered a great deal of injustice and died without ever obtaining redress for the wrong done to them. This means there has to be another life, other than the present life, where the righteous will be rewarded and the evildoers will be punished, everyone getting the reward or punishment they deserve.

> Islam teaches us to save ourselves from Hellfire by showing kindness to others even by giving half of a date-fruit in charity.

What Does Belief in the Last Day Include?

Belief in the Last Day includes a number of things, some of which are as follow:

1. **Belief in the Ultimate Resurrection and Gathering:** This means that Almighty Allah will raise people to life from their graves, and each soul will return to its respective body. People will then stand before the Lord of all the worlds for judgement. They will be gathered on a huge level plain, naked and barefooted just as Allah first created them.

Indeed, belief in the resurrection of the dead is confirmed by textual evidence from the Qur'an and the *Sunnah* and has been proven rationally as well as through the inner nature (*fitrah*). We therefore firmly believe that Allah will raise the dead from their graves, their souls will return to their respective bodies and all people will stand before the Lord of the worlds for judgement.

The Qur'an says, "Then subsequently you will certainly die. Then on the Day of Rising you will be raised again." (*Soorat Al-Mu'minoon*, 23:15-16)

All divine books have confirmed this fact, stating that part of Allah's wisdom behind creating people is to set an ultimate day on which He will judge them for obeying or rejecting His commands which he sent down to them through His messengers, as the Qur'an states, "Did you suppose that We created you for amusement and that you would not return to Us?'" (*Soorat Al-Mu'minoon*, 23:115)

Some Textual Evidence from the Qur'an Regarding Resurrection

- It was Allah who created mankind the first time, and He is able to bring them back to life, as the Qur'an states, "And it is He who originates creation, then brings it back again, and it is easier for Him." (*Soorat Ar-Room*, 30:27) Refuting the false claim that it is impossible for bones to be restored to life when they are decayed, Almighty Allah says, "Say, 'He who made them in the first place will bring them back to life.'" (*Soorat Yaa Seen*, 36:79)

- When the earth is barren and lifeless, Allah pours rain down upon it, and it stirs and swells and brings forth every kind of lovely plant. The One who can bring it to life is certainly able to bring the dead back to life, as the Qur'an states, "And We sent down blessed water from the sky and made gardens grow by it and grain for harvesting, and tall palm-trees with their

thickly-clustered dates, as provision for Our slaves; by it We brought a dead land to life. Thus will be the resurrection." (*Soorat Qaaf,* 50:9-11)

* Every sensible person admits that if someone can do something hard, then he can, with all the more reason, do something easier than that. Therefore, if Almighty Allah was able to create the wonderful heavens, the vast earth and all the mighty stars, then He can, with all the more reason, easily bring bones that have decayed, back to life, as the Qur'an states, "Does He who created the heavens and earth not have the power to create [from rotten bones] the like of them again? Yes indeed! He is the Creator, the All-Knowing." (*Soorat Yaa Seen,* 36:81)

2. Belief in the Judgement and the Balance of Deeds: Almighty Allah will judge people according to their deeds which they did in the life of the world. Those who worship Allah alone and obey Him and His Messenger Muhammad ﷺ will receive an easy reckoning. As for those who commit the unforgivable sin of *shirk* and disobey Him, they will receive a severe reckoning.

People's deeds will be weighed in a huge balance. The good deeds will be placed on one weighing pan, while the bad deeds will be placed on the pan at the other end of the Balance. Those whose good deeds outweigh their bad deeds will be admitted into Paradise, while those whose bad deeds outweigh their good deeds will be sent to Hellfire, and Allah does not wrong anyone.

Allah ﷻ say, "We will set up the Just Balance on the Day of Rising and no one will be wronged in any way. Even if it is no more than the weight of a grain of mustard-seed, We will produce it. We are sufficient as a Reckoner." (*Soorat Al-Anbiyyaa',* 21:47)

3. Paradise and Hellfire: Paradise is the abode of eternal bliss which Allah ﷻ has prepared for the pious people who have obeyed Allah and His Messenger ﷺ. In it they will find all that their hearts desire and their eyes find delight in.

Awakening His servants' desire to vie with one another in obeying Him so that they will be admitted into Paradise, Almighty Allah says, "Race each other to forgiveness from your Lord and a Garden as wide as the heavens and the earth, prepared for the righteous." (*Soorat Aal-'Imraan,* 3:133)

As for Hellfire, it is the abode of eternal punishment which Allah has prepared for the unbelievers who have rejected Allah and disobeyed His messengers. In it they will find all kinds of unimaginable terrifying punishments and suffering.

Warning His servants against the Hellfire, Almighty Allah says, "Fear the Fire whose fuel is people and stones, made ready for the unbelievers." (*Soorat Al-Baqarah,* 2:24)

We ask You, O Allah, to admit us into Paradise and to assist us in saying words and doing deeds that are bound to bring us closer to it, and we seek refuge with You from the Hellfire and from words and deeds that are bound to bring us closer to it.

4. Punishment and Bliss in the Grave: We believe that death is a fact, as the Qur'an states, "Say: 'The Angel of Death, who has been given charge of you, will take you back and then you will be sent back to your Lord.'" (*Soorat As-Sajdah,* 32:11)

In fact, no one can deny death; we believe that when someone dies or is killed by any means whatsoever, it is because his appointed time has come, which he can neither delay nor bring forward, as the Qur'an states, "When the end of the term falls, they can neither delay it by a single moment, nor can they hasten it." (*Soorat Al-A'raaf,* 7:34)

- We also believe that whoever dies has actually moved to life hereafter.

- There are numerous authentic traditions attributed to Prophet Muḥammad ﷺ in which he mentions punishment in the grave for the unbelievers and the wicked people and bliss for the believers and upright people. We believe in all this, but we abstain from trying to find out how this may happen, for the human mind cannot possibly comprehend its manner or reality, being part of the unseen world, such as Hellfire and Paradise, and not part of the material, visible world. The human mind can only carry out analogical reasoning and deductive arguments and reach judgements in matters which have the same relationship and whose laws are known in the visible world.

- Life in the grave is part of the unseen world which cannot be perceived by the senses. Were this possible, belief in the unseen would be of no benefit whatsoever, there would be no wisdom behind observance of religious duties and people would not find it necessary to bury the dead. As the Prophet ﷺ once observed, "Were it not that you would not bury one another, I would pray to Allah to make you hear the punishment in the grave which I can hear." (*Saḥeeḥ Muslim:* 2868; *Sunan An-Nasaa'ee:* 2058). It is because animals are exempt from religious duties that they can hear the voices of those punished in their graves.

Benefits of Belief in the Last Day

1. Belief in the Last Day prompts people to lead a pious life, do righteous deeds, fear Allah ﷻ and stay away from selfishness and arrogance.

   It is for this reason that the Qur'an frequently links belief in the Last Day with righteous deeds. The following verses are examples showing this: "The mosques of Allah should only be frequented by those who believe in Allah and the Last Day." (*Soorat At-Tawbah*, 9:18)

   "Those who believe in the hereafter do believe in it, and they are ever-mindful of their prayers." (*Soorat Al-Ana'am*, 6:92)

2. It reminds those who are totally absorbed in the life of the world and its transitory pleasures of the importance of vying with one another to obey Allah, urging them to do as many good deeds as long as they are alive and showing them that the worldly life is fleeting and that the hereafter is the everlasting abode.

   After praising His messengers in the Qur'an and mentioning their righteous deeds, Allah ﷻ mentions the reason that prompted them to do such virtuous acts: "We purified their sincerity through sincere remembrance of the Abode." (*Soorat Saad*, 38:46)

   This means that their constant remembrance of the hereafter was the reason behind their performance of such acts.

   When some of the Muslims became too sluggish to obey Allah and His Messenger ﷺ on one occasion, Allah ﷻ revealed the following verse, "Do you prefer the life of this world to the hereafter? But little is the comfort of this life, compared to that of the hereafter." (*Soorat At-Tawbah*, 9:38)

   Belief in the hereafter makes a person realise that all worldly comforts cannot be possibly compared to the eternal bliss in Paradise, nor is it worth one single dip in Hellfire; conversely, it makes one realise that all worldly discomforts and hardships for the sake of Allah cannot be possibly compared to punishment, in Hellfire, nor will it be compared to even one dip in Paradise.

3. It makes a person satisfied with his lot in life. He does not feel sad or lose heart if he misses a worldly opportunity. Rather, he does what he can possibly do, knowing for certain that Allah will not let the reward of anyone who does a good deed go to waste. If anything has been unjustly or deceitfully taken away from him, even if it is smaller than an atom, he will certainly get it back on the Day of Judgement when he will be in dire need of it. How then can someone feel sad when he knows for sure that he will get his rightful dues at a very critical moment on the Day of Judgement? How can he possibly grieve or be worried when he knows that it is the Best of Judges who will judge between him and his adversaries?

> Belief in the Divine Decree

What Does Belief in the Divine decree Mean?

This means firm belief that everything, good and bad, takes place by the will of Allah, who does whatever He desires. Nothing can happen without His will, and not even the like of a weight of an atom in the heavens or the earth escapes His knowledge. However, He commands His servants to do certain acts and forbids them to do certain others, giving them free will to do whatever they please without being forced to do anything against their will. He created them as well as their ability to do things. He guides whomever He wills in His mercy and misguides whomever He wills in His absolute wisdom. He will not be questioned about what He does, but people will be questioned for what they do.

> Belief in the divine decree is one of the pillars of faith. When the Prophet ﷺ was once asked about faith, he said, "It is to believe in Allah, His angels, His books, His messengers, the Last Day and to believe in the divine decree, the good and the bad of it."
> (_Saheeh_ Muslim: 8)

What Does Belief in the Divine Decree Include?

Belief in Allah's decree includes the following:

* The belief that Allah ﷻ knows everything and that He knew everything about His creation even before He brought them into being. His foreknowledge includes their provisions, their appointed time in life, their words and deeds, all their doings, whatever they conceal and reveal, those who will be admitted into Paradise as well as those who will be sent to Hellfire. The Qur'an says, "He is Allah, other than Whom there is no other god, the Knower of the Invisible and the Visible." (_Soorat Al-Hashr_, 59:22)

* The belief that He recorded everything that will exist according to His prior knowledge in the Preserved Tablet (Book of Decrees), as the Qur'an states, "No misfortune can happen on earth or in yourselves but is recorded in a Book before We bring it into being." (_Soorat Al-Hadeed_, 57:22) The Prophet ﷺ also said in this connection, "Allah recorded the measurement of all matters pertaining to creation fifty thousand years before He created the heavens and the earth." (_Saheeh Muslim:_ 2653)

* The belief that Allah's will is absolute and cannot be frustrated or challenged by any power whatsoever. Indeed, everything takes place according to His will. Whatever He wills certainly takes place and whatever He does not will cannot possibly take place. The Qur'an says, "But you will not will unless Allah wills, the Lord of all the Worlds." (_Soorat At-Takweer_, 81:29)

- The belief that Allah is the originator of everything, that He is the only Creator besides whom there is no creator, that everything in existence was created by Him and that He has power over all things, as the Qur'an states, "He created everything and determined it most exactly." (*Soorat Al-Furqaan*, 25:2)

Man Has Free Will, Free Choice and the Ability to Do as He Pleases

Belief in the divine decree in no way implies that man does not have free will or that he cannot choose his own actions. This can be proven by Islamic textual evidence as well as by concrete evidence in the real world.

The Qur'an says, "That is the Day of Truth. So whoever wills should take the path that leads to his Lord." (*Soorat An-Naba'*, 78:39)

Regarding man's power and will to do as he chooses, the Qur'an states, "Allah will not force any soul beyond its capacity: It shall have the good which it has gained, and it shall suffer the evil which it has gained." (*Soorat Al-Baqarah*, 2:286)

Based on concrete evidence in the real world, every person knows that he has the free will and ability to do whatever he wants. With these, he can choose between things. He can do some things willingly, such as walking, but he cannot possibly do some other things willingly, such as shivering or a sudden fall. It remains to be said that man's will and ability can only take place following those of Almighty Allah, as the Qur'an states, "It is nothing but a Reminder to all the worlds to whoever among you wishes to go straight. But you will not will unless Allah wills, the Lord of all the Worlds." (*Soorat At-Takweer*, 81:27-9)

> "We have shown him the way, whether he be grateful or ungrateful." (*Soorat Al-Insaan*, 76:3)

Using Divine Decree as an Excuse to Commit Sins

The obligations of observing religious duties, abiding by divine commands and avoiding divine prohibitions is conditional upon man's free will and ability to do as he chooses. Accordingly, the virtuous will be rewarded for choosing the path of righteousness, and the evil will be punished for choosing the path of wickedness.

Almighty Allah does not impose a duty upon us that is beyond our capacity, and He does not want any one of us to neglect his religious duties by using divine decree as an excuse.

Besides, Allah has endowed us with free will and the ability to choose our own actions and has clearly pointed to us the path of righteousness and that of wickedness. Therefore, if we disobey Allah, such disobedience comes only of our own choosing and thus we will have to bear the consequences of this choice.

> If a person assaulted you, harmed you and robbed you of your money, claiming that he had done this because it had been decreed by Allah, you would certainly consider his excuse completely absurd and unacceptable, and you would definitely punish him and claim your money because he had actually done this entirely of his own volition.

Benefits of Belief in the Divine Decree

1. Belief in the divine decree has numerous benefits in people's lives, including the following:

   It is one of the best incentives to act in a manner that is pleasing to Almighty Allah in this life.

   The believers are commanded to do what they can possibly do, to the best of their ability, relying upon Allah ﷻ. They believe that whatever they do cannot possibly yield any results without Allah's will, because Allah is the Creator of the causes and effects.

   The Prophet ﷺ once said, "Cherish that which gives you benefit [in the hereafter], seek help from Allah and do not lose heart. If anything unpleasant happens to you, do not say, 'If I had done such-and-such, such-and-such would have happened instead.' Rather say, '*Qaddarallaahu wa maa shaa'a fa'ala* (This is Allah's decree, and He does whatever He wills)', for the words 'if only' begin the work of Satan." (*Saheeh Muslim:* 2664)

2. Belief in divine decree prompts man to realise his own self-worth, and so he tries to avoid self-conceit and arrogance, for he knows that he does not know what has been decreed for him. This makes him admit his weakness and need for Allah ﷻ and thus urges him to turn to Him constantly.

   Generally, man becomes conceited when something good happens to him and becomes rather sad and dejected when something bad befalls him. Only belief in the divine decree will protect man from such arrogance in times of ease and dejection in times of hardship, for he knows that things happen according to Allah's decree and His foreknowledge.

3. Belief in divine decree helps overcome the vice of envy. A true believer does not envy people for the bounties Allah has bestowed upon them, for He knows that it is Allah ﷻ who has granted them such bounties in the first place and that envying others is tantamount to objecting to Allah's decree.

4. It fills the believer's heart with courage and strengthens his determination in the face of hardships, for he knows that his worldly provision and appointed time to depart the world has already been decreed by Allah ﷻ and that nothing will happen to him except what Allah has decreed for him.

5. It instills in him the numerous realities of faith. Consequently, he constantly seeks Allah's assistance, places his trust in Allah after doing what is required of him and always shows his need for Allah from whom he derives support to stay on the straight path.

6. It provides him with reassurance and fills his heart with peace and contentment, for he knows that what has passed him by was not going to befall him and that what has befallen him was not going to pass him by.

Your Purification (Tahaarah)

Allah ﷻ commands Muslims to purify themselves inwardly from the sin of *shirk* as well as from diseases, such as envy, pride and hatred, of the heart and outwardly from dirt and all kinds of impurities. Once they do so, they become worthy of His love, as the Qur'an states, "Allah loves those who turn to Him constantly and He loves those who keep themselves pure and clean ."(*Soorat Al-Baqarah*, 2:222)

Contents

The Meaning of Purification
Purification from Physical Impurity
- Removing Physical Impurity
- Toilet Etiquette

Ritual Impurity (*Hadath*)
- The Minor Ritual Impurity and How to Remove It

Manner of Performing the Partial Ablution (*Wudoo'*)
- How to Perform Wudoo' and Remove the Minor Ritual Impurity
- The Major Ritual Impurity and the Full Ablution (*Ghusl*)
- How to Remove the Major Ritual Impurity
- What to Do if One Is Unable to Use Water

> The Meaning of Purification

The Arabic word *tahaarah* (purification) denotes purity and cleanliness.

Allah ﷻ commands Muslims to purify themselves outwardly from forbidden appearances and all types of physical impurities, and inwardly from the unpardonable sin of *shirk* as well as diseases of the heart such as envy, pride and hatred. Once they do so, they become worthy of His love, as the Qur'an states, "Allah loves those who turn to Him constantly and He loves those who keep themselves pure and clean." (*Soorat Al-Baqarah*, 2:222)

Allah ﷻ also commands them to purify themselves prior to standing before Him in prayer. If man generally cleans himself and puts on his finest clothes before meeting a person who has a worldly position of authority, such as being a king or a president, then, surely he has to do so before standing before the King of kings.

What is the Required Purification for Performing the Prayer?

Allah ﷻ commands Muslims to purify themselves and perform the partial ablution (*wudoo'*) before engaging in such ritual acts as performing the prayer, touching the Qur'an and circumambulating the Ka'bah in Makkah. He also recommends them to perform *wudoo'* before doing a number of things, such as reciting the Qur'an from memory, supplicating and sleeping.

Therefore, before a Muslim offers a prayer, he must remove two things:

| ① Physical impurity (*najaasah*) | ② Ritual impurity (*hadath*) |

> Allah ﷻ commands Muslims to purify themselves inwardly from the unpardonable sin of *shirk* as well as diseases of the heart such as envy, pride and hatred, and outwardly from forbidden appearances and all types of physical impurities.

> Purification from Physical Impurity

- The Arabic word *najaasah* denotes all physical substances which Islam considers impure and commands us to remove them before engaging in an act of worship.

- The general rule in Islamic law (*Sharee'ah*) is that all things are considered pure, and physical impurity (*najaasah*) is only an intervening factor. Thus, if a person has doubts as to whether or not his trousers, for instance, are clean or not but there is no proof for any type of physical impurity on them, then they should be assumed to be clean, following the general rule.

- If we want to pray, we must first remove all physical impurities from the body, clothing and the place where we intend to offer the prayer.

Things that are considered impure include the following:

1	Human urine and faeces
2	Blood (except if it constitutes an insignificant amount)
3	Urine and dung of animals that are considered unlawful for human consumption (See page 189)
4	Dogs and pigs
5	Dead animals (except for those ones that are considered fit and lawful for human consumption and have been slaughtered according to Islamic rules (See page 190)). Human corpses, fish and insects are considered pure.

Removing Physical Impurity

Physical impurity on the body, clothes, place where the prayer is intended to be performed, or anything or anywhere for that matter, can be removed with anything, be it water or otherwise, for Islam commands removing it. It is not stipulated as to how many times it must be washed off, except in the case of the physical impurity of a dog (i.e. its saliva, urine and faeces), where it must be washed seven times, one of which must be done with earth. For the rest of physical impurities, they must be washed off, and if some smell or stubborn stains remain after washing, they may be ignored. Once a woman asked the Prophet ﷺ about washing off menstrual blood, and he said, "It would suffice to wash it off, and you do not have to worry about any stains that are left." (*Sunan Abu Daawood*: 365)

> Physical impurity can be removed with water or any other cleanser.

Toilet Etiquette

- **A Muslim is recommended** to enter the toilet with the left foot first after saying, *Bismillaah. Allaahumma inneea'oodhu bika min-al-khubthi wal-khabaa'ith* (I seek refuge with You, O Allah, from the male and fema le jinn).

- **He is also recommended** to leave the toilet with the right foot first and then say, "*Ghufraa-nak*" (I seek Your forgiveness, O Allah).

- **He must cover his** private parts while answering the call of nature.

- **He must not answer** the call of nature in a place where he may be seen or where he may offend people. Doing so is strictly forbidden.

- **If he is out in an open space,** such as the desert, he must not relieve himself in a hole, as he may either harm creatures that live in holes in the ground or be harmed by them. Doing so is strictly forbidden.

- **He must not face the *qiblah*,** the direction of the Ka'bah in Makkah towards which Muslims pray, or turn his back towards it, for the Prophet ﷺ said, "When you are answering the call of nature, you should not face the *qiblah* or turn your back towards it."(*Saheeh Al-Bukhaaree: 386; Saheeh Muslim:* 264).This mainly applies if one is out in an open space. There is no harm, however, to do so in buildings, such as in present-day toilets.

- **He must try to be careful** not to have any impurities splashed onto his body or clothes. If this happens accidentally, then he must wash the impurity off the affected place thoroughly.

- **Once he has relieved himself, he must:**

either clean his private parts thoroughly with water. This act is called *istinjaa'* in Arabic.

or

clean them three or times or more with anything that would serve the purpose, such as toilet tissue or stones. This act is called *istijmaar* in Arabic.

It is recommended to use the left hand for cleaning the private parts.

> Ritual Impurity (Ḥadath)

- Ritual impurity (*Ḥadath*) refers to the state of intangible uncleanliness that prevents a Muslim from offering the prayer until he removes it. It is not physical like *najaasah*.

- This ritual impurity can be removed by performing the partial ablution (*wuḍoo'*) or a full ablution (*ghusl*/bath) using pure water. Pure water is water that has not been in contact with any physical impurities that might otherwise change its colour, taste or smell. If he performs *wuḍoo'*, then he can perform as many prayers as he wishes as long as he does not break it.

Ritual impurity is of two types:

> Minor ritual impurity: This can be removed by performing *wuḍoo'* (partial ablution).

> Major ritual impurity: This can be removed by performing (*ghusl*/ritual bath).

The Minor Ritual Impurity and *Wuḍoo'*:

The partial ablution (*wuḍoo'*), becomes invalid with any of the following:

1 Natural discharges from the private parts (both the external genital and excretory organs), such as urine, excrement and wind. Detailing things which invalidate ablution, the Qur'an states, "...or have just satisfied a want of nature." (*Soorat An-Nisaa'*, 4:43)

When the Prophet ﷺ was informed about a man who had doubts as to whether he has passed wind or not (i.e. whether he had broken his *wuḍoo'* or not) during the prayer, he advised, "He should not turn away or leave the prayer unless he hears a noise or smells something." (*Ṣaḥeeḥ Al-Bukhaaree*: 175; *Ṣaḥeeḥ Muslim*: 361)

2 Lustfully touching the private parts with bare hands, for the Prophet ﷺ said, "Whoever touches his private parts must perform *wuḍoo'* again." (*Sunan Abu Daawood*, 181)

3 Eating camel meat: The Prophet ﷺ was once asked, "Should we perform *wuḍoo'* after eating camel meat?" he replied, "Yes." (*Ṣaḥeeḥ Muslim*: 360)

4 Loss of consciousness because of sleep, insanity or drunkenness.

> Loss of consciousness as a result of sleep, insanity or drunkenness is one of the things which render *wuḍoo'* invalid.

> Manner of Performing the partial Ablution (Wudoo')

Performing *wudoo'*, and purification for that matter, is one of the best and most exalted deeds because of which Allah ﷻ forgives one's sins. As the Prophet ﷺ said, "When a Muslim servant [of Allah] washes his face [in the course of performing *wudoo*], every sin he has committed with his eyes is washed away from his face along with the water; when he washes his hands, every sin his hands have committed is washed away from his hands with the water; when he washes his feet, every sin towards which his feet have walked is washed away with water, with the result that he comes out cleansed of all sins." (*Saheeh Muslim:* 244)

How to Perform Wudoo' and Remove the Minor Ritual Impurity

If a Muslim wants to perform *wudoo'*, he intends to do so for the purpose of offering the prayer but without making a verbal declaration, for the intention is a condition for all acts in Islam. The Prophet ﷺ said, "Actions are but by intentions." (*Saheeh Al-Bukhaaree:* 1; *Saheeh Muslim:* 1907) Then he starts the ablution, washing each part in a continuous manner, without long intervals and in the following sequence:

1

He says *bismillaah* (In the name of Allah).

2

He washes his hands up to the wrists three times. It is recommended to do so three times.

3

He rinses out his mouth thoroughly by moving water around in the mouth and then spitting it out. He uses his right hand to take in water. It is obligatory to rinse out the mouth once, but it is recommended to do so three times.

4

He cleans his nose by sniffing water into the nostrils and ejecting it out. It is recommended to snuff up water deeply without causing any harm to himself. It is obligatory to clean the nose once, but it is recommended to do so three times.

5

He washes the entire face with both hands from the top of the forehead to the bottom of the chin and from ear to ear. The ears are not included in washing the face. It is obligatory to wash the face once, but it is recommended to wash it three times.

6

He washes the right hand up the far end of the elbow, and then he does the same thing with the left hand and forearm. It is obligatory to wash the hands up to the elbows once, but it is recommended to do so three times.

7

With wet hands, and starting with his hands flat on the top of the head near the hairline, he wipes it to the back of the neck. It is *Sunnah* to wipe it back to the front. This should be done only once, unlike the case with other parts.

8

With wet fingers, he wipes the inner sides of the ears with the forefingers and their outer sides with the thumbs. This is also done once.

9

He washes his feet up to the ankles, beginning with the right foot. It is obligatory to wash the feet only once, but it is recommended to wash them three times. If he is wearing a pair of socks, he can wipe over them with wet hands but only under certain conditions. (See page 99)

The Major Ritual Impurity and the Full Ablution (*Ghusl*/Ritual Bath):

Things which Require a Person to Perform Full Ablution:

There are certain things which require an adult Muslim to perform full ablution (*ghusl*) before engaging in the prayer or circumambulating the Ka'bah. Before he performs such ablution, he is said to be in a state of a major ritual impurity.

These things are as follows

1. **Ejaculation with** pleasure and by any means, while asleep or awake.

    Ejaculation involves the expulsion of seminal fluid, a thick whitish fluid, from the urethra of the penis during orgasm, which is generally followed by a feeling of lethargy and inertia.

2. **Sexual intercourse:** This involves penetration even if it does not lead to ejaculation. In fact, mere penetration of the glans into the vagina provides sufficient grounds for performing *ghusl*, i.e. taking a ritual bath. The Qur'an says, "If you are in a state of major impurity, then purify yourselves."(*Soorat Al-Maa'idah*, 5:6)

3. **Menstrual blood and post-natal bleeding**

    * Menstrual blood is a natural type of blood, which flows from the uterus of women and occurs at roughly monthly intervals during a woman's reproductive years. It usually lasts more or less seven days with some variation from one woman to another.

    * Post-natal bleeding: This bleeding takes place following a delivery in the post-natal period and lasts for a number of days.

> To perform the full ablution, the entire body must be washed with water.

Menstruating women and women experiencing their post-natal bleeding are exempt from fasting as well as from performing the prayers. They must, however, make up for their missed fasts but not for the missed prayers. During this period, a husband and wife can satisfy their sexual desire but without having an intercourse. At the end of menstruation and post-natal bleeding, women must take a ritual bath (*ghusl*).

As the Qur'an states, "They will ask you about menstruation. Say, 'It is an impurity, so keep apart from women during menstruation and do not approach them until they have purified themselves. But once they have purified themselves, then go to them in the way that Allah has enjoined on you.'" (*Soorat Al-Baqarah*, 2:222)

How to Remove the Major Ritual Impurity (*Janaabah*)

To perform the full ablution, It would be sufficient for a Muslim to wash the entire body with water with the intention that it is for the purpose of purity and worship.

- However, the best method of taking a ritual bath is to wash oneself in the same way one cleans oneself after answering nature's call, perform *wudoo'* and then wash the entire body with water. Doing so increases one's rewards, as it is in accordance with the guidance of the Prophet ﷺ.

- After taking a ritual bath that way, there is no need to perform *wudoo' along* with it. However, the best method of removing the major ritual impurity is to perform the full ablution which includes *wudoo'*, for this was the very practice of the Prophet ﷺ.

Wiping over the Socks

Islam is so practical that it allows a Muslim to wipe over the top of his socks or shoes with wet hands (but not over the soles) instead of washing his feet when renewing his *wudoo'* on condition that he has put them on after having performed *wudoo'*. He can continue doing so for a period not exceeding 24 hours for a resident and 72 hours for a traveller.

The feet must, however, be washed when performing a ritual bath to remove *janaabah*.

What to Do in Case One Is Unable to Use Water

If a Muslim is unable to use water to perform *wudoo'* or take a ritual bath (*ghusl*) due to illness, when water is not readily available or when using the available water for *wudoo'* or *ghusl* would leave insufficient water for drinking, he can resort to pure earth as a substitute for ablution. This is called *tayammum*, and he can continue to do so until he finds sufficient water or becomes able to use it.

Manner of Performing *Tayammum*: (1) Strike both hands slightly on pure earth once, (2) wipe the face with them, (3) wipe the back of the right hand with the palm of the left, and then the back of the left hand with the palm of the right hand.

Your Prayer

The prayer *(salaat)* is the very foundation of religion and a 'link' between a servant and his Lord, hence its exalted position as the greatest act of worship in Islam. Almighty Allah commands Muslims to observe it under all circumstances—whether they are residents or travellers, sick or in good health.

Contents

Position and Virtues of the Prayer in Islam
Virtues of the Prayer
The Five Obligatory Prayers and their Times
The Place of the Prayer
Performing the Prayer
How to Pray
The Pillars and the Obligatory Acts of the Prayer
- Acts which Invalidate the Prayer
- Acts which Are Disliked During the Prayer

The Recommended Voluntary Prayers
The Congregational Prayer
The Call to Prayer (*Adhaan*)
Humility and Attentiveness in Prayer
The Friday prayer (*Salaat-ul-Jumu'ah*)
The Traveller's Prayer
The Prayer of the Sick

The Prayer

The Arabic word *salaat* (commonly translated prayer) literally means supplication. It is the connection a Muslim establishes with his Lord and Creator and comprises the loftiest manifestations of total submissiveness to Allah, turning to Him and seeking His assistance and support. When a Muslim stands in prayer before his Lord, invokes and remembers Him, his mind becomes serene. He realises his true and deep sense of nothingness, the worthlessness and transitory nature of this life, and recognises the greatness of his Lord and the immense mercy He has shown him. This prayer then prompts him to adhere to the principles of the divine law and to shun injustice, indecency and wrongdoing, as the Qur'an states, "The prayer restrains from shameful and unjust deeds." (*Soorat Al-'Ankaboot,*29:45)

>Position and Virtues of Salaat in Islam

The prayer (*salaat*) is undeniably the greatest and most exalted act of worship. It is an act of worship which engages not only the body but also the heart, the mind and the tongue. Its immeasurable significance can be perceived in a number of aspects including the following:

It Occupies the Loftiest Position in Islam

1. It is the second pillar of Islam, as the Prophet ﷺ said, "Islam has been built on five [pillars]: Testifying that there is no god but Allah and that Muhammad is the messenger of Allah, performing the prayers, paying the *zakaat*, making the pilgrimage to the House, and fasting in Ramadaan." (*Saheeh Al-Bukhaaree:* 8; *Saheeh Muslim:* 16) These pillars are the foundations upon which Islam is firmly established, and a pillar is a post that is used to support a building, without which it will certainly collapse.

2. Textual evidence from the Qur'an and the Prophet's traditions considers performance of the prayer to be the act which distinguishes Muslims from non-Muslims. The Prophet ﷺ said, "What makes a person become an unbeliever or a polytheist is his abandonment of the prayer." (*Saheeh Al-Bukhaaree:* 8; *Saheeh Muslim:* 16) He also said, "The criterion between us and the polytheists is performance of the prayer. Thus, whoever abandons it is an unbeliever." *(Sunan At-Tirmidhee:* 2621; *Sunan An-Nasaa'ee:* 463)

3. Allah ﷻ commands the believers to perform it under all circumstances—whether travelling or residing, in times of war and peace, and whether they are sick or in good health, according to their ability. The Qur'an says, "Strictly observe the prayers." (*Soorat Al-Baqarah,* 2:238). Almighty Allah describes His faithful servants as those "who consistently observe the prayers." (*Soorat Al-Mu'minoon,* 23:9)

It Has Numerous Virtues

Textual evidence from the Qur'an and the Prophet's traditions attests to the numerous virtues of the prayer. The following are some of them:

1. It wipes off the minor sins, as the Prophet ﷺ said, "The five daily prayers and the Friday prayer to the next Friday prayer wipe off whatever minor sins may be committed in between, so long as the major sins are avoided." (*Saheeh Muslim:* 233; *Sunan At-Tirmidhee:* 214)

2. It is a light that enlightens a Muslim's life, guides him to all that is good and keeps him away from evil, as the Qur'an states, "The prayer restrains from shameful and unjust deeds."(*Soorat Al-'Ankaboot,* 29:45) The Prophet ﷺ also said, "The prayer is a light." (*Saheeh Muslim:* 223)

3. It will be the first act people will be questioned about on the Day of Judgement: If it is accepted, the rest of their acts will be accepted; if, however, it is not accepted, none of the other acts will be accepted, as the Prophet ﷺ said, "The first act that the servant of Allah will be accountable for on the Day of Judgement will be his prayers. If they are good, the rest of his acts will be good. But if they are bad, the rest of his acts will be bad." (*At-Tabaraanee's Al-Mu'jam Al-Awsat:* 1859)

> Allah ﷻ commands the believers to observe the prayers under all circumstances, even in times of war and disasters.

The sweetest moments a believer experiences is during the prayer, for when he engages in making humble and devout supplication to his Lord, he experiences peace and tranquillity in His presence.

Indeed, it was the greatest joy for the Prophet ﷺ who once observed, "The prayer is the source of my greatest joy." (*Sunan An-Nasaa'ee:* 3940)

He would even ask Bilaal ؓ, his caller to the prayer, to call the prayer so he would experience spiritual peace and tranquillity. "Call [the people] to prayer, Bilaal," he would say to him. "Let us be comforted by it." (*Sunan Abu Daawood:* 4985)

Also, whenever something distressed him, he would turn to prayer. (*Sunan Abu Daawood:* 1319)

For Whom Is It Obligatory?

It is obligatory for every adult, sane and responsible Muslim, male or female to offer the prayer. However, menstruating women or women in their post-natal bleeding are exempt from offering the prayers and are not required to make up for the prayers they have missed after their bleeding ceases and they have purified themselves. (See page 98)

Maturity or puberty can be determined by the following indicators:

Turning fifteen

Appearance of pubic hair

Seminal discharge while sleeping or when awake

Menstruation and conception (for women)

>What Are the Conditions that Must Be Met before Engaging in Prayer?

1 Removing physical impurity and ritual impurity (See page 93)

2 Covering the intimate parts of the body (*'awrah*)

The *'awrah* must be covered with clothing that is neither skin-tight, nor skimpy, nor see-through.

The *'awrah* during the prayer is of three types:

For an adult woman: All her body is considered *'awrah* except for the face and hands.

For a small child: His *'awrah* includes his private parts and the buttocks.

For a man: His *'awrah* is from the navel to the knees.

As Allah ﷻ says in the Qur'an, "Children of Adam! Wear fine clothing for every prayer." (*Soorat Al-A'raaf*, 7:31) In fact, covering the intimate parts of the body is the minimum amount of clothing.

> When a Muslim woman offers the prayer, she must cover her entire body except for the face and hands.

3 Facing the *qiblah*

Allah ﷻ says, "Wherever you come from, turn your face to the Holy Mosque [in Makkah]." (*Soorat Al-Baqarah*, 2:149)

- The direction Muslims face in prayer (*qiblah*) is the Ka'bah, a cube-shaped building located inside the Holy Mosque in Makkah, which was originally constructed by Abraham ﷺ and to which the prophets had made a pilgrimage. It is true that it is a stone structure which can do neither harm nor good, but Allah ﷻ commands the Muslims to face it during the prayer to serve as a focal and unifying point among them.

- A Muslim is required to face the Ka'bah if he can see it in front of him. However, if he is far away from it and cannot see it, being in a different country, for instance, he can only face Makkah. The prayer is still considered valid with slight deviation from the direction of the *qiblah*, for the Prophet ﷺ said, "Whatever is between the east and the west is the *qiblah*." (*Sunan At-Tirmidhee*: 342)

- If he cannot possibly face it due to illness, for instance, then he does not have to do so, for all obligatory acts are normally dropped in case of inability, as the Qur'an states, "Therefore, do your duty towards Allah to the best of your ability." (*Soorat At-Taghaabun*, 64:16)

4 When its Appointed time Becomes Due

The prayer will not be valid if it is offered before its time has started, and delaying it beyond its designated time is strictly forbidden, as the Qur'an states, "The prayers are enjoined on the believers at stated times." (*Soorat An-Nisaa'*, 4:103)

The following facts must be stressed regarding this point:

- It is better to offer the prayer as soon as its actual time becomes due.

- It must be offered at its stated times

- If a prayer is missed due to sleep or forgetfulness, it must be made up for as soon as it is remembered.

> "The prayers are enjoined on the believers at stated times." (4:103)

> The Five Obligatory Prayers and Their Times

Allah ﷻ has enjoined upon Muslims five prayers throughout the day and night and has specified the following times for them:

The Dawn Prayer (_Salaat-ul-Fajr_): It consists of two units (*rak'aat*, singular: *rak'ah*); it begins at daybreak, the time of day when light first appears, and lasts until sunrise.

The Afternoon Prayer (_Salaat-udh-Dhuhr_): It consists of four units; its time begins when the sun declines westward from the middle of the sky and ends when the shadow of an object becomes equal in length to the object itself plus the length of its shadow when the sun was at its zenith.

The Late Afternoon Prayer (_Salaat-ul-'Asr_): It consists of four units; its time begins after the time of *Dhuhr* ends and ends with the setting of the sun. Hence, if the shadow of an object becomes equal to the length of that object plus its length when the sun was at its zenith, then the time of *Dhuhr* ends and the *'Asr* time begins. A Muslim must perform it before the sun loses some of its intensity and turns yellow.

The Sunset Prayer (_Salaat-ul-Maghrib_): It consists of three units; its time begins with sunset, that is, when the sun disappears below the horizon and finishes with the disappearance of the red glow (evening twilight) in the western horizon.

The Late Evening Prayer (_Salaat-ul-'Ishaa'_): It consists of four units; its time begins when the twilight has completely faded away and lasts until midnight. It could be offered, however, a little before dawn, if need be, and the reason is acceptable in Islam.

> A Muslim may use prayer timetables and does not have to find out if the prayer appointed time has become due by himself.

> The Place of Prayer

Islam commands men to perform congregational prayers and encourages them to do so in the mosque, which provides a social forum for Muslims. Congregational prayers help increase and strengthen the bonds of brotherhood, unity and togetherness between them. In fact, Islam promises greater rewards for those who join the congregational prayers, as the Prophet ﷺ said, "The reward for a prayer a man offers in congregation is twenty-seven times greater than that for a prayer he offers by himself." (*Saheeh Al-Bukhaaree: 619, Saheeh Muslim: 650, and Musnad Ahmad: 5921*)

The prayer can, however, be performed anywhere. This reflects one of the favours Allah ﷻ has bestowed upon us, making this religion easy and practical. The Prophet ﷺ said, "The earth has been made a place of prayer for me, and it is pure (i.e. suitable for performing *tayammum* when there is no water available or when one is unable to use it). Therefore, anyone from my community who is overtaken by the time of prayer can pray wherever they may be." (*Saheeh Al-Bukhaaree:* 328; *Saheeh Muslim:* 521)

Criteria That Must Be Met Regarding the Place of Prayer

Islam stipulates that the place where we intend to offer the prayer must be pure and clean, as the Qur'an states, "We commanded Abraham and Ishmael: 'Purify My House for those who walk round it, those who stay there, and those who bow and prostrate themselves in worship.'"(*Soorat Al-Baqarah,* 2:125) As a general rule, wherever we intend to pray must be clean and pure unless it is clear beyond any doubt that it has been smeared by some impurity. Therefore, if there is nothing that might otherwise render a place impure, it must be considered clean, and we are allowed to offer our prayer on it without the need of using a prayer mat.

There are a number of criteria and conditions that must be met regarding the place where we intend to pray. These include the following:

1. One must not pray in a place where one may disturb people, such as busy public areas, passageways and places where one is not allowed to stand or sit, as this can lead to crowdedness and cause a great deal of inconvenience. The Prophet ﷺ said, "There should be neither harming, nor reciprocating harm." (*Sunan Ibn Maajah:* 2340, *Musnad Ahmad:* 2865)

2. The place must be free from things which may otherwise cause distraction, such as pictures (like the ones found on some prayer mats), loud noises and music.

3. One must not pray in a place where worship is ridiculed, such as a place where there are drunken people or fanatics. Almighty Allah forbids Muslims to abuse the false deities of non-Muslims so that they may not in revenge abuse Allah ﷻ in their ignorance: "Do not insult those they call upon besides Allah in case that makes them insult Allah in animosity, without knowledge ." (*Soorat Al-An'aam,* 6:108)

4. One must not pray in a place specifically designed for committing sinful acts, such as ballrooms and nightclubs.

> The Place of Prayer

Can you offer the congregational prayer in the mosque?

- **Yes** → A man must offer the congregational prayer in the mosque, for doing so is one of the virtuous acts that are dearest to Allah. Women are also allowed to join the congregational prayer in the mosque.
- **No** ↓

If you cannot possibly offer it in the mosque, is the place where you want to pray pure and clean?

- **No** → Offering the prayer in a place that is not clean and pure is strictly forbidden, for Allah commands us to choose a clean spot for our prayer.
- **Yes** ↓

If the place where you want to pray is clean, will your prayer in it inconvenience people, being a passageway, for instance?

- **Yes** → Offering the prayer in a place where you are bound to inconvenience and disturb people is forbidden, and so you must find a more suitable place.
- **No** ↓

Is there anything in the place where you want to pray that is bound to distract your attention, such as pictures and loud noises?

- **Yes** → you must avoid places where your prayer may be distracted.
- **No** → Offering the prayer anywhere in the world is absolutely valid. This is one of Allah's gifts to the Muslims and one of the favours He has bestowed upon them.

> Performing the Prayer

1 The Intention

The intention (*niyyah*) is one of the conditions of the prayer, without which the prayer will not be valid. The intention is the object for which the prayer is offered. Before offering the prayer, one must have in mind the intention to offer the specified prayer, as being the sunset prayer or the late evening prayer, for instance, for the purpose of worshipping Allah ﷻ. A Muslim must not announce the intention, and doing so is a mistake, for neither the Prophet ﷺ, nor his noble companions ever declared it.

2 He then stands
in reverence and humility, raising his hands up to the level of the shoulders or a little above them, with the palms of his hands facing the *qiblah*, and says, as he does so, *Allaahu akbar* (Allah is Most Great).

The *takbeer* (that is, the Arabic phrase *Allaahu akbar*) is a way of extolling and glorifying Allah ﷻ. Indeed, Allah is greater than everyone and everything else. He is greater than the life of this world and all its transitory desires. When we declare the *takbeer*, we leave the worldly concerns and earthly desires behind us and turn towards Allah, Most High, the All-Exalted, in great reverence and utmost humility.

3 Then he places
his right hand on the left hand, having both of them on his chest. He maintains this whenever he is in a standing position.

4 Then He recites
the opening supplication: *Subhaanak-Allaahumma wa bi hamdika, wa tabaarak-asmuka, wa ta'aalaa jadduka, wa laa ilaaha ghayruka* (Glory be to You, Allah; Yours is the praise, blessed is Your name, exalted is Your majesty, and there is no god besides You). This supplication is recommended but not obligatory.

5 Then he says:
A'oodhu billaahi min-ash-shaytaan-ir-rajeem (I seek Allah's protection from Satan, who has been expelled from His mercy).

6 Then he says:
Bismillaah-ir-rahmaan-ir-raheem (In the name of Allah, Most Beneficent, Most Merciful).

What Should a Person Who Does not Know *Soorat Al-Faatihah* and the Post-Obligatory Prayer Supplications by Heart Do?

A new Muslim who does not know *Soorat Al-Faatihah* and the post-obligatory prayer supplications by heart must do the following:

* He must do his best to memorise the obligatory supplications in the prayer, for the prayer will not be valid except by reciting these supplications in the Arabic language. These supplications are:

Soorat Al-Faatihah, Allaahu akbar (Allah is Most Great), *Subhaana rabbiyal-'adheem* (Glory be to my Lord, the Almighty), *Sami'allaahu li man hamidah* (Allah listens to him who praises Him), *Rabbanaa wa lakal-hamd* (Our Lord, to You is due all praise), *Subhaana rabbiyal-a'laa* (Glory be to my Lord, Most High), *Rabbighfir lee,* (O Lord, forgive me), the first *tashahhud*, the final *tashahhud*, and *Assalaamu 'alaykum wa rahmatullaah* (Peace and mercy of Allah be on you).

* He must, before completing memorisation of these utterances, repeat, to the best of his ability, whatever of them he has committed to memory during the prayer and repeat whatever part of *Soorat Al-Faatihah* he has memorised, which is normally recited in the standing posture, for the Qur'an states, "Keep your duty to Allah as best you can." (*Soorat At-Taghaabun*, 64:16)

* It is recommended that he attends the congregational prayers during this period so he can perfect his prayers and because the prayer leader (*imaam*) covers part of the shortcomings in the prayer of those praying behind him.

7 **Then he recites** *Soorat Al-Faatihah*, the greatest soorah in the Qur'an.

* Allah reminds the Prophet of His favour upon him by revealing it to him: "We have given you the seven oft-repeated verses and the Magnificent Qur'an." (*Soorat Al-Hijr*,15:87)

* A Muslim must learn it by heart, for reciting it in prayer constitutes one of the pillars of the prayer for those who pray alone or behind the *imaam* in prayers during which Qur'anic verses are recited in a low voice, such as the afternoon and late afternoon prayers.

8 He says after reciting *Soorat Al-Faatihah* or listening to it behind the *imaam: Aameen*, which means "O Allah, answer my prayers."

9 After reciting *Soorat Al-Faatihah*, he recites another *soorah* or some other Qur'anic verses. In the third and fourth units of the prayer he recites only *Soorat Al-Faatihah*.

* *Soorat Al-Faatihah* and whatever Qur'anic verses are recited after it are normally recited aloud in the dawn (*Fajr*), sunset (*Maghrib*) and late evening prayers (*'Ishaa'*). As for the afternoon (*Dhuhr*) and late afternoon prayers (*'Asr*), they are recited in a low voice.

* All the supplications are normally recited in a low voice.

Soorat Al-Faatihah Explained

Al-hamdu lillaahi rabbil-'aalameen "Praise be to Allah, the Lord of all the worlds." (1:2): I extol Allah with all His attributes, acts and apparent and hidden blessings, with due love and reverence. *Rabb* (translated here 'Lord') refers to Almighty Allah, the Creator, Owner, Provider and Disposer of all affairs. The 'worlds' refers to anything apart from Allah ﷻ and includes, among other things, the world of human beings, that of the jinn, that of the angels and that of animals.

Ar-Rahmaan-ir-Raheem "The Beneficent, the Merciful." (1:3): *Ar-Rahmaan* (Most Beneficent) and *Raheem* (Most Merciful) are two of Allah's names. *Ar-Rahmaan* is more intensive, in that Allah's mercy includes in its objects the believers and the unbelievers, while *Ar-Raheem* has for its peculiar object the believers only.

Maaliki yawmid-Deen "Master of the Day of Judgement." (1:4): He is the only Judge on the Day of Judgement. This statement reminds the believers of the Last Day and prompts them to do righteous deeds.

Iyyaaka na'budu wa iyyaaka nasta'een "You alone we worship. You alone we ask for help." (1:5): We worship none but You, and we do not associate anyone with You in worship. We also seek only Your assistance and support in all our affairs, for the power of decision rests with you alone.

Ihdinassiraat-al-mustaqeem "Guide us on the Straight Path." (1:6): Show us the Straight Path and help us adhere to it until we meet You. The Straight Path (*as-siraat al-mustaqeem*) is nothing but Islam, the clear religion that leads to Allah's good pleasure and Paradise. It was Muhammad ﷺ, the Seal of Prophets, who guided us to it, and man's happiness entirely depends on adhering to it.

Siraatalladheena an'amta 'alayhim "The path of those You have blessed;" (1:7): That is, the path to which You have guided the prophets, the righteous people who know the truth and follow it.

Ghayril maghdoobi 'alayhim waladh-daalleen "not of those who have incurred Your wrath, nor of those who have gone astray." (1:7): Keep us away from the path of those with whom You are angry because they know the truth but have chosen not to follow it, also keep us away from the path of those who have not been guided to the truth due to their ignorance,.

10 Then he recites the *takbeer* while raising his hands up to the level of the shoulders or a little above them, with the palms of his hands facing the *qiblah*, just as he has done upon reciting the first *takbeer*.

11 Then he bows down, lowering his head and back and keeping them straight at a right angle, placing the palms of his hands on the knees. He says three times while in this position, called *rukoo', Subhaana rabbiy-al-'adheem* (Glory be to my Lord, the Almighty). It is obligatory to say this only once, but it is recommended to say it three times. In the *rukoo'* position, we must glorify and extoll Allah ﷻ.

Subhaana rabbiy-al-'adheem : I declare Him free from all defects and to recognise His absolute perfection. He recites the words *Subhaana rabbiyal-'adheem*, whilst bowing, in complete humility and in total submission to Almighty Allah.

12 Then he resumes the standing position, raising his hands up to the level of the shoulders or a little above them, with the palms of his hands facing the *qiblah*, saying *Sami'allaahu li man hamidah* (Allah listens to him who praises Him). He says this whether he is praying alone or is the prayer leader (*imaam*). Then each one says: *Rabbanaa wa lakal-hamd* (Our Lord, to You is due all praise). It is recommended to say after this: *hamdan katheeran tayyiban mubaarakan feehi. Mil'assamaawaati wa mil'al-ardi wa mil'a maa shi'ta min shay'in ba'd* (An abundant, beautiful and blessed praise. A praise that fills the heavens, the earth and all that You will thereafter).

13 Then he recites the *takbeer* and prostrates himself, with the toes of both feet, the knees, the hands and the forehead and the nose touching the floor. He is recommended not to bring the arms close to the sides nor the abdomen close to the thighs, making sure that his forearms are not in contact with the floor.

14 He says in this position, called *sujood*, *Sub<u>h</u>aana rabbiyal-a'laa* (Glory be to my Lord, Most High). It is obligatory to say this only once, but it is recommended to say it three times.

The prostrate position (*sujood*) is the noblest state where supplications must be made to Almighty Allah. Thus, after reciting the obligatory supplication mentioned above, a Muslim is recommended to invoke Allah and humbly and earnestly ask Him for anything which he wants in this life or in the hereafter. The Prophet ﷺ said, "The nearest a servant can be to his Lord is when he prostrates himself in prayer. So invoke Allah much in this state." (<u>Sa<u>h</u>ee<u>h</u> Muslim:</u> 482)

Sub<u>h</u>aana rabbiyal-a'laa means: I declare Allah, Most High, the Almighty, above the heavens, free from all defects. This statement reminds the worshipper, who is humbly prostrating himself before Allah, of the difference between him and his Creator, Most High, prompting him to humbly submit to Him.

15 Then he recites the *takbeer* and sits between the two prostrations. He is recommended to sit on the left leg while keeping the right foot upright with the toes pointing towards the *qiblah* and resting his hands on his thighs close to the knees.

- In fact, all the sitting postures during the prayer should be done in this way, except for the sitting posture where the final *tashahhud* is recited, in which case it is recommended to sit with the left buttock on the ground, the right foot placed vertically with the toes pointing towards the *qiblah*, and the left foot on its side emerging from underneath the right foot.

- If he cannot sit in this manner for the first *tashahhud* or the second one due to some knee pain or because he is not used to such postures, then he can sit in a similarly comfortable manner.

16 He says between the two prostrations: *Rabbighfir lee, warhamnee, wahdinee, warzuqnee, wajburnee wa 'aafinee* (O Lord, forgive me, have mercy on me, guide me, provide for me, support me and protect me.).

17 Then he recites the *takbeer* and prostrates himself in the same way as before. This completes one unit (*rak'ah*) of the prayer.

18 Then he rises to the standing position again, for the second unit, reciting the *takbeer* as he does so.

19 He performs the second unit in exactly the same way as the first one.

20 After the second prostration in the second unit, he takes a sitting posture and recites the first *tashahhud*: *Attahiyyaatu lillaah, wassalawaatu wattayyibaat, assalaamu 'alayka ayyuhannabiyyu wa rahmatullaahi wa barakaatuh, assalaamu 'alaynaa wa 'alaa 'ibaad-illaah-issaaliheen, ash hadu an laa ilaaha illallaah, wa ash hadu anna Muhammadan 'abduhu wa rasooluh* (All reverence, all worship, all sanctity are due to Allah. Peace be on you, O Prophet, and the mercy of Allah and His blessings. Peace be on us and all the righteous servants of Allah. I bear witness that none is worthy of worship except Allah, and I bear witness that Muhammad is His servant and His Messenger.)

21 Then he rises, reciting the *takbeer*, to assume a standing position and complete the rest of the prayer units if the prayer consists of three units (*Maghrib*) or four units (*Dhuhr, 'Asr and 'Ishaa'*). In the third and fourth units, however, he recites only *Soorat Al-Faatihah*.

If the prayer consists of two units (*Fajr*), he recites the final *tashahhud* after completing the first *tashahhud*.

22 In the last unit after the second prostration, he takes a sitting posture and recites the final *tashahhud*. This consists of the first *tashahhud* mentioned earlier, which is immediately followed by the following: *Allaahumma salli 'alaa Muhammad, wa 'alaa aali Muhammad, kamaa sallayta 'alaa Ibraaheema wa 'alaa aali Ibraaheema, innaka hameedun majeed.*

Wa baarik 'alaa Muhammad, wa 'alaa aali Muhammad, kamaa baarakta 'alaa Ibraaheema wa 'alaa aali Ibraaheema, innaka hameedun majeed (O Allah, exalt Muhammad and the family of Muhammad, as You have exalted Abraham and the family of Abraham. Verily, You are Praiseworthy and Glorious. O Allah, bless Muhammad and the family of Muhammad, as You have blessed Abraham and the family of Abraham. Verily, You are Praiseworthy and Glorious.)

After this, he is recommended to recite the following supplication: *Allaahumma innee a'oodhu bika min 'adhaabi jahannama, wa min 'adhaab-il-qabri, wa min fitnat-il-mahyaa wal mamaati, wa min fitnat-il-maseeh-id-Dajjaal* (O Allah, I take refuge in You from the punishment of the Fire, from the torment of the grave, from the trials and tribulations of life and death and from the mischief of the false Messiah.)

23 Finally, he turns his face to the right side, saying: Assalaamu 'alaykum wa rahmatullaah (Peace, and mercy of Allah be on you). Then he turns his face to the left side and says the same thing.

With these greetings he concludes his prayer, as the Prophet ﷺ said, "The prayer begins with the *takbeer* and ends with the *tasleem*." (*Sunan Abu Daawood:* 61; *Sunan At-Tirmidhee:* 3) The *takbeer* refers to the words *Allaahu akbar* (Allah is the greatest of all), and the tasleem refers to the words *Assalaamu 'alaykum wa rahmatullaah* (Peace and mercy of Allah be on you).

24 It is recommended that a Muslim recites the following supplications after completing any of the five obligatory daily prayers:

1. *Astaghfirullaah,* (I seek Allah's forgiveness) three times.

2. *Allaahumma antas-Salaam, wa mink-as-Salaam, tabaarakta yaa dhal-jalaali wal-ikraam* (O Allah, You are Peace and from You comes peace. Blessed are You, Owner of might and honour). *Allaahumma laa maani'a limaa a'tayta, wa laa mu'tiya limaa mana'ta, wa laa yanfa'u dhal-jaddi, minkal-jadd* (O Allah, no one can withhold what You give, nor can anyone give what You withhold; and the might of the mighty person cannot benefit him against You.)

3. *Subhaanallaah* (Glory be to Allah) 33 times, *Al-hamdu lillaah* (Praise be to Allah) 33 times and *Allaahu akbar* (Allah is the greatest of all) 33 times. He completes the total of one hundred by saying: *Laa ilaaha illallaahu, wahdahu laa shareeka lahu, lahul-mulku, wa lahul-hamdul, wa huwa 'alaa kulli shay'in qadeer* (There is no god worthy of worship but Allah; He has no partners; the kingdom and praise belong to Him and He has power over everything)

> How to Pray (The Standing, Bowing and Prostrate Postures)

1

Assume a standing position and recite the *takbeer* while raising your hands up to the level of the shoulders or a little above them, with the palms of your hands facing the *qiblah*.

2

Place your right hand on the left hand, having both of them on your chest, recite *Soorat Al-Faatihah* and as much of the Qur'an as may be easy for you. Do this in the first and second units of prayer.

3

Recite the *takbeer* while raising your hands up to the level of the shoulders or a little above them, with the palms of your hands facing the *qiblah*, then bow down, lowering your head and back and keeping them straight at a right angle, placing the palms of your hands on the knees. Say three times, while in this position: *Subhaana rabbiy-al-'adheem* (Glory be to my Lord, the Almighty).

4 Resume the standing position, raising your hands up to the level of the shoulders or a little above them, with the palms of your hands *facing* the *qiblah*, saying *Sami'allaahu li man hamidah* (Allah listens to him who praises Him). Say this whether you are praying alone or you are the prayer leader (*imaam*). Then say: *Rabbanaa wa lakal-hamd* (Our Lord, to You is due all praise).

5 Recite the *takbeer* and prostrate yourself, with the toes of both feet, the knees, the hands and the forehead touching the floor. It is recommended that you do not bring the arms close to the sides, nor the abdomen close to the thighs, making sure that your forearms are not in contact with the floor. Say three times, while in this position: *Subhaana rabbiyal-a'laa* (Glory be to my Lord, Most High).

6 Say between the two prostrations: *Rabbighfir lee, warhamnee*, (O Lord, forgive me and have mercy on me).

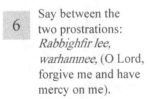

> How to Pray (The Second Rak'ah, the Tashahhud and the Tasleem)

7

Rise, while reciting the *takbeer*, from the prostrate position to the standing position again to perform the second unit, and do exactly as you have done in the first *rak'ah* (standing, reciting, bowing, rising from the bowing position and assuming the standing position, prostration and the relevant recitations and utterances).

8

After the second prostration in the second unit, take a sitting posture similar to the one taken between the two prostrations, and recite the first *tashahhud: Attahiyyaatu lillaah, wassalawaatu wattayyibaat, assalaamu 'alayka ayyuhannabiyyu wa rahmatullaahi wa barakaatuh, assalaamu 'alaynaa wa 'alaa 'ibaad-illaah-issaaliheen, ash hadu an laa ilaaha illallaah, wa ash hadu anna Muhammadan 'abduhu wa rasooluh* (All reverence, all worship, all sanctity are due to Allah. Peace be on you, O Prophet, and the mercy of Allah and His blessings. Peace be on us and all the righteous servants of Allah. I bear witness that none is worthy of worship except Allah, and I bear witness that Muhammad is His servant and His Messenger).

9 If the prayer consists of three units (*Maghrib*) or four units (*Dhuhr*, *'Asr* and *'Ishaa'*), rise, reciting the *takbeer*, to assume a standing position for the third unit and do exactly as you have done in the previous two units. In the third and fourth units, however, recite only *Soorat Al-Faatihah*. If the prayer consists of two units (*Fajr*), recite the final *tashahhud* after completing the first *tashahhud*.

10. After the second prostration of the final unit, take a sitting posture and recite the first *tashahhud* and follow it up with the final *tashahhud*: *Allaahumma salli 'alaa Muhammad, wa 'alaa aali Muhammad, kamaa sallayta 'alaa Ibraaheema wa 'alaa aali Ibraaheema, innaka hameedun majeed. Wa baarik 'alaa Muhammad, wa 'alaa aali Muhammad, kamaa baarakta 'alaa Ibraaheema wa 'alaa aali Ibraaheema, innaka hameedun majeed* (O Allah, exalt Muhammad and the family of Muhammad, as You exalted Abraham and the family of Abraham. Verily, You are Praiseworthy and Glorious. O Allah, bless Muhammad and the family of Muhammad, as You blessed Abraham and the family of Abraham. Verily, You are Praiseworthy, and Glorious).

11. Finally, turn your face to the right side, saying: *Assalaamu 'alaykum wa rahmatullaah* (Peace, and mercy of Allah be on you). Then turn your face to the left side and say the same thing.

> The Pillars and the Obligatory Acts of the Prayer

The pillars (*arkaan;* singular: *rukn*) of the prayer are its essential parts that are necessary for its validity. If any of these pillars is left out due to forgetfulness or deliberate omission, the prayer becomes invalid.

They are as follows:

The opening *takbeer;* assuming the standing position, if one has the ability to do so; reciting *Soorat Al-Faatihah* (in the case of performing the prayer alone, i.e., not being led by an *imaam*); bowing; rising from the bowing position; prostrating; sitting between the two prostrations, the final *tashahhud*, sitting while reciting the *tashahhud*; the *tasleem*.; and making certain that each body part assumes the appropriate position before one moves from one position to another.

The obligatory acts of the prayer (*waajibaat*, singular: *waajib*) are those acts that must be done in the prayer. If they are deliberately omitted, the prayer becomes invalid. However, if they are left out due to inattention or forgetfulness, the prayer is still valid, but the acts that are left out can be compensated for with the two prostrations of forgetfulness, as will be explained later.

The obligatory acts of the prayer are as follows:

Recitation of *takbeer* throughout the prayer other than the opening *takbeer*; saying *Subhaana rabbiy-al-'adheem* (Glory be to my Lord, the Almighty) once; saying *Sami'allaahu li man hamidah* (Allah listens to him who praises Him), whether one is praying alone or one is the prayer leader (*imaam*); saying *Rabbanaa wa lakal-hamd* (Our Lord, to You is due all praise); *Subhaana rabbiyal-a'laa* (Glory be to my Lord, Most High) once; saying *Rabbighfir lee,* (O Lord, forgive me) while sitting between the two prostrations once; and reciting the first *tashahhud*. These obligatory acts can be made up for with the two prostrations of forgetfulness.

The recommended acts of the prayer (*sunan as-salaat*) are those words and acts other than the pillars and the obligatory acts of the prayer. They serve to complement the prayer and it is recommended to observe them. Omission of any of these acts, however, does not render the prayer invalid.

> The more a person keeps distractions away by concentrating in prayer and humbling himself before his Lord, the more rewards he will get and the higher his grade in Paradise will be.

The Two Prostrations of Forgetfulness

These prostrations are generally performed to make up for any deficiency in the prayer.

When can they be performed?

They can be performed in the following cases:

1. If a person forgetfully adds an extra act in the prayer, whether this act consists of assuming an extra standing position, prostrate position, bowing position or sitting position, then he has to perform the two prostrations of forgetfulness at the end of the prayer.

2. If he unintentionally leaves out any of the pillars of the prayer (*arkaan*), he must add the missing pillar and then perform the two prostrations of forgetfulness at the end of the prayer.

3. If he unintentionally leaves out any of the obligatory acts of prayer (*waajibaat*), such as the first *tashahhud*, he must perform the prostrations of forgetfulness.

4. If he is in doubt as to the number of the prayer units he has performed, he simply assumes he has performed the lesser number to be on the safe side and performs the two prostrations of forgetfulness at the end of the prayer.

Manner of Performing the Two Prostrations due to Forgetfulness: These can be performed in exactly the same manner he normally performs them in the prayer; that is, by performing two prostrations and sitting between them.

When to Perform the Two Prostrations of Forgetfulness: They can be performed:

- After the final *tashahhud* and before reciting the *tasleem*, he performs the two prostrations of forgetfulness and then recites the *tasleem* as he normally does to conclude the prayer.

- After reciting the *tasleem*, he performs the two prostrations of forgetfulness and then recites the *tasleem* again.

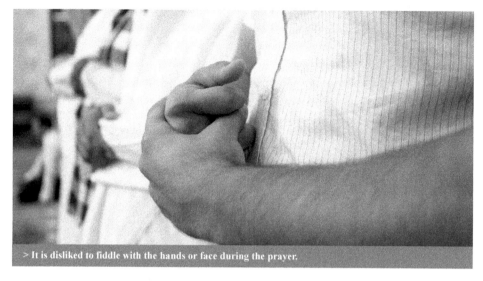
> It is disliked to fiddle with the hands or face during the prayer.

Acts which Invalidate the Prayer

The prayer becomes invalid in the following cases:

1. If any of its pillars (*arkaan*) or obligatory acts (*waajibaat*) are intentionally or forgetfully omitted despite one's ability.

2. If any of its obligatory acts (*waajibaat*) are intentionally left out.

3. Deliberately speaking whilst in prayer.

4. Laughing out loud whilst in prayer.

5. Making unnecessary, continuous movements.

Acts which Are Disliked During the Prayer

These are the acts which are bound to decrease the reward for one's prayer and negatively affect humility, concentration and attentiveness in it. They are as follows:

1. Turning the head around during prayer, When the Prophet ﷺ was asked about this act, he said, "It is a way of stealing by which Satan takes away a portion from a person's prayer." (*Saheeh Al-Bukhaaree:* 718)

2. Fiddling with one's hands or face, placing one's hands on the hips, clasping one's hands together and cracking one's fingers.

3. Engaging in prayer when one is distracted by something, such as one's need to answer the call of nature, for the Prophet ﷺ said, "No prayer can be correctly offered when the food is served before the worshipper, or when they is prompted by the call of nature." (*Saheeh Muslim:* 560)

> The Recommended Voluntary Prayers

Muslims are required to offer only five prayers a day.

However, Islam encourages them to offer other recommended prayers, for doing so makes them worthy of Allah's love and serve to make up for any deficiencies in the performance of the obligatory prayers.

The following are some of the most important supererogatory prayers:

1. **The Supererogatory Prayers Accompanying the Obligatory Prayers (*As-Sunan Ar-Rawaatib*):** These are the prayers that are offered before or after the obligatory prayers and Muslims generally do not neglect them.

Regarding the reward for performing these prayers, the Prophet ﷺ said, "Allah will build a house in Paradise for any Muslim who prays twelve units of voluntary prayer during the night and day." (*Saheeh Muslim:* 728)

They are as follows:

1	Two units before the *Fajr* prayer
2	Four units before the *Dhuhr* prayer, reciting the *tasleem* after each two units; and two other units after the *Dhuhr* prayer
3	Two units after the *Maghrib* prayer
4	Two units after the *'Ishaa'* prayer

2. **The *Witr* Prayer:** the Arabic word *witr* means "odd number" and refers to odd-numbered prayer offered after the *'Ishaa'* prayer. It is considered to be one of the best and most meritorious of all supererogatory prayers. The Prophet ﷺ once commanded the Muslims, "Followers of the Qur'an! Perform the *witr* prayer." (*Sunan At-Tirmidhee:* 453; *Sunan Ibn Maajah:* 1170)

The best time to offer the *witr* prayer is in the later part of the night before the *Fajr* prayer, but a Muslim may perform it at any time between the *'Ishaa'* and the *Fajr* prayers.

The minimum number of units for the *witr* prayer is one, but it is better to offer three. A Muslim may offer more if he wishes, but the maximum number of units which the Prophet ﷺ used to perform was eleven.

The units of the supererogatory prayers are generally offered two by two, followed by the *tasleem*. The *witr* prayer is no exception. However, if a Muslim wants to conclude his prayer, he must add one single unit, during which he may recite a special supplication, known as *qunoot* supplication. This supplication is recited after rising from the bowing position and before prostrating. After this supplication, he may pray to Allah and ask Him for whatever he wishes, holding his hands in front of him with both palms up.

Times During Which It Is Not Permissible to Offer the Supererogatory Prayers

A Muslim may offer a supererogatory prayer at any time, except at such times during which it is prohibited to offer them, as they are generally times specified for prayers offered by some non-Muslims. During these times, he is only allowed to make up for the obligatory prayers he may have missed or the supererogatory prayers which are offered for a reason, such as the prayer of *tahiyyatul-masjid*, "greeting the mosque", a prayer which consists of two units and is performed upon entering the mosque and there is enough time to perform it before the obligatory prayer commences. A Muslim may, however, invoke Allah and recite supplications at any time.

These times are as follows:

1	From the time following the *Fajr* prayer until the sunrises above the horizon by the length of a spear, a short period of time specified in Islamic Law and is equal to approximately twenty minutes in countries with a temperate climate.
2	From the time the sun is at its zenith until it declines westward from the middle of the sky. This is a short period of time preceding the beginning of the time of the *Dhuhr* prayer.
3	From the time following the *'Asr* prayer until sunset

> It is strictly prohibited to offer the optional prayers from the time following the *'Asr* prayer until sunset.

> The Congregational Prayer

Allah commands Muslim men to perform the five obligatory prayers in congregation and promises them a great reward for doing so. Mentioning the reward of the congregational prayer, the Prophet once said, "The reward for a prayer offered in congregation is twenty-seven times greater than that offered by a person alone." (*Saheeh Al-Bukhaaree:* 619; *Saheeh Muslim:* 650)

The congregational prayer can be established by at least two people, one of them acts as the prayer leader (*imaam*). However, the larger the congregation, the dearer it is to Allah.

Following the Imam in Prayer

This means that those praying behind the *imaam* must do the same as he does during the prayer by observing all the prayer movements and taking all the prayer postures, such as bowing and prostrating, immediately after him. They must not engage in any movement or posture before him or differ with him in this respect in anything whatsoever.

The Prophet said, "The *imaam* is to be followed. Say *Allaahu akbar* when he says it, and do not say it until he says it first. Bow when he bows, and do not bow until he has done so first. When he says, *sami'-Allaahu liman hamidah* (Allah listens to him who praises Him),' say, *"Rabbanaa wa lak-al-hamd* (Our Lord, to You is due all praise).' Prostrate when he prostrates, and do not prostrate until he has done so first." (*Saheeh Al-Bukhaaree:* 710, *Saheeh Muslim:* 414 and *Sunan Abu Daawood:* 603)

Who Should Lead the Prayer?

Generally speaking, the person who knows the Qur'an the best should be given preference in leading the prayer. If those present are equal in that respect, then the one who is best informed in the rules of religion, as the Prophet said, "Let him act as *imaam* to a congregation who knows the Qur'an by heart the best; and if all present should be equal in that respect, then let him perform who has the deepest knowledge of the *Sunnah*..."(*Saheeh Muslim:* 673)

Where Does the *Imaam* and Those He Leads Stand in Prayer?

The *imaam* stands in front of those he leads in prayer (*ma'moomoon;* singular: *ma'moom* /follower). The followers, standing shoulder to shoulder, form straight lines behind him, and the front rows should be filled and completed first. If there is only one follower (*ma'moom*), he positions himself to the right of the *imaam*.

127

How to Make up for Missed Prayer Units

If the prayer has already started, the latecomer should join in the congregation in the very position in which he finds the *imaam*. For example, if he finds the *imaam* in the prostrate position, he must recite the *takbeer* and then prostrate himself. When the *imaam* concludes the congregational prayer by reciting the *tasleem*, the latecomer rises, reciting the *takbeer*, to assume a standing position and complete the rest of the prayer individually, by making up for the units he has missed.

The unit (*rak'ah*) that he catches up with the *imaam* when he first joins the congregation counts as the beginning of his own prayer, and whatever he makes up for after the *imaam* concludes the congregational prayer counts as the rest of his prayer.

How to Determine that a Complete *Rak'ah* Is Offered

The prayer is determined by the number of units offered in it; if a latecomer joins the congregation while the *imaam* is in the bowing position, he is considered to have offered a complete unit (*rak'ah*) even though he has not recited *Soorat Al- Faatihah* in that particular *rak'ah* in the standing position. If, however, he misses the bowing position, then he must trecite the *takbeer* and join the congregation. In this case, he is considered to have missed this particular *rak'ah*, and whatever movements and postures in it do not count.

Examples Illustrating Ways of Making up for Missed Prayer Units

If someone joins the congregation during the *Fajr* prayer while the *imaam* is in the second *rak'ah*, he must, after the *imaam* concludes the prayer with the *tasleem*, rise, reciting the *takbeer*, to assume a standing position and make up for the other *rak'ah* which he has missed. He must not recite the *tasleem* until he completes the prayer, for the *Fajr* prayer consists of two units and he has only offered one unit with the *imaam*.

If he joins the congregation during the *Maghrib* prayer while the *imaam* is in the sitting position reciting the final *tashahhud*, he must, after the *imaam* concludes the prayer with the *tasleem*, rise, reciting the *takbeer*, to assume a standing position and offer three complete units of prayer. The reason for this is that he has joined the congregation only at its end while the *imaam* is reciting the final *tashahhud*. A unit (*rak'ah*) only counts as complete if one joins the congregation while the *imaam* is in the bowing posture.

If he joins the congregation during the *Dhuhr* prayer while the *imaam* is in the bowing position of the third *rak'ah*, then this means that he has offered two complete units of prayer, which count for him as his two first units. As soon as the *imaam* concludes the prayer with the *tasleem*, he must then rise, reciting the takbeer, to assume a standing position and offer two more units, namely the third and fourth units, considering that the *Dhuhr* prayer consists of four units of prayer.

> The Call to Prayer (Adhaan)

> The *adhaan* is one of the most meritorious acts in the sight of Allah.

The *adhaan* serves the purpose of calling people to prayer and signalling the beginning of the time of an obligatory prayer. Another call, called the *iqaamah*, serves the purpose of summoning Muslims to line up for the beginning of the obligatory prayers. Muslims used to meet up and seek to know the time of prayer, but no one summoned them. One day they were discussing how to gather everyone for prayer.

Some suggested using a bell as the Christians do, and others recommended using a ram's horn, following an ancient Jewish practice. Then 'Umar ibn Al-Khattaab, one of the Prophet's companions, suggested appointing someone to call people to prayer. The Prophet agreed, so he turned to Bilaal, and said, "Get up, Bilaal, and call the people to prayer." (*Saheeh Al-Bukhaaree:* 579; *Saheeh Muslim:* 377)

The Manner of Reciting the *Adhaan* and the *Iqaamah*

- Both the *adhaan* and the *iqaamah* must be recited in the case of a group of people (congregation) but it is not the case with an individual. If a congregation intentionally leave it out, their prayer will still be valid but they will be considered sinners.

- The *adhaan* ought to be recited in a nice and loud voice so people can hear it and come to the mosque and perform the congregational prayer.

- The *adhaan* has different formulas, all approved by the Prophet. The following is the common formula:

The Adhaan

1. *Allaahu akbar* "Allah is the greatest of all" (four times)

2. *Ash hadu an laa ilaaha illallaah* " I bear witness that there is no god worthy of worship except Allah" (twice)

3. *Ash hadu anna Muhammadan rasoolullaah* "I bear witness that *Muhammad is the Messenger of Allah*" (twice)

4. *Hayya 'alassalaah* "Come to prayer" (twice)

5. *Hayya 'alal-falaah* "Come to success" (twice)

6. *Allaahu akbar* "Allah is the greatest of all" (twice)

7. *laa ilaaha illallaah* " There is no god worthy of worship except Allah" (once)

The *Iqaamah*

1. *Allaahu akbar, Allaahu akbar* "Allah is the greatest of all, Allah is the greatest of all".

2. *Ash hadu an laa ilaaha illallaah* " I bear witness that there is no God worthy of worship except Allah".

3. *Ash hadu anna Muhammadan rasoolullaah* " I bear witness that Muhammad is the Messenger of Allah".

4. *Hayya 'alassalaah* "Come to prayer"

5. *Hayya 'alal-falaah* "Come to success"

6. *Qad qaamat-issalaatu, qad qaamat-issalaah* " The prayer is about to begin, the prayer is about to begin"

7. *Allaahu akbar, Allaahu akbar* "Allah is the greatest of all, Allah is the greatest of all"

8. *laa ilaaha illallaah* "There is no god worthy of worship except Allah"

Responding to the *Adhaan*

It is recommended, upon hearing each statement of the *adhaan*, to repeat after the *mu'adh-dhin* (the caller to prayer) and say exactly as he says, except when he says *Hayya 'alassalaah* "Come to prayer" or *Hayya 'alal-falaah* "Come to success", in which case one must say: *Laa hawla wa laa quwwata illaa billaah*, which means "There is neither might nor power except with Allah".

It is recommended to recite the following supplication after the *adhaan*: *Allaahumma rabba haadhih-id-da'wat-it-taammati, wassalaat-il-qaa'imati, aati Muhammadan-il-waseelata wal-fadeelata, wab'athu maqaaman mahmoodan alladhee wa'adtah*

(O Allah! Lord of this perfect call and this established prayer, grant Muhammad the intercession and favour, and raise him to the Praiseworthy Station which You have promised him).

> Allah rewards for every step one takes to the mosque.

> Humility and Attentiveness in Prayer

Humility and attentiveness (***khushoo'***) constitute the essence of the prayer and involve deep concentration and total humility before Almighty Allah, trying one's best to concentrate and understand the Qur'anic verses and supplications recited in the prayer.

Being one of the most meritorious acts of worship, Allah ﷻ considers it to be one of the characteristics of the believers: "Successful indeed are the believers; they are those who humble themselves in their prayer." (*Al-Mu'minoon,* 23:1-2)

> The nearest a servant can be to his Lord is when he prostrates himself in prayer.

Those who observe *khushoo'* in their prayer taste the sweetness of worship and faith, hence the Prophet's saying, "The prayer is the source of my greatest joy." (*Sunan An-Nasaa'ee:* 3940)

Means of Observing *Khushoo'* in Prayer

There are a number of means which help develop this state of humility and attentiveness in prayer including the following:

1. Making the Necessary Preparations for the Prayer

This can be done by going early to the mosque (for men), observing the recommended acts that precede it, wearing appropriate and fine clothes and walking to the mosque humbly and in a dignified manner.

2. Keeping Distractions away

One must not engage in prayer while there are some distractions that are bound to affect his concentration, such as pictures, loud noises, the need to answer the call of nature and hunger and thirst after food has been served. By keeping such distractions away, one develops a serene mind that paves the way for better concentration in this great act of worship one is about to offer.

3. *Tuma'neenah*

Tuma'neenah has no equivalent in English, and it generally means avoiding haste and not moving from one posture to another until it has lasted at least the time that it took for the bones to settle. The Prophet ﷺ never offered his prayer hurriedly. He would perform all the prayer postures and movements perfectly and would not move from one posture to another until it lasted at least the time that it took for the bones to settle. He would also order those of his companions who rushed their prayers to take their time in all the prayer postures and movements and to complete them properly. He did not like them to rush it and compared the act of hurriedly offering the prayer to that of the pecking of crows.

He once said to his companions, "The worst kind of thief is one who steals from his prayer." They asked him, "How can someone steal from this prayer?" He replied, "By not completing its bowing and prostrate postures properly." (*Musnad Ahmad:* 22642)

Those who rush their prayer cannot possibly offer it with deep concentration and total humility before Almighty Allah, for haste undoubtedly affects attentiveness and humility in prayer, reducing one's rewards.

4. Contemplating Allah's Greatness

We must contemplate the greatness of the Creator, recognising His perfection and acknowledging our own weaknesses and defects. Those who contemplate the greatness of Allah cannot help but notice that they are rather worthless by comparison. This increases their reverence of Allah and makes them invoke Allah and humbly and earnestly ask Him for anything. We must also remember the eternal bliss Allah ﷻ has prepared for the obedient believers and the severe punishment He has prepared for the unbelievers. We also must think about the day when we will stand before Allah for the final judgement.

Allah ﷻ mentions in the Qur'an that those who do so are indeed those who are certain they will meet Him: "Seek Allah's help with patient perseverance and prayer; and truly it is a very hard thing except for the humble, those who know that they will have to meet their Lord, and that to Him they are returning." (*Soorat Al-Baqarah,* 2:45-6)

The more conscious awareness we have that Allah can hear us, give us and respond to our prayers, the more humbleness we develop and the more we will contemplate Allah's greatness.

5. Meditating on the Qur'anic Verses and Other Prayer Utterances and Responding to Them

The Qur'an was revealed to be reflected on, as the Qur'an states, "It is a Book We have sent down to you, full of blessing, so let people of intelligence ponder its signs and take heed." (*Soorat Saad,* 38:29) This cannot be possibly achieved without understanding the meaning of the invocations, supplications and Qur'anic verses recited in prayer. Meditation on the meaning of what one recites as well as on one's own condition is bound to increase one's concentration and humility in prayer and even move one to tears and ecstasy. Such emotional effect becomes evident with every verse to which one listens, as the Qur'an states, "Those who, when they are reminded of the verses of their Lord, they do not turn a blind eye and a deaf ear to them." (*Soorat Al-Furqaan,* 25:73)

> The Friday Prayer (Salaat-ul-Jumu'ah)

The Friday prayer (*salaat-ul-jumu'ah*) is a religious obligation which takes the place of the daily afternoon prayer (*salaat-udh-Dhuhr*) on Friday. It is one of the most exalted Islamic rituals and one of its confirmed obligatory acts. On this day, Muslims gather once a week, listen to the sermon which the *imaam* delivers, and then offer the Friday prayer.

Virtues of Friday

Friday is the best and most exalted day of the week, for Allah ﷻ has favoured it over other days due to a number of virtues including the following:

> Worshippers must listen attentively to the Friday sermon and must not engage in anything which is bound to distract them from it.

- Allah ﷻ has specifically chosen it for the Muslims, as the Prophet ﷺ said, "Allah led those who came before us away from Friday. The Jews had Saturday, and the Christians had Sunday. Then Allah brought us and He guided us to Friday." (*Saheeh Muslim:* 856)

- Allah created Adam on it, and on this very day the Day of Judgement will take place, as the Prophet ﷺ said, "Friday is the best day on which the sun rises. On this day, Adam was created; on it he was admitted into Paradise and on it he was turned out of it. The Day of Judgement will also take place on Friday." (*Saheeh Muslim:* 854)

Who Must Perform the Friday Prayer?

The Friday prayer is a religious obligation that is binding on those who meet these conditions:

1. **They must be men:** Women do not have to offer it.

2. **They must be legally accountable (*mukallaf*)** for their actions: It is not obligatory for insane or children who have not reached puberty.

3. **They must be resident:** It is not obligatory for travellers or those who live in the countryside, outside towns and cities.

The Friday Prayer: Manner and Rulings

1. It is recommended that a Muslim should take a ritual bath (*ghusl*), wear nice and clean clothes and proceed early to the mosque.

2. Muslims gather in the mosque. The *imaam* mounts the pulpit *(minbar)*, faces the worshippers and delivers the *khutbah (sermon)*, which normally consists of two sections, between which he sits briefly. In this sermon, he reminds them of being conscious of Allah, offers them advice, preaches to them and recites to them verses from the Qur'an.

3. Muslims must listen attentively to the *khutbah*. They are not allowed to engage in talking or do anything which will otherwise deprive them of benefiting from the *khutbah*, even if it is fiddling with the carpet, stones or sand.

4. The *imaam* then descends from the pulpit, takes his position and leads the people in a two-rak'ah prayer in which he recites the Qur'an aloud.

5. The Friday prayer can only be performed if a certain number of people are present. If any person misses it for a valid reason, he cannot make up for it; and if he offers it on his own, it will not be valid. Instead, he must offer the daily afternoon prayer (*salaat-udh-Dhuhr*).

6. If a person comes late to the mosque and catches up with the *imaam* in less than one unit (*rak'ah*), he must complete his prayer after the *imaam* concludes the prayer, treating it as the afternoon prayer (*salaat-udh-Dhuhr*).

7. Those who are exempt from offering the Friday prayer, such as women and travellers, do not have to offer the daily afternoon prayer (*salaat-udh-Dhuhr*) if they have already performed the Friday prayer in the mosque.

Those who Are Exempt from Attending the Friday Prayer

Islam stresses that Muslims who are not exempt from offering the Friday prayer must perform it and warns them against occupying themselves with worldly pursuits: "O you who believe, when the call is proclaimed to prayer on Friday, hasten earnestly to the remembrance of Allah and leave off business and traffic. That is best for you if you only knew." (*Soorat Al-Jumu'ah*, 62:9)

It also warns that Allah will set a seal on the hearts of those who miss it without a valid excuse, as the Prophet ﷺ said, "Allah will seal up the hearts of those who

miss three Friday prayers consecutively, out of sheer negligence and without an excuse." (*Sunan Abu Daawood:* 1052; *Musnad Ahmad:* 15498) This means that He will cover their hearts and place ignorance in them, just like the hearts of hypocrites and disobedient people.

An excuse that is considered genuinely valid for missing a Friday prayer is one which involves unusually great hardship or one which is bound to cause serious harm to one's health or is detrimental to one's livelihood.

> "Say, 'What is with Allah is better than trade or entertainment.'" (*Soorat Al-Jumu'ah, 62:11*)

Can a career that requires one to work at the time of the Friday prayer be considered a valid excuse to miss it?

Generally, taking up careers that require one to carry on working at the time of the Friday prayer is not a valid excuse for missing the Friday prayer, for Allah ﷻ commands us to leave our worldly pursuits when we are called to the Friday prayer: "O you who believe, when the call is proclaimed to prayer on Friday, hasten earnestly to the remembrance of Allah and leave off business and traffic." (*Soorat Al-Jumu'ah,* 62:9) Therefore, a Muslim is required to take up jobs that will not prevent him from observing religious obligations even if such jobs are with less pay.

The Qur'an also states, "For those who fear Allah, He ever prepares a way out, and He provides for them from sources they never could imagine. And if any one puts his trust in Allah, sufficient is Allah for him." (*Soorat At-Talaaq,* 65:2-3)

When Can a Career Be Considered a Valid Excuse to Miss the Friday Prayer?

A career which requires us to carry on working during the time of the Friday prayer can only be considered a valid excuse in the following two cases:

1. Such a career must provide a great benefit which cannot be possibly realised if a person leaves the job and attends the Friday prayer. By the same token, leaving it will certainly cause great harm, especially when there is no one else to replace him.

   Examples:
   - Doctors who treat emergency cases.
   - Guards or police officers who protect people and their property from theft and criminal activity.
   - People who hold supervisory positions in large firms and the like which require constant supervision.

2. If such a career is the sole source of income which covers his basic expenses, such as food, drink and other necessary matters, for him and his family, then he may not attend the Friday prayer and may continue his work until he finds an alternative job or until he finds a source of food, drink and necessary matters that are sufficient for himself and his dependents. However, he must keep looking for another source of income.

> The Prayer of the Sick

A Muslim must offer the obligatory prayers under all circumstances as long as he is fully conscious and in full possession of his mental faculties. Islam does, however, take into account people's various situations and special needs, hence its legislation regarding sick people.

To clarify this point:

- If he is too sick to stand up, or if offering the prayer in a standing posture is bound to delay recovery, he is allowed to offer it in a sitting posture. If he cannot possibly do so, then he can offer it while lying down on his side. The Prophet ﷺ said, "Pray standing; if you cannot do so, pray in a sitting position; if you cannot do so either, then pray on your side." (*Saheeh Al-Bukhaaree:* 1066)

- If he cannot bow or prostrate, he may only lean forward as far as he can.

- If he cannot sit down on the floor, he may sit on a chair or anything similar.

- If he cannot perform *wudoo'* for every prayer due to his sickness, he may combine the afternoon prayer (*Dhuhr*) and the late afternoon prayer (*'Asr*), and the sunset prayer (*Maghrib*) and late evening prayer (*Ishaa'*)

- If he cannot use water due to his illness, he may perform *tayammum* (dry ablution) instead and then offer the prayer.

> The Traveller's Prayer

- **A traveller may,** when moving from one place to another or during his temporary residence which lasts less than four days, shorten the four-*rak'ah* prayers to two each. Thus, he offers two units (*rak'aat*, singular: *rak'ah*) instead of four for the afternoon prayer (*Dhuhr*), the late afternoon prayer (*'Asr*) and the late evening prayer (*'Ishaa'*), unless he prays behind a resident prayer leader (*imaam*), in which case he must follow suit.

- **He may leave** off the supererogatory prayers that are regularly offered with the obligatory ones (*as-sunan ar-rawaatib*) with the exception of the supererogatory prayer of the Fajr prayer.

- **He may combine** the afternoon prayer (*Dhuhr*) and the late afternoon prayer (*'Asr*), and the sunset prayer (*Maghrib*) and the late evening prayer (*'Ishaa'*) at the due time of either of them. This serves to ease the hardship he undergoes while travelling.

Your Fast

4

Allah ﷻ commands Muslims to observe a strict fast for one lunar month every year, namely, *Ramadaan*, which is the fourth pillar of Islam. As the Qur'an states, "O you who believe, fasting has been prescribed for you, just as it was prescribed for those before you, so that you may become righteous." (*Soorat Al-Baqarah*, 2:183)

Contents

Definition

Virtues of the Month of *Ramadaan*

The Wisdom behind Fasting

Virtues of Fasting

Things which Break the Fast

Those Who Are Exempt from Fasting
- The Sick
- The Infirm
- Travellers
- Menstruating Women and Women Experiencing Post-Natal Bleeding
- Pregnant and Nursing Women

Voluntary Fasting

The Festival of Fast Breaking (*'Eed-ul-Fitr*)
- What Should Be Done On *'Eed* Day?

Fasting Ramadaan

Definition

Fasting (*siyyaam* or *sawm*) is an act of worship which involves abstaining from all food, drink, sexual activity and anything which is bound to break the fast from dawn (the time of calling to the *Fajr* prayer) till sunset (the time of calling to the *Maghrib* prayer).

> Virtues of the Month of Ramadaan

Ramadaan is the ninth month of the Islamic lunar calendar. It is the best month of the year and has a number of virtues, including the following:

1 It was the month in which the greatest and most exalted of all divine books, the Holy Qur'an, was revealed: "It was in the month of *Ramadaan* that the Qur'an was revealed, with clear signs of guidance and a criterion of right and wrong. Therefore, those of you who are resident for the month must fast it." (*Soorat Al-Baqarah*, 2:185)

2 The Prophet ﷺ said, "When the month of *Ramadaan* comes, the gates of Paradise are opened, the gates of Hellfire are closed and the devils are chained." (*Saheeh Al-Bukhaaree*: 3103, *Saheeh Muslim*: 1079) Thus, it provides an opportunity for the faithful to do their utmost to get closer to Allah by doing righteous deeds and avoiding evil ones.

3 Whoever fasts during the daylight hours and stands in prayer at night throughout this month will have his past sins forgiven, as the Prophet ﷺ said, "Whoever fasts in the month of *Ramadaan*, out of sincere faith and in anticipation of Allah's rewards [in the hereafter], will have all his past sins forgiven." (*Saheeh Al-Bukhaaree*: 1910, *Saheeh Muslim*: 760) He also said, "Whoever offers the voluntary night prayers with sincere faith and hoping to attain Allah's rewards [in the hereafter] will have all his past sins forgiven." (*Saheeh Al-Bukhaaree*: 1905; *Saheeh Muslim*: 759)

4 L*aylat-ul-Qadr* (The Night of Decree; also called the Night of Power) occurs in this month. The Qur'an informs us that doing righteous deeds during this night is far better than doing them for many years: "The Night of Power is better than a thousand months." (*Soorat Al-Qadr*, 97:3) A person who prays on this night out of sincere faith and in anticipation of Allah's rewards in the hereafter will obtain Allah's forgiveness of all past sins. This night falls on one of the last ten odd-numbered nights of *Ramadaan* and no one knows its exact time.

> The Wisdom behind Fasting

Allah ﷻ commands the believers to observe the fast for numerous reasons pertaining to this world and the hereafter. These include the following:

① It helps realise *taqwaa* (righteousness, piety, consciousness of Allah, guarding against evil)

Fasting is an act of worship through which the faithful seek closeness to their Lord by giving up their passionate desires and placing themselves in opposition to physical temptations at all times and places, in secret and in public, knowing that Allah is watching them. As the Qur'an states, "O you who believe, fasting has been prescribed for you, just as it was prescribed for those before you, so that you may become righteous." (*Soorat Al-Baqarah,* 2:183)

② It provides ample training in refraining from sin and wrongdoing

When a fasting person desists from engaging in permissible acts, in total obedience to Allah, he will certainly be able to bring his whims and desires under control, easily avoid sins and will not persist in falsehood and deviation from the truth. The Prophet ﷺ said, "A person who does not desist form deceitful speech and actions [while fasting] must know that Allah is not in need of him leaving his food and drink." (*Saheeh Al-Bukhaaree:* 1804) This means that those who do not desist from telling lies and deceiving others do not actually perceive the purpose of fasting.

③ It helps us remember the needy and the distressed and encourages us to sympathise with them

Because the fasting person experiences the pangs of deprivation and hunger, which are only temporary, he realises the severe effects of such pains on his fellow Muslim brothers and sisters who might be deprived of the essentials of life for a long time and undergo extreme hunger and thirst. This prompts him to feel more compassion for them and help them.

> The fasting person has two moments of joy: one when he breaks his fast and the other one when he meets his Lord.

> Virtues of Fasting

Fasting has numerous virtues including the following:

1 A person who fasts during this month, sincerely believing in Allah, in obedience to His commands and is certain of His rewards in the hereafter for doing so, will have all his past sins forgiven. The Prophet ﷺ said, "Whoever fasts in the month of Ramadaan, out of sincere faith and in anticipation of Allah's rewards [in the hereafter], will have all his past sins forgiven." (Saheeh Al-Bukhaaree: 1910; Saheeh Muslim: 760)

2 The fasting person will experience great joy in the hereafter for the great rewards he will get and the bliss he will enjoy for fasting. The Prophet ﷺ said, "The fasting person has two moments of joy: one when he breaks his fast and the other one when he meets his Lord." (Saheeh Al-Bukhaaree: 1805; Saheeh Muslim: 1151)

3 Paradise has a gate called Ar-Rayyaan through which only those who used to fast will enter, as the Prophet ﷺ said, "In Paradise there is a gate called Ar-Rayyaan, through which only those who fast will enter on the Day of Resurrection, and no one but they will enter it. It will be said, 'Where are those who fasted?' They will then get up, and none will enter it but them. When they enter, it will be closed, and no one else will enter." (Saheeh Al-Bukhaaree: 1797; Saheeh Muslim: 1152)

4 Every act of worship has a certain reward except for fasting, for which Allah, in His boundless bounty and mercy, will reward those who observe it abundantly. The Prophet ﷺ said, "Allah said, 'All the deeds of the children of Adam are for them except for fasting, which is for Me, and I will reward it.'" (Saheeh Al-Bukhaaree: 1805, Saheeh Muslim: 1151)

> *Ramadaan* is the ninth month of the Islamic lunar calendar.

> Things which Break the Fast

A fasting person must avoid a number of things which are bound to break the fast. They are as follows:

1. Food and drink, as the Qur'an states, "Eat and drink until you can clearly discern the white thread from the black thread of the dawn, then strictly observe the fast until nightfall." (*Soorat Al-Baqarah,* 2:187)

However, if a person forgets that he is fasting and so he eats or drinks, his fast is still valid and he is not considered sinful for absent-mindedly doing so. The Prophet ﷺ said, "Whoever forgets he is fasting and so he eats or drinks, let him complete his fast for it is Allah who has fed him and given him to drink." (*Saheeh Al-Bukhaaree:* 1831; *Saheeh Muslim:* 1155)

2. Anything that is classified as being in some way similar to eating and drinking. This includes the following:

- Injections which have some nutritional value: These serve to supply the body with the necessary minerals and nutrients it needs, hence their similarity to eating and drinking.

- Having a blood transfusion: Blood is like the body's transportation system, and as it circulates, it delivers oxygen and nutrients throughout the body, hence its resemblance to eating and drinking.

- Smoking in all its forms renders the fast void, for inhaling smoke introduces numerous toxic substances into the body.

3. Sexual activity in which a man puts his penis into a woman's vagina, whether or not this results in ejaculation.

4. Deliberate seminal emission through sexual contact, masturbation or any other means.

However, wet dreams, sexually exciting dreams that result in an orgasm, do not break the fast.

A man may kiss his wife if he knows he can easily control himself and does not engage in intercourse or any act that may lead to seminal emission.

5. Deliberate vomiting: Involuntary vomiting, however, does not the break the fast. The Prophet ﷺ said, "If a person vomits unintentionally while observing a fast, he does not have to make up for this by fasting another day; however, if he deliberately vomits, then he must fast another day for breaking his [obligatory] fast." (*Sunan At-Tirmidhee:* 720; *Sunan Abu Daawood:* 2380)

6. Beginning of menstruation or post-natal bleeding regardless of the time or part of the day when such bleeding begins. Whenever such bleeding begins, even if it takes place just before sunset, a woman's fast is automatically broken. If a menstruating woman becomes clean after dawn, her fast is also broken. The Prophet ﷺ said, "Isn't it true that a woman can neither pray nor fast during her menses?"(*Saheeh Al-Bukhaaree:* 1850)

Nevertheless, apart from menstrual bleeding and post-natal bleeding, abnormal uterine bleeding which some women experience does not prevent them from fasting.

> Those Who Are Exempt from Fasting

To make it easy for people, Allah has exempted some of them from fasting. They are:

1 **Sick people** whose medical condition is bound to be further worsened by fasting are permitted to break the fast but must make up for the missed fasts after *Ramadaan*.

2 **People who cannot possibly observe a fast** due to old age or sick people for whom there is no hope of recovery may also break the fast but must feed a needy person for every day missed, by giving him 1.5 kg of the staple food common in the country.

3 **Travellers,** while moving from one place to another or during their temporary residence which lasts less than four days, are allowed to break the fast but have to make up for the fast days they have missed after Ramadaan. As the Qur'an states, "But those of you who are sick or are on a journey must fast an equal number of other days. Allah wants ease for you, not hardship." (*Soorat Al-Baqarah:* 185)

4 **Menstruating women and women experiencing post-natal bleeding** are forbidden to fast but must make up an equal number of days after *Ramadaan*. Even if they fast, it will not be valid. (See page 98)

5 **Pregnant and nursing** women are permitted to break the fast if they fear it would be dangerous for them or for their babies if they fast. They must, however, make up for the fast days they have missed after *Ramadaan*.

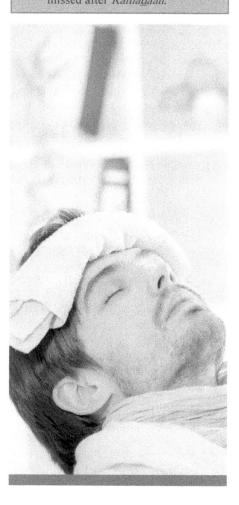

The Islamic Ruling Regarding Those who Deliberately Break the Fast

Breaking the fast without a valid excuse is a grave sin which clearly testifies to its doer's disobedience to Allah ﷻ. Therefore, those who commit such a sin must sincerely repent to Allah in addition to making up for the fast days they have omitted. Those who engage in sexual intercourse during the day in *Ramadaan* must, in addition to expressing sincere repentance and making up that day, expiate for doing so by freeing a Muslim slave, hence the importance Islam attaches to liberating people from the shackles of servitude. If they cannot find any slaves to set free, as is the case today, they must fast for two consecutive months; if they are unable do so, then they have to feed sixty poor people.

> Voluntary Fasting

Muslims are required to observe a strict month-long fast once a year, that is, during the month of *Ramadaan*. They are also recommended, as long as they are able to do so, to fast on other days in order to gain more rewards. These days include the following:

1. The day of *'Aashuraa'*, as well as a day before it or after it: *'Aashuraa'* is the tenth day of the lunar month of *Muharram*, the first month of the Islamic calendar. It is the very day Allah ﷻ saved Moses ﷺ and drowned Pharaoh and his army. A Muslim fasts it as an expression of gratitude to Allah for saving Moses and to follow in the footsteps of our Prophet ﷺ who not only fasted on this day but also asked his companions to fast a day before it or a day after it. (*Musnad Ahmad:* 2154). When he was asked about fasting on it, he replied, "It expiates [the sins committed in] the previous year."(*Saheeh Muslim:*1162)

2. The Day of *'Arafah: 'Arafah* is the ninth day of the lunar month of *Dhul-Hijjah*, the twelfth month of the Islamic calendar. On this day, pilgrims who perform the *hajj*, the annual Muslim pilgrimage, gather in the wide open plain of 'Arafah and engage in invoking Allah, praising Him and glorifying Him. *'Arafah* is the best day of the year, and those who are not performing the *hajj* may fast on it. When the Prophet ﷺ was asked about fasting on this day, he replied, "It atones for the sins committed the preceding year and the coming year." (*Saheeh Muslim:* 1162)

3. Six days of *Shawwaal: Shawwaal* is the tenth month of the Islamic calendar. The Prophet ﷺ said, "Whoever fasts in *Ramadaan* then follows it up with six days of the month of *Shawwaal* will obtain the rewards of fasting for the entire year." (*Saheeh Muslim:* 1164)

> The Festival of Fast Breaking ('Eed-ul-Fitr)

Festivals represent apparent rituals of religion. When the Prophet ﷺ arrived in Madeenah, he found that the people there had set aside two days in the year for fun. He asked them, "What are these two days?" "We used to play and have fun on these days before the advent of Islam," they replied. The Prophet ﷺ then said, "Allah has given you two better days: *'Eed-ul-Fitr* and *'Eed-ul-Adhaa*." (*Sunan Abu Daawood:* 1134) Explaining that festivals represent the religion of their followers, he once observed, "Every nation has a festival, and this is our festival." (*Saheeh Al-Bukhaaree:* 909; *Saheeh Muslim:* 892)

The Meaning of *'Eed* in Islam

'Eed is a day of festivity and rejoicing. On this day, Muslims express their happiness and their gratitude to Allah for guiding them to the truth and for assisting them in completing the fast of *Ramadaan*. They share happiness with everyone by putting on their best clothes, giving charity to the poor and the needy and engaging in permissible celebrations and festivities which make everyone happy and remind them of Allah's favours upon them.

Muslim Festivals

There are only two annual festivals in Islam, and Muslims must not celebrate any other day apart from them. They are: (1) The Festival of Fast Breaking (*'Eed-ul-Fitr*), which is celebrated on the first day of the lunar month of *Shawwaal*, and (2) the Festival of *Sacrifice* (*'Eed-ul-Adhaa*), which is celebrated on the tenth day of the lunar month of *Dhul-Hijjah*.

The Festival of Fast Breaking (*'Eed-ul-Fitr*)

'Eed-ul-Fitr falls on the first day of the lunar month of *Shawwaal*, marking the end of the month-long *Ramadaan* fast. Just as fasting during the month of *Ramadaan* is an act of worship, celebrating *'Eed-ul-Fitr* is also an act of worship whereby Muslims express their gratitude to Allah for enabling them to perform this act of worship and for completing His grace upon them. As the Qur'an states, "You should complete the number of days and proclaim Allah's greatness for the guidance He has given you so that you will be thankful." (*Soorat Al-Baqarah*, 2:185)

What Should Be Done On the *'Eed Day*?

1 **Offering the *'Eed* Prayer:** Islam stresses that the *'Eed* prayer should be performed. In fact, it was one of those practices which the Prophet ﷺ observed consistently and even encouraged not only men but also women and children to observe. Its time starts after the sun has risen to the length of a spear above the horizon (just over 1 metre) and lasts until it has crossed the meridian.

Description: The *'Eed* prayer consists of two units (*rak'aat;* singular *rak'ah*) in which the *imaam* recites the Qur'an loudly, after which he delivers a sermon (*khutbah*) in two parts. This prayer contains several *takbeeraat* (singular *takbeerah*, one's saying *Allaahu akbar*) at the beginning of each unit more than the ordinary prayer: The *imaam* says *Allaahu akbar* and, before he starts reciting the Qur'an, repeats the same utterance six more times; also, after rising from the prostrate position to the standing position to perform the second unit, he repeats the same utterance five more times in addition to the *takbeer* he has recited while rising to the second unit. The worshippers follow the *imaam* in these movements, doing and saying exactly the same.

2 Paying *Zakaat-ul-Fitr*: Allah has enjoined *zakaat-ul-fitr* (literally, the purifying obligatory charity of the breaking of the fast) on anyone who possesses a day's and night's worth of food. It consists of one *saa'* of the most common staple food of the country, be it rice, wheat or dates, and must be given to the Muslim poor and needy so that there would be no person in need of food on the *'Eed day*. It is permissible, however, to pay the value of *zakaat-ul-fitr* in money instead if it appears that this will be more beneficial to the poor.

Time of Its Payment: *Zakaat-ul-fitr* is to be paid from the time the sun sets on the last day of *Ramadaan* up to the time of the *'Eed* prayer. It may, however, be paid a day or two before the *'Eed* day as well.

The amount of *zakaat-ul-fitr* is one *saa'* of the usual foods tufs of the country, be it rice, wheat or dates. One *saa'* is equivalent to approximately 3 kg.

A Muslim must pay it for himself and all the persons he is legally bound to support, such as his wife and children. It is recommended to pay it on behalf of an unborn child.

The Prophet ﷺ enjoined it as "atonement for any obscene language used while observing the fast and for providing food for the needy. It would be accepted as *zakaat* from those who pay it before the *'Eed* prayer, but it would be considered as mere *sadaqah* (voluntary charity) for those who pay it after the *'Eed* prayer." (*Sunan Abu Daawood:* 1609)

3 Muslims on this occasion spread joy and merriment to all family members, young and old, men and women, providing all possible types of lawful amusements. They wear their best and most beautiful clothes and eat and drink, as doing so is an act of worship. Fasting on this day is strictly forbidden.

4 They recite the *takbeer* on this special occasion on the night preceding the *'Eed day* and on the way to the *'Eed* prayer, and continue doing so until the *imaam* appears for the *'Eed* prayer starts, expressing gratitude to Allah ﷻ for enabling them to complete the fast of *Ramadaan*. The Qur'an states, "He wants you to complete the prescribed period and to glorify Him for having guided you, so that you may be thankful." (*Soorat Al-Baqarah*, 2:185)

The manner of *takbeer* pronounced on this occasion is as follows: *Allaahu akbar, Allaahu akbar, laa ilaaha ill allaah, Allaahu akbar, Allaahu akbar, walillaahil-hamd* (Allah is the Greatest, Allah is the Greatest; there is no god worthy of worship except Allah; Allah is the Greatest, Allah is the Greatest; all praise belongs to Allah).

One may also recite the following: *Allaah uakbaru kabeeran, wal-hamdu lillaahi katheeran, wa subhaan-Allaahi bukratan wa aseelaa* (Allah is the Greatest;His is the abundant praise, and glory be to Him day and night).

Men generally pronounce the *takbeer* aloud, but without disturbing other people; women, however, pronounce it quietly.

> Muslims leaving the mosque after offering the *'Eid prayer*.

Your Zakaat

5

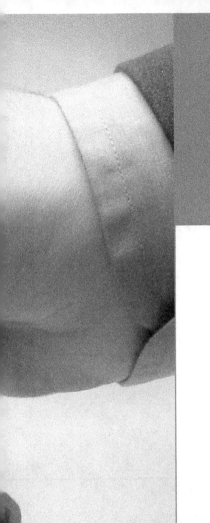

Allah ﷻ has enjoined *zakaat* upon the faithful, making it the third pillar of Islam, and warned those who do not pay it against severe punishment. Indeed, He links brotherhood of faith with sincere repentance, offering the prayers and paying the *zakaat*, as the Qur'an states, "Yet if they repent and establish regular prayers and pay the *zakaat*, then they are your brothers in faith." (*Soorat At-Tawbah,* 9:11)

The Prophet ﷺ also said, "Islam has been built on five [pillars]: Testifying that there is no god but Allah and that *Muhammad* is the messenger of Allah, performing the prayers, paying the *zakaat*, making the pilgrimage to the House, and fasting in *Ramadaan*."(*Saheeh Al-Bukhaaree*.8; *Saheeh Muslim:* 16)

Contents

The Ultimate Objectives of *Zakaat*

Types of Wealth upon which *Zakaat* Is Due

- Gold and Silver
- All Types of Currency.
- Commercial commodities
- Agricultural Produce
- Livestock

Recipients of *Zakaat*

Zakaat

The Ultimate Objectives of *Zakaat*

Allah has enjoined *zakaat* on the Muslims for a number of reasons including the following:

1. Love of wealth is an innate human tendency, and man does whatever he possibly can to acquire it. It is for this reason that Islam requires him to pay *zakaat* to purify his heart from selfishness and greed, as the Qur'an states, "Take *zakaat* from their wealth to purify and cleanse them." (*Soorat At-Tawbah*, 9:103)

2. Paying *zakaat* nurtures feelings of affection and harmony and fosters community cohesion. Because people generally have a disposition to like those who do them a good turn, members of the Muslim society become so close-knit that they resemble bricks of a building, supporting one another. Crimes such as theft and robbery tend to drop off.

3. Paying *zakaat* is a vivid expression of true worship and total submission to Allah . When the wealthy pay *zakaat* they actually obey Allah's commands, recognising that all prosperity ultimately comes from Allah's favour and grace. By doing so, they also show thankfulness to Him for having bestowed His blessings upon them: "If you are grateful, I will certainly give you increase." (*Soorat Ibraaheem*, 14:7)

4. By paying *zakaat* the concept of social security and relative equality among members of society is realised. When the wealthy distribute the annual amount of *zakaat* among the rightful beneficiaries, wealth ceases to build up in a few hands and is instead kept in constant circulation. As the Qur'an states, "This is so that they do not just circulate among those of you who are rich." (*Soorat Al-Hashr*, 59:7)

> Love of wealth is an innate human tendency, and Islam requires its followers not to be obsessively attached to wealth and to pay *zakaat* in order to purify their hearts from selfish greed.

Types of Wealth upon which *Zakaat* Is Due

Zakaat is not due on the necessities of life, such as food, drink, clothing, the house one lives in, even if it is a high-priced house, and the car one drives, even if it is a luxurious car.

It is only due on types of wealth which are not kept for immediate use and which are bound to increase, such as the following:

❶ Gold and silver (with the exception of gold and silver ornaments used by women for their personal use)

Zakaat is due on gold and silver only if their value has reached or exceeded an established minimum threshold for this particular kind of wealth (*nisaab*) and after one has been in possession of this for a complete lunar year (354 days).

The minimum prescribed limit on which *zakaat* becomes obligatory (*nisaab*) on this type of wealth is as follows:

Zakaat due on gold is approximately 85 grams and that due on silver is 595 grams.

Therefore, if a Muslim has held such an amount for a whole year, he must pay *zakaat* at the minimum rate of two and a half per cent (2.5%).

❷ All types of currency (banknotes and coins) held as cash in hand or bank balances

The *nisaab* liable to *zakaat* on cash, banknotes and coins is to be determined according to its corresponding value of gold (85 grams of pure gold) at the time *zakaat* falls due, based on the current rates of the country in which the payer of *zakaat* is resident. If such currency has been held in one's possession for an entire lunar year, two and a half per cent (2.5%) of its value must be given out as *zakaat*.

To illustrate, if one gram of pure gold at the time *zakaat* falls due is worth, say $25, the *nisaab* of the currency will be as follows:

25 (price of one gram of gold, which is unstable) x85 (number of grams, which is stable) = $2125 is the minimum exemption limit (*nisaab*).

It is worth noting that estimating the *nisaab* liable to *zakaat* on banknotes, coins and commercial commodities is generally based on their corresponding minimum amount of gold, since the value of gold is more stable than any other kind of property.

③ Commercial commodities

This term stands for all properties owned with the aim of investing them in trade. They generally include assets, such as real property, and commodities, such as consumer goods and foodstuffs.

The value of commercial assets, which have been held in one's possession for an entire lunar year, must be estimated according to the current market value on the day *zakaat* falls due. If the commercial commodities reach the *nisaab*, two and a half per cent (2.5%) of their value must be given out as *zakaat*.

④ Farm produce

The Qur'an states, "O you who believe, give away some of the good things you have earned and some of what We have produced for you from the earth." (*Soorat Al-Baqarah*, 2:267)

Zakaat is due only on certain types of agricultural produce on condition *zakaatable* produce has reached the minimum amount on which *zakaat* is due (*nisaab*)

In consideration of people's different circumstances, the amount of *zakaat* payable on farm produce varies according to costs spent and effort exerted in irrigation.

⑤ Livestock:
Zakaat is due on livestock, such as cows, camels and sheep, only if the animals graze on pasture and the owner does not take a lot of trouble to supply them with fodder.

If he supplies them with fodder all or most of the year, *zakaat* is not due on them.

Details as to the minimum amount upon which *zakaat* is due (*nisaab*) on livestock are available in books on Islamic jurisprudence (*fiqh*).

Recipients of *Zakaat*

Islam has specified the beneficiaries of *zakaat*, and a Muslim may pay it to one or more categories or simply give it to charitable societies which undertake to distribute it to those entitled to it. It is more appropriate, however, to pay it in the country where one lives.

Those who qualify to receive *zakaat* funds are as follows:

1. **The destitute** who live in absolute poverty as well as those who cannot meet their basic needs.

2. **Those employed** to collect and distribute *zakaat*.

3. **Slaves** who need money to purchase their freedom.

4. **Those who have run into debt and cannot possibly pay it off,** regardless of whether they have assumed debt for public or personal interest.

5. **Those who struggle in the cause of Allah:** This includes those who fight in defence of their religion and country as well as those who engage in any activity which aims to support and propagate Islam.

6. **Those whose hearts are to be reconciled:** These are those who have recently embraced Islam or those expected to embrace it. The duty of giving *zakaat* to this category of recipients does not belong to individuals but rather to government bodies, Islamic centres and charitable organisations that determine the real benefit behind that.

7. **The travellers who are undergoing financial difficulties** even if they are very rich back home.

Regarding the deserving beneficiaries of *zakaat*, the Qur'an states, "*Zakaat* is for the poor, the destitute, those who collect it, those whose hearts are to be reconciled, for those in debt, for the cause of Allah and the stranded travellers. It is a legal obligation from Allah. Allah is All-Knowing, All-Wise." (*Soorat At-Tawbah,* 9:60)

> The poor and the needy are those who cannot meet their basic needs.

Your Pilgrimage

Hajj, the annual Muslim pilgrimage to Makkah, is the fifth pillar of Islam. It is an act of worship which not only involves the heart but also requires physical and financial ability and must be carried out by every able-bodied Muslim who can afford to do so once in his lifetime.

As the Qur'an states, "Pilgrimage to the House is a duty owed to Allah by people who are able to undertake it. Those who reject this [should know that] Allah has no need of anyone." (*Soorat Aal-'Imraan*, 3:97)

Contents

The Importance and Virtues of Makkah and the Sacred Mosque

The Meaning of *Hajj*

The Ability to Perform *Hajj*: Different Circumstances

A Woman Needs a *Mahram* as a Companion to Perform *Hajj*

Virtues of *Hajj*

The Ultimate Goals of *Hajj*

'Umrah

The Festival of Sacrifice (*'Eed-ul-Adhaa*)
- What Should Be Done On *'Eed Day*?
- The Conditions that the Sacrificial Animal Must Satisfy
- What Should Be Done with the Sacrificial Animal?

Visiting Madeenah

*H*ajj

The Importance and Virtues of Makkah and the Sacred Mosque

The Sacred Mosque (*Al-Masjid Al-Haraam*) is located in Makkah, a city on the western side of the Arabian Peninsula, and has numerous virtues including the following:

1. It houses the Ka'bah

The Ka'bah is a cube-shaped building located at the centre of the Sacred Mosque in Makkah.

It is the direction towards which Muslims turn in prayer as well as during some other acts of worship which Allah ﷻ commands them to do.

It was built by Prophet Abraham ﷺ and his son Ishmael ﷺ following Allah's command to do so, and was rebuilt several times throughout history.

As the Qur'an states, "And when Abraham and Ishmael were raising the foundations of the House (the Ka'bah), [they prayed:] 'Our Lord, accept this from us, for You are the All-Hearing, the All-Knowing.'" (*Soorat Al-Baqarah,* 2:127)

Prophet Mu*h*ammad ﷺ himself took part in laying the Black Stone in its proper place along with the various Makkan tribes when they rebuilt the Ka'bah.

> The door of the Ka'bah, lavishly inscribed with quotations from the Holy Qur'an

2. It was the first mosque ever built on earth

Abu Dharr ؓ, one of the Prophet's noble companions, once asked the Prophet ﷺ, "Messenger of Allah, which mosque was built first on earth?" "The Sacred Mosque [in Makkah]" he replied. Abu Dharr again asked, "Which was next?" "Al-Aqsaa Mosque [in Jerusalem]," he replied. "How long was the period between them?" Abu Dharr further enquired, "Forty years," the Prophet ﷺ replied. "Wherever you may be and the prayer time becomes due," he continued, "offer the prayer there, for virtue lies in offering the prayers at their due times." (*Saheeh Al-Bukhaaree:* 3186; *Saheeh Muslim:* 520)

3. The reward for offering prayers in it is multiplied many times over

The Prophet ﷺ said, "One prayer in this mosque of mine [in Madeenah] is better than a thousand prayers in any other, except the Sacred Mosque [in Makkah], and one prayer in the Sacred Mosque is better than one hundred thousand prayers anywhere else." (*Sunan Ibn Maajah:* 1406; *Musnad Ahmad:* 14694)

4. Allah ﷻ and His Messenger ﷺ have declared it sacred

As the Qur'an states, "I have been ordered to worship the Lord of this city which He has declared sacred; everything belongs to Him; and I have been ordered to be one of the Muslims." (*Soorat An-Naml*, 27:91)

This verse makes it plain that Allah has declared Makkah a sanctuary and has thus forbidden people from committing injustices or shedding blood in it, chasing its game or cutting down its trees or grass.

The Prophet ﷺ once observed, "Allah, not the people, has made Makkah a sanctuary; therefore, any person who believes in Allah and the Last Day should neither shed blood in it nor cut down its trees." (*Saheeh Al-Bukhaaree:* 104; *Saheeh Muslim:* 1354)

5. It is the dearest of all lands to Allah ﷻ and His Messenger ﷺ

One of the Prophet's companions once said, "I saw Allah's Messenger ﷺ sitting on his camel in the Al-Hazwarah market, addressing Makkah thus, "By Allah, you are the best and the dearest of all lands of Allah to Him. Had I not been driven out of you, I would have never left you." (*Sunan At-Tirmidhee:* 3925; *An-Nasaa'ee's As-Sunan Al-Kubraa:* 4252)

6. Allah ﷻ has made pilgrimage to the Sacred House obligatory upon all those who are able to do so

Abraham ﷺ proclaimed pilgrimage to the people and they came to perform it from distant places. According to a Prophetic tradition, all the prophets performed *hajj* to the Sacred House. Regarding Allah's command to Abraham ﷺ in this respect, the Qur'an states, "Announce *hajj* to mankind. They will come to you on foot and on every sort of lean animal, coming by every distant road." (*Soorat Al-Hajj*, 22:27)

> Walking around the Ka'bah (*tawaaf*) seven times is one of the 'pillars' of *hajj* and *'umrah*.

> The Meaning of Hajj

Hajj is the religious journey undertaken to the Sacred Mosque in Makkah and some of the surrounding areas with the intention of performing the pilgrimage rituals. This journey involves a series of activities taught by the Prophet ﷺ, which include, among other things, assuming the condition of ritual purity (*ihraam*), walking seven times around the Ka'bah, walking seven times between the hills of As-Safaa and Al-Marwah, staying in the Plain of 'Arafah and throwing pebbles at the stone pillars in Mina.

Indeed, *Hajj* provides pilgrims with huge benefits, including, among other things, declaration of the oneness of Allah, immense forgiveness, getting to know one another and learning the rulings of Islam.

The *hajj* rites are usually performed between the eighth and thirteenth of *Dhul-Hijjah*, the twelfth month of the Islamic lunar calendar.

Who must perform it?

For a Muslim to perform *Hajj*, he has to be legally accountable for his actions (*mukallaf*) and able to do so. Legal accountability (*takleef*) means he has to be mature and sane.

What does ability mean?

Ability here involves the ability to undertake the journey to the Sacred Mosque through legitimate means and to perform the *Hajj* rites without undergoing unusually strenuous hardships and without risking personal safety and property. This also means that the expenses the pilgrim requires for *Hajj* must be in excess of his needs and the needs of his dependents.

>The Ability to Perform _Hajj_: Different Circumstances

1. **The ability to perform _Hajj_ in person:** This ability allows a Muslim to undertake the journey to the Sacred House without undergoing unusually strenuous hardships while having sufficient means to do so. He must, in this case, perform it in person.

2. **The financial ability to authorise someone else to perform _Hajj_ on one's behalf:** This applies to a Muslim who is unable to perform _Hajj_ in person due to illness or old age but who has the means to authorise someone else to perform it on his behalf. He must, in this case, offer the proxy the necessary expenses to perform it on his behalf.

3. **Lack of ability to perform _Hajj_ in person or by proxy:** A person who cannot possibly do so is exempt from performing _Hajj_ altogether. To illustrate, a person who does not have expenses in excess of his needs and the needs of his dependents with which he can perform _Hajj_ does not have to perform it at all. Nor is he required to raise or collect money in order to perform it. However, he must perform it as soon as he becomes physically and financially able to do so.

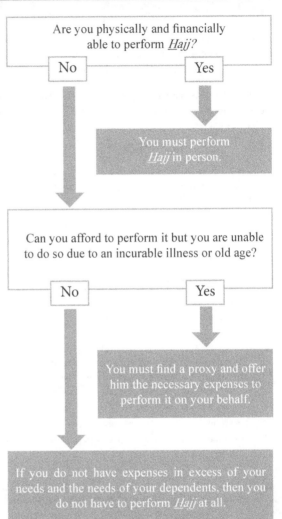

A Woman Needs a Mahram as a Companion to Perform Hajj

For a woman to perform _Hajj_, she has to be with her husband or any of her male relatives whom she is not permitted to marry because of their close blood relationship (_mahram_), such as her father, grandfather, sons, grandsons, brothers, nephews and uncles. (See page 207)

However, if a woman performs _Hajj_ without a _mahram_ in such a way that she is not exposed to any danger whatsoever, her _Hajj_ is valid and would certainly suffice.

Virtues of Hajj

Performing _Hajj_ has numerous virtues including the following:

1. It is one of the best deeds in the sight of Allah. The Prophet ﷺ was once asked, "What is the best deed?" He replied, "Belief in Allah and His Messenger." He was then asked, "What next?" "Fighting in the way of Allah," he replied. He was further asked, "What next?" He replied, "_Hajj_ that is performed correctly and is accepted by Allah." (_Saheeh Al-Bukhaaree_: 1447; _Saheeh Muslim_: 83)

2. It is a season of great forgiveness. The Prophet ﷺ said, "Whoever performs the pilgrimage for Allah's sake, avoids intimate relations [with his wife], does not fight with anyone nor abuse anyone, he will return home free from sins like the day his mother gave birth to him." (_Saheeh Al-Bukhaaree_: 1449; _Saheeh Muslim_: 1350)

3. It provides a great opportunity to be saved from the hellfire. The Prophet ﷺ said, "There is no day on which Allah frees people from the Fire as He does on the Day of 'Arafah." (_Saheeh Muslim_: 1348)

4. The reward for it is Paradise, as evidenced by the saying of the Prophet ﷺ: "There is no reward for a _Hajj_ that is preformed correctly and is accepted by Allah except Paradise." (_Saheeh Muslim_: 1349)

However, these and other merits will be enjoyed only by those who perform it solely for the sake of Allah and follow in the footsteps of the Prophet ﷺ.

> The Ultimate Goals of Hajj

Hajj has numerous goals and objectives. After instructing pilgrims about what to do regarding the sacrificial animal they have to slaughter to seek closeness to Allah, Allah ﷻ states, "Their flesh and blood does not reach Allah: it is your piety that reaches Him." (*Soorat Al-Hajj*, 22:37) The Prophet ﷺ also said in this connection, "Going round the Ka'bah, running between the hills of A*s*-*S*afaa and Al-Marwah and the stoning of the pillars are only meant for the remembrance of Allah." (*Sunan Abu Daawood:* 1888)

These goals and objectives include the following:

1 A demonstration of total submission and humility to Allah

This is realised when pilgrims forsake all forms of luxury and adornment and wear simple seamless garments before assuming the condition of ritual purity (*ihraam*), showing their total need and dependence on their Lord and ridding themselves of all worldly concerns and pursuits that may otherwise distract them from demonstrating total devotion to Him, which is bound to invite His mercy and forgiveness. This demonstration of total submission becomes all the more vivid on the Day of 'Arafah when they stand before their Lord, in a state of awe and reverence, giving thanks to Him for His countless blessings and seeking His forgiveness for their slips and failings.

2 A demonstration of gratefulness to Allah

Gratefulness to Allah for performing *hajj* is shown for both the money and good health Allah ﷻ has provided, which are amongst the greatest worldly blessings Allah has bestowed on man. When a Muslim performs *Hajj*, he actually demonstrates gratefulness to Allah for these two blessings by undergoing great physical hardships and spending his money to seek closeness to Allah, in total obedience to Him. Showing gratefulness is a duty that is not only established and affirmed by reasoning but also ordained by divine law.

> A person who intends to perform *Hajj* or *'umrah* must learn about the Islamic rulings relating to them.

A wholesome demonstration of the universality of Islam

Muslims from the four corners of the world gather in the holy land in response to the call of Allah. They get to know one another, and the barriers of race, colour, language and social class are set aside in this fraternity of faith that unites all Muslims in the largest, annual human gathering in which they help one another in furthering virtue and God-consciousness.

It is a reminder of the Day of Judgement

Hajj reminds those who perform it, of the Day of Resurrection when all human beings will stand equal before Allah for the final judgement. When pilgrims stand in the plain of 'Arafah, after assuming the state of ritual purity (*ihraam*) by replacing their ordinary clothes with simple garments and expressing their readiness to serve Allah, and perceive the countless multitudes of pilgrims, all dressed in what looks like shrouds, this will open their eyes to what they will go through after death and will prompt them to strive harder in preparation for the Hereafter.

 It is a demonstration of true worship of Allah alone

This is realised through the pilgrims' recitation of the *talbiyah: Labbayk-Allaahumma labbayk, labbayka laa shareeka laka labbayk, innal-hamda wanni'mata laka wal-mulk, laa shareeka lak* (Here I am at Your service O Allah, here I am. Here I am at Your service. You have no partners. Yours alone is all praise and all bounty, and Yours alone is the sovereignty. You have no partners." Describing *talbiyah* Prophet ﷺ one of the Prophet's companions once referred to them as words of "pure monotheism". (*Saheeh Muslim:* 1218) Indeed, pure monotheism is apparent in all the *Hajj* rites, words and deeds without exception.

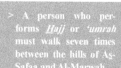

> A person who performs *Hajj* or *'umrah* must walk seven times between the hills of As-Safaa and Al-Marwah.

> 'Umrah

'*Umrah*, or minor pilgrimage (*Hajj* being the major pilgrimage), is an act of worship which consists of ritual practices that are confined to the Sacred Mosque area only, namely entering the sacred state of purity (*ihraam*), walking seven times round the Ka'bah, walking seven times between the hills of As-Safaa and Al-Marwah, and then having one's head shaved off or one's hair cut short.

The Islamic ruling regarding '*Umrah*: It is obligatory for those who can afford it once in their lifetime and it is recommended to perform it again and again.

Its time: It may be undertaken anytime throughout the year, but performing it during the month of *Ramadaan* has a special merit, as the Prophet ﷺ states, "Performing '*Umrah* during the month of *Ramadaan* is equal to performing *Hajj* (pilgrimage) in merit and excellence." (*Saheeh Al-Bukhaaree:* 3186; *Saheeh Muslim:* 520)

> Muslims are required to perform '*Umrah* once in their lifetime if they are able to do so.

The Festival of Sacrifice ('Eed-ul-Adhaa)

The Festival of Sacrifice (*'Eed-ul-Adhaa*), which is celebrated on the tenth day of the lunar month of *Dhul-Hijjah*, the twelfth month of the Islamic calendar, has numerous merits including the following:

1. It is one of the best days of the year, being amongst the first ten days of the lunar month of *Dhul-Hijjah*, as the Prophet ﷺ said, "There are no days in which good deeds are dearer to Allah than these ten days [of *Dhul-Hijjah*]." His companions enquired, "Not even *jihaad* in the way of Allah?" He replied, "Not even *jihaad* in the way of Allah, except for someone who goes out for *jihaad*, sacrificing both his life and property, and returns with neither of them." (*Saheeh Al-Bukhaaree*: 926; *Sunan At-Tirmidhee*: 757)

2. It is "the day of the greater pilgrimage" in which the greatest *Hajj* rites are carried out, the foremost and most exalted of which are walking round the Ka'bah (*tawaaf*), slaughtering sacrificial animals and throwing pebbles at the largest pillar in Mina, known as *Jamrat-ul-'Aqabah*.

What Should Be Done On *'Eed Day*?

On this day, a Muslim who is not performing *hajj* engages in the same activities he normally does on the Festival of Fast Breaking (*'Eed-ul-Fitr*), with the exception of paying *Zakaat-ul-Fitr*, which applies only to *'Eed-ul-Fitr*.

A distinctive feature of *'Eed-ul-Adhaa* is the slaughtering of a sacrificial animal, which is considered to be a highly recommended act of worship.

Ud-hiyah, or sacrificial animal, refers to any of the pastoral animals (sheep, cows or camels) that are slaughtered during the Festival of Sacrifice (*'Eed-ul-Adhaa*) with the intention of seeking closeness to Allah. The time for offering a sacrifice begins after the *'Eed-ul-Adhaa* prayer and lasts until the sunset of the 13th day of *Dhul-Hijjah*. As the Qur'an states, "Pray to your Lord and sacrifice to Him alone." (*Soorat Al-Kawthar*, 108:2) Prayer mentioned here has been interpreted to mean the *'Eed-ul-Adhaa* prayer and sacrifice has been interpreted to refer to *ud-hiyah*, or the sacrificial animal.

Islamic ruling regarding *ud-hiyah*:

Slaughtering a sacrificial animal during the Festival of Sacrifice (*'Eed-ul-Adhaa*) is a practice which the Prophet ﷺ regularly did and encouraged (*sunnah mu'akkadah*) for those who can afford to do so. The head of the household may offer a sacrifice for himself and on behalf of his dependents.

A Muslim who intends to offer a sacrifice must refrain from cutting his hair, clipping his nails or picking his skin from the first day of *Dhul-Hijjah* until he slaughters the sacrificial animal on the 10th of *Dhul-Hijjah*.

The Conditions that the Sacrificial Animal Must Satisfy

1 It is not lawful to offer a sacrifice of any animal or bird except pastoral animals, namely sheep, cows or camels.

One sheep or goat would suffice for a man and his household, and seven different households may share a cow or a camel.

2 The sacrificial animal must be of the right age. A sheep must be at least six months, a goat one year old, a cow two years old, and a camel five years old.

3 It should be free from apparent defects, because the Prophet ﷺ said, "There are four [types of animals] that will not do for sacrifice: a one-eyed or blind animal whose defect is obvious, a sick animal whose sickness is obvious, a lame animal whose lameness is obvious and an emaciated animal that has no marrow in its bones." (*Sunan An-Nasaa'ee:* 4371; *Sunan At-Tirmidhee,* 1497)

What Should Be Done with the Sacrificial Animal?

- It is forbidden to sell any part of the sacrificial animal.

- It is recommended to divide it into three parts: one third for eating, one third to be given as gifts and one third to be given in charity to the poor and the needy.

- It is permissible to authorise someone to slaughter a sacrificial animal on one's behalf, such as trustworthy charitable societies that undertake the slaughter of sacrificial animals and distribute them to the needy.

> Islam stipulates that sacrificial animals must be free from defects.

Visiting Madeenah

Madeenah is the city to which Prophet Muhammad ﷺ emigrated, leaving his native city of Makkah after he had suffered at the hands of the polytheists there.

Upon reaching Madeenah, the Prophet ﷺ set about constructing his mosque which became a major centre of knowledge and served to call people to Islam and teach them its lofty principles.

It is highly recommended to visit the Prophet's Mosque in Madeenah during the _Hajj_ season or any other time of the year.

It is worth noting, however, that visiting the Prophet's Mosque has nothing to do with the _Hajj_ rituals and is not confined to any particular time.

The Prophet ﷺ said, "There are only three mosques to which you should embark on a journey: the Sacred Mosque [in Makkah], this mosque of mine [in Madeenah] and Al-Aqsaa Mosque [in Jerusalem]." (_Saheeh Al-Bukhaaree:_ 1139; _Saheeh Muslim:_ 1397; _Sunan Abu Daawood:_ 2033)

He also said on a different occasion, "One prayer in my mosque is better than one thousand prayers in any other mosque except in the Sacred Mosque [in Makkah]." (_Saheeh Al-Bukhaaree:_ 1133; _Saheeh Muslim:_ 1394)

Places in Madeenah that Are Worth Visiting

A Muslim who visits Madeenah must intend to visit the Prophet's Mosque there and offer prayers in it. He may also visit other places including the following:

1 The heart of the Prophet's Mosque houses a very special but small area known as _ar-Rawdah ash-Shareefah_ (Literally, 'the noble garden'), which extends from the Prophet's tomb, where one of his rooms used to be, to his pulpit. Offering prayers in this area has great merits, as the Prophet ﷺ said, "Between my house and my pulpit lies a garden from the gardens of Paradise." (_Saheeh Al-Bukhaaree:_ 1137; _Saheeh Muslim:_ 1390)

2 Sending greetings of peace to Allah's Messenger ﷺ: One should stand in front of the grave of the Prophet ﷺ, facing the grave with one's back to the _qiblah_ and say, with all graciousness and in a quiet voice: _Assalaamu 'alayka yaa rasoolallaahi wa rahmatullaahi wa barakaatuhu. Ash-hadu annaka qad ballaght-ar-risaalata, wa addayt-al-amaanata, wa nasaht-al-ummata, wa jaahadta fillaahi haqqa jihaadih, fa jazaak-Allaahu 'an *ummatika afdala maa jazaa nabiyyan 'an ummatih* (May Allah's peace, blessings and mercy be upon you, O Messenger of Allah. I bear witness that you have conveyed the message, fulfilled the trust, sincerely advised the Muslim community and striven hard for the sake of Allah as is His due. May Allah reward you on our behalf better than the reward that any prophet received on behalf of his community).

The Prophet ﷺ said in this respect, "No one sends greetings of peace upon me but Allah returns my soul to me so that I may return his greetings." (*Sunan Abu Daawood:* 2041)

One then takes one step to the right and sends greetings of peace to Abu Bakr As-Siddeeq ☬, the Prophet's successor and the best of all his companions.

Then one takes one further step to the right and sends greetings of peace to 'Umar ibn Al-Khattaab ☬, the second rightly-guided caliph and the best of all the Prophet's companions after Abu Bakr As-Siddeeq ☬.

It is worth noting here that despite the fact Allah's Messenger ﷺ is the best of all mankind, he can do neither harm nor good and thus one must not invoke him or seek his help. Instead, one must invoke Allah and direct all forms of worship to Him alone.

3 Visiting Qubaa' Mosque: Qubaa' Mosque is the first mosque built in Islam; indeed, it was built even before the Prophet ﷺ built his own mosque in Madeenah. Pilgrims visiting Madeenah are highly recommended to visit it, as was the practice of the Prophet ﷺ who once said "Whoever makes ablutions (*wudoo*') at home and then goes to Qubaa' Mosque and prays in it, he will have a reward like that of performing *'umrah.*" (*Sunan Ibn Maajah:* 1412)

> A pilgrim visiting Madeenah is highly recommended to visit *Qubaa'* Mosque and pray in it, as was the practice of the Prophet ﷺ.

Your Financial Transactions

Islam has laid down all legislation that takes into account man's interest, protects his professional and financial rights, whether he is rich or poor, creates a close-knit society and helps develop it in all aspects of life.

Contents

All Types of Transactions Are Generally Allowed in Islam

Things That Are prohibited Due to Their Innate Impurity

Things That Are prohibited Due to the Manner They Are Acquired

Usury (*Ribaa*)

- *Ribaa* on Debts
- *Ribaa* on Loans
- The Islamic Ruling on *Ribaa*
- Detrimental Effects of *Ribaa*

Deception through Ignorance and Uncertainty (*Gharar*)

Injustice and Wrongfully Taking Other People's Property

Gambling

- Detrimental Effects of Gambling on the Individual and Society

Examples of Business Ethics which Islam Has Stressed

- Honesty
- Truthfulness
- Efficiency

Your Financial Transactions

Allah ﷻ commands and encourages Muslims to earn their livelihood. This is clear in a number of aspects including the following:

- The Prophet ﷺ has forbidden us from begging as long as we are able to earn a livelihood and informs us that those who engage in begging despite their ability to scrape a living, lose their dignity in the sight of Allah and that of people: "A person who unnecessarily continues to beg will stand before Almighty Allah [on the Day of Judgement] without a shred of flesh on his face." (*Saheeh Al-Bukhaaree:* 1405; *Saheeh Muslim:* 1040)

  He also said, "If a person who is afflicted with poverty refers it to people, his poverty will not be brought to an end; but if he refers it to Allah, Allah will soon give him sufficiency." (*Sunan Ahmad: 3869; Sunan Abu Daawood:* 1645)

- Islam respects all types of occupations in any field, trade, industry, services, investment or in any other field, as long as they are lawful and do not involve any wrongdoing whatsoever. Indeed, Islam informs us that prophets engaged in decent occupations prevalent in their societies. As the Prophet ﷺ said, "Allah did not send a prophet who did not tend sheep." (*Saheeh Al-Bukhaaree:* 2143) He mentioned once that Prophet Zachariah ﷺ was a carpenter. (*Saheeh Muslim:* 2379)

- A person who engages in an occupation with the intention of supporting himself and his family and helping the needy will be abundantly rewarded for his effort.

> Islam respects all types of occupations as long as they are lawful and do not involve any wrongdoing whatsoever.

All Types of Transactions Are Generally Allowed in Islam

All types of transactions are, as a general rule, allowed in Islam. These include selling, buying, leasing and all kinds of transactions which people need in their everyday lives, with the exception of those things which are forbidden due to their innate impurity or the manner they are acquired.

Things That Are prohibited Due to Their Innate Impurity

These are things which Allah has declared unlawful due to their innate impurity and therefore must not be sold, purchased, leased, manufactured or put into circulation.

Examples of things which Islam has prohibited due to their innate impurity

- The flesh of dogs and pigs
- Dead animals or any part of them
- Alcoholic drinks

- Drugs and all other substances which are injurious to health
- materials that aim to spread immorality, such as pornographic tapes, magazines and websites
- Idols or anything that is worshipped besides or instead of Allah

Things That Are prohibited Due to the Manner They Are Acquired

These are things which are naturally lawful but have become unlawful due to the manner in which they are acquired, causing harm to the individual and society at large. Things which generally render transactions unlawful are:

Usury (*ribaa*), deception, injustice and gambling.

We will clarify these in the following pages.

> Usury (Ribaa)

Usury (*ribaa*) is the practice of assigning a fee on credit and other borrowed assets on top of the principal borrowed amount, thus making a profit on the loan, which is strictly prohibited in Islam due to the harm and injustice involved in it.

Ribaa is of different types, but the most serious type of *ribaa*, and thus the one that is all the more unlawful, is one relating to loans and debts. It covers any stipulated additional amount over the principal in a transaction of loan or debt and is of two types.

> Every loan or debt from which the lender makes a profit is a form of *ribaa*.

▪ *Ribaa* on Debts

This type of *ribaa* exists in every debt, which carries a stipulation binding the debtor to pay to the creditor any sum of money in excess of the principal sum of the debt.

Example: John borrows £1000 from Martin and promises to pay it back after a month. However, John finds himself unable to pay the debt off after a month and so Martin, the creditor, stipulates that John either pays the debt off without any excess of the principal sum of the debt or pay £1100 after another month. If, however, he still cannot possibly pay that sum off either after a month, Martin will defer payment another month on condition that John pays £1200.

▪ *Ribaa* on Loans

In this type of *ribaa*, a person takes out a loan from another person or from a bank with the stipulation at the time of the contract that the borrower must pay an annual interest both parties agree upon of, say 5%, on the borrowed amount to the lender.

Example: John is interested in a house which is worth £100,000 but does not have enough money to purchase it, so he takes out a loan from the bank on condition that he must pay the bank £150,000 in monthly instalments over a period of five years.

Ribaa is strictly forbidden in Islam and is one of the major sins as long as the loan is taken out with interest, whether it is an investment loan for financing a business or industry or purchasing a vital asset such as a house or property, or a consumer loan for personal, family or household purposes.

However, purchasing goods in instalments at a price higher than the actual price paid in cash is not considered a form of *ribaa*.

Example: A person has the choice to purchase a kitchen appliance for £1000 and pay for it in cash or for £1200 in monthly instalments, paying a monthly amount of £100 to the owner of the store from which he purchased the appliance.

The Islamic Ruling on *Ribaa*

Textual evidence from the Qur'an and the Prophet's traditions, points out that *ribaa* is strictly forbidden in Islam, that it is one of the major sins and that Allah has not declared war on any one of the sinners except those who deal with *ribaa*. In fact, *ribaa* is forbidden, not only in Islam but also in all previous divine religions. Such a ruling, however, was changed after numerous distortions crept into the religious texts of such religions, and altered many other rulings. Allah mentions that he inflicted punishment on a group of the People of the Book "for their taking usury although it had been forbidden to them." (*Soorat An-Nisaa'*, 4:161)

Punishment for *Ribaa*

1. Those who engage in usurious transactions expose themselves to a war which Allah and His Messenger have declared on those who deal with *ribaa*, thereby becoming their enemies. As the Qur'an states, "If you do not do so, be warned of war from Allah and His Messenger. But if you repent, you may have your capital, without wronging and without being wronged." (*Soorat Al-Baqarah*, 2: 279) Indeed, such a war leaves devastating physical and psychological effects, and the numerous forms of deep anxiety and depression that have afflicted people these days are some signs of such a war which Allah has declared on those who disobey His commands by engaging in usurious transactions. The effects of such war in the hereafter will be far worse than one can possibly imagine.

2. Those who engage in usurious transactions in any way are deprived of Allah's mercy. Jaabir ibn 'Abdullaah narrated: "Allah's Messenger cursed the person who accepts usury (interest), the one who gives it, the one who records it and the two witnesses to it." He said, "They are all sinners." (*Saheeh Muslim:* 1598)

3. They will be resurrected on the Day of Judgement in such an unsightly manner that they will be staggering, jerking and shaking like someone suffering from madness or experiencing epileptic seizures, as the Qur'an states, "Those who take unlawful interest will stand before Allah [on the Day of Judgement] as those who suffer from a mental imbalance because of Satan's touch." (*Soorat Al-Baqarah*, 2: 275)

4. Profits made from usurious transactions, no matter how massive they may look, will be deprived of all blessing, and those who make use of such profits will find neither happiness, nor peace of mind, as the Qur'an states, "Allah deprives usurious gains of all blessing, whereas He blesses charitable deeds with manifold increase." (*Soorat Al-Baqarah*, 2: 276)

Detrimental Effects of Ribaa on the Individual and Society

Islam has strictly forbidden *ribaa* due to the great deal of harm it is bound to inflict on both the individual and society. Such detrimental effects include the following:

1. It causes a severe disorder in the distribution of wealth and widens the gulf between the rich and the poor

Because *ribaa* tends to concentrate wealth in the hands of a few individuals and prevents it from being used for the general good of the community, it causes an inequitable distribution of wealth and resources and divides society into a tiny super-rich minority and a large poor or deprived large majority, a state of affairs which normally gives rise to hatred and crimes in society.

2. It encourages wasteful extravagance

The fact that taking out loans from financial institutions that charge interest on such loans has become more readily available than ever before has encouraged many people to become big wasters. Finding a financial institution from which to borrow money to meet all kinds of needs, they tend to spend lavishly on luxury items, only to find themselves burdened by debts which cause them depression, anxiety and stress and which they cannot possibly pay off.

3. It dissuades investors from investing in domestic beneficial projects

Lured by the interest gains the usurious system has allowed investors to derive from their capital, they desist from investing their capital in domestic industrial, agricultural and commercial projects, no matter how beneficial such projects may be to society, as they believe these projects involve some risk and require a great deal of effort.

4. It deprives wealth of all blessing and leads to economic crises

All economic crises undergone by financial institutions and individuals alike are, in the main, caused by persistence in engaging in usurious transactions and are some of the reasons why such transactions are deprived of all blessing, as opposed to charitable deeds which are bound to bless wealth and increase it. As the Qur'an states, "Allah deprives usurious gains of all blessing, whereas He blesses charitable deeds with manifold increase." (*Soorat Al-Baqarah*, 2: 276)

> *Ribaa* deprives wealth of all blessing and is bound to lead to economic crises.

What is the ruling regarding a person who embraces Islam while he is a party to a usurious contract?

This involves two cases:

1. If he is the party that takes interest, he is only entitled to his capital and must desist, as soon as he embraces Islam, from taking any interest whatsoever, as the Qur'an states, "But if you repent, you may have your capital, without wronging and without being wronged." (*Soorat Al-Baqarah*, 2: 279) If he receives any further interest after embracing Islam, he can get rid of it by donating it to charity to support charitable causes.

2. If he is the party that pays interest, two cases are involved here:

   • If he can cancel the contract without incurring huge losses, then he must do so.

   • If, however, he cannot cancel the contract except by incurring huge losses, he may fulfil the terms of the contract but must show strong determination not to enter into such contracts ever again in the future, as the Qur'an states, "Whoever is given a warning by his Lord and then desists, may keep what he received in the past and his affair is Allah's concern. As for those who return to it, they will be the Companions of the Fire, remaining in it timelessly, for ever." (*Soorat Al-Baqarah*, 2: 275)

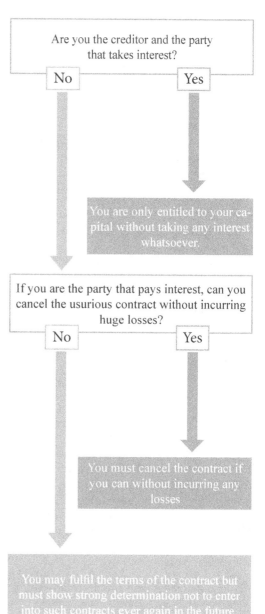

Deception through Ignorance and Uncertainty (Gharar)

Examples of sales contracts that involve deception through ignorance

1. Selling fruits before they ripen and become ready for picking. Indeed, the Prophet ﷺ has forbidden the sale of dates until their benefit becomes evident and suitable for eating, for there is a chance that they may become decayed and never ripen.

2. Paying a certain amount of money to purchase a box without knowing whether its contents are valuable or worthless.

Circumstances under which *gharar* (ignorance and uncertainty) may affect the contract

Ignorance and uncertainty (*gharar*) may only affect the contract and render it impermissible if the contract involves a great deal of it and if it relates to the object of the contract.

Therefore, a Muslim may purchase a house even if he is not aware of such things as the type of building materials used in the construction of the house and the type of paint used in painting it, for such ignorance is rather trivial and does not affect the object of the contract.

> A contract that is based on uncertainty and ignorance (*gharar*) is one which involves a certain amount of risk or deception which is bound to lead to disagreements and disputes between the parties to the contract or cause one of them to wrong the other.

Islam has strictly forbidden this type of contract in order to block the means to disputes and all forms of injustice. In fact, it declares it prohibited even if it may be an acceptable practice amongst people, for the Prophet ﷺ has forbidden sales which involve deception through ignorance. (*Saheeh Muslim:* 1513)

>Injustice and Wrongfully Taking Other People's Property

Injustice is one of the most heinous deeds against which Islam has vehemently warned. The Prophet ﷺ said in this connection, "Beware of injustice, for indeed injustice will be darkness on the Day of Judegment."(*Saheeh Al-Bukhaaree:* 2315; *Saheeh Muslim:* 2579)

Indeed, Islam considers the act of taking other people's property wrongfully, no matter how small this property may be, one of the most odious sins and warns those who commit it against severe punishment in the hereafter. As the Prophet ﷺ said, "If anyone takes a span of land unjustly, its extent taken from seven earths will be tied round his neck on the Day of Resurrection." (*Saheeh Al-Bukhaaree:* 2321; *Saheeh Muslim:* 1610)

Examples of forms of injustice committed in business transactions

1 Coercion: A transaction that is conducted under coercion in any form whatsoever invalidates the contract. Indeed, mutual consent between the parties to the contract is a necessary condition for the validity of a business transaction, as the Prophet ﷺ once observed, "A sale is a sale only if it is made through mutual consent. (*Sunan Ibn Maajah:* 2185)

2 Dishonesty: deceiving other people to take their property wrongfully is one of the major sins, as the Prophet ﷺ said, "Whoever cheats us is not one of us." (*Saheeh Muslim:* 101). Once, while the Prophet ﷺ was walking in the market, he passed by a pile of food and put his hands inside it. Feeling water on his fingers, he turned to the seller of the food and said, "What is this?" "It was left out in the rain, Messenger of Allah," he replied. "Why don't you put the wet food on top of the pile so that people can see it?" the Prophet ﷺ disapprovingly said, "Whoever deceives us is not one of us." (*Sunan At-Tirmidhee:* 1315)

3 Manipulating the Law: Some cunning people, when presenting their cases in court, speak in honeyed tones and in a convincing manner in order to take other people's property wrongfully, not realising that even if the judge rules in their favour he cannot possibly turn falsehood into truth. Addressing some of his companions once, the Prophet ﷺ said, "I am only a human being, and litigants come to me to settle their disputes. It may be that one of you may present his case more eloquently and in a more convincing way than his opponent, whereby I may consider him to be in the right and thus pass a judgement in his favour based on what I have heard. Therefore, if I ever

> Taking other people's property wrongfully, no matter how small it may be, is one of the most heinous sins in Islam.

give the right of a Muslim to another by mistake [while he knows that he is in the wrong], then the one in the wrong must not take, it for I will actually be giving him only a piece of Fire." (*Saheeh Al-Bukhaaree:* 6748; *Saheeh Muslim:* 1713)

4. **Bribery:** Bribery is a sum of money given or a service rendered in order to influence the judgement or conduct of a person in a position of trust and thus get something illegally. Islam considers bribery one of the most atrocious forms of injustice and the most heinous sins. The Prophet ﷺ went as far as to curse those who give bribes and those who accept them." (*Sunan At-Tirmidhee:* 1337)

When bribery becomes widespread, it destroys the very fabric of society and affects its development and prosperity.

What is the Islamic ruling regarding a person who has taken people's property before embracing Islam?

If a person embraces Islam while he is still in possession of money which he has acquired as a result of deceiving or assaulting others through theft or embezzlement, for instance, then he must return it to its legal owners as long as he knows them and can do so without incurring any harm whatsoever upon himself.

Even if he has committed such an injustice before embracing Islam, the money he has taken from other people wrongfully is still in his possession and he must thus return it to its legitimate owners, as the Qur'an states, "Allah commands you to deliver trusts back to their owners." (*Soorat An-Nisaa',* 4:58)

If, however, he does not know its rightful owners after exhausting all possible ways to find out who they are, he can get rid of it by giving it away to charity.

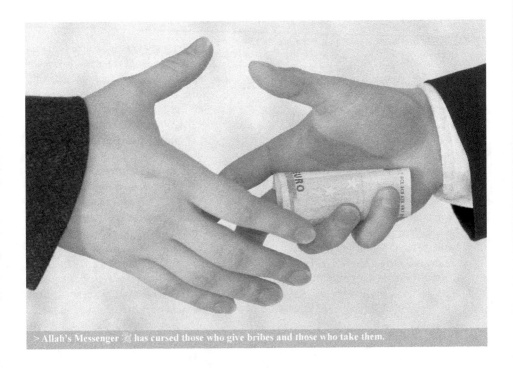

> Allah's Messenger ﷺ has cursed those who give bribes and those who take them.

> Gambling

What is Gambling?

Gambling is the act of risking money upon the outcome of a contest of chance. In this way, a person risks money upon an agreement that he or someone else will receive something of value in the event of a certain outcome. Put simply, gambling involves betting that must result either in a gain or a loss, and the gambler profits solely at another person's loss.

The Islamic Ruling on Gambling

Gambling is strictly forbidden, as supported by textual evidence from the Qur'an and the Prophet's traditions, including the following:

> Gambling gets gamblers caught in the grip of addiction.

1. Allah ﷻ considers the sin of engaging in gambling to be far greater than the profit gained from it, as the Qur'an states, "They will ask you about alcoholic drinks and gambling. Say, 'There is great wrong in both of them and also certain benefits for mankind. But the wrong in them is greater than the benefit.'" (*Soorat Al-Baqarah*, 2: 219)

2. Allah ﷻ considers it to be a type of filth and abomination due to its detrimental effects on the individual and society and commands the faithful to avoid it as it sows enmity and hatred amongst them and turns them away from the remembrance of Allah and from prayer, as the Qur'an states, "O you who believe, intoxicants, gambling, stone altars and divining arrows are abominations devised by Satan. Avoid them so that you may be successful. Satan only seeks to sow enmity and hatred among you by means of wine and gambling, and to keep you from the remembrance of God and from your prayers. Will you not then abstain?" (*Soorat Al-Maa'idah*, 5:90-1)

Detrimental Effects of Gambling on the Individual and Society

Gambling has numerous adverse effects on the individual and society including the following:

1. It precipitates enmity and hatred among gamblers, for when friends gamble and one of them wins and takes their money they will undoubtedly feel hatred towards him and hold grudges against him and even plot against him and harm him. This is a known fact that is based upon observation. The Qur'an states in this context, "Satan only seeks to sow enmity and hatred among you by means of wine and gambling." Besides, it distracts from the obligatory prayers and the remembrance of Allah, as the Qur'an states in the context of mentioning Satan's tireless effort to make gambling look good to man, "and to keep you from the remembrance of Allah and from your prayers. Will you not then abstain?" (*Soorat Al-Maa'idah*, 5:90-1)

2. It destroys wealth and causes gamblers to suffer heavy financial losses and personal or legal problems.

3. The thrill of gambling and the possibility of winning becomes addictive. If the gambler wins, he becomes greedier and gets carried away, hopeful to acquire more ill-gotten gains. If he loses, he does not give up easily and carries on gambling in the hope of getting back what he has lost. Both gain and loss stand in the way of productive work and constitute a creeping evil that destroys society.

Types of Gambling

Types of gambling, past and present, are many, and modern forms of gambling include the following:

1. Playing a game in which players stipulate that the winner will take some money. For instance, a group of people have a game of cards, each one of them setting aside a certain amount of money, and the winner takes all of it.

2. Betting, which is the act of risking money on the unknown result of an event. For instance, each gambler places a bet on a certain team in, say, a football match, and one can only win the bet if the team on which the bet is placed wins, otherwise the bet is lost, which means loss of money.

3. Lottery, which is a type of gambling that has the element of chance. In a lottery, lots, usually in the form of tickets, are purchased and a lot is randomly selected to win a prize, usually a large sum of money. For instance, one purchases a ticket for £1 in the hope of winning £1000.

4. All types of gambling without exception, casino or non-casino gambling games, such as electronic and online gambling, involve money that gamblers can either win or lose.

> Islam forbids all types of gambling without exception and considers gambling a major sin.

Examples of Business Ethics which Islam Has Stressed

Islam instructs its followers to observe certain ethics when they engage in financial transactions, including the following:

Honesty

Islam requires its adherents to be honest in their dealings with Muslims and non-Muslims alike. Indeed, honesty is one of the most important moral principles which testifies to a Muslim's devoutness. Its importance is indicated in a number of Qur'anic verses and traditions of the Prophet ﷺ, including the following:

- Allah says, "Allah commands you to deliver trusts back to their owners." (*Soorat An-Nisaa'*, 4:58)

- The Prophet ﷺ considers betraying the trust as one of the signs of hypocrisy: "The signs of the hypocrite are three: when he speaks he lies, when he promises he breaks his promise and when he is entrusted he betrays the trust." (*Saheeh Al-Bukhaaree:* 33; *Saheeh Muslim:* 59)

- Honesty is among the characteristics of the believers whom Allah calls "successful" because they "honour their trusts and their contracts", among other traits. (*Soorat Al-Mu'minoon*, 23:8)

- It is for this reason that the Prophet ﷺ considers those who do not fulfil the terms and conditions of the trusts which are placed in their charge to have no faith: "The person who does not fulfil the terms of his trust has no faith." (*Sunan Ahmad:* 12567)

- The Prophet ﷺ was known by his honorific title of *As-Saadiq al-Ameen* (the truthful and trustworthy) before the advent of Islam, for he was the epitome of honesty in all his dealings.

Truthfulness

Truthfulness and transparency are among the virtues that Islam has stressed

- The Prophet ﷺ said, "The seller and the buyer have the right to keep or return goods as long as they have not parted; and if both parties speak the truth and describe the defects and qualities of the goods, their transaction will be blessed; however, if they tell lies or hide something, their transaction will be deprived of all blessings." (*Saheeh Al-Bukhaaree:* 1973; *Saheeh Muslim:* 1532)

- He also said, "Be truthful, for truthfulness leads to righteousness, and righteousness leads to Paradise. A man keeps on telling the truth until he becomes known as a truthful person." (*Saheeh Muslim:* 2607)

- Some traders often have recourse to swearing falsely claiming that their merchandise is of good quality in order to persuade the buyers to purchase it. Islam considers such an act one of the major sins, as the Prophet ﷺ said, "Allah will not speak to three types of people on the Day of Judgement, nor will He look at them, nor purify them and they will have a severe punishment." Amongst these types he mentioned those who "swear falsely in order to sell their goods."(*Saheeh Muslim:* 106)

Proficiency

A Muslim, no matter what his occupation may be, must carry out his duties with efficiency and to the best of his ability, making efficiency his guiding principle in all his endeavours

- Allah ﷻ has prescribed proficiency in all things and requires Muslims to observe it in all aspects of life, even when doing things that may, on the surface, seem unimportant, such as hunting and slaughtering. The Prophet ﷺ said in this regard, "Allah has prescribed proficiency in all things. Thus, if you kill, kill well; and if you slaughter, slaughter well. Let each one of you sharpen his blade and let him spare suffering to the animal he slaughters." (*Saheeh Muslim:* 1955)

- Once, he attended the funeral of a man and gave instructions to his companions to level the grave and carry out the burial process efficiently. Then he turned to them and said, "Doing so will neither benefit the deceased, nor harm him; however, if a worker does any work, Allah loves to see him do it well and with efficiency." (*Al-Bayhaqee's Shu'ab Al-Eemaan:* 5315) Another narration reads, "If any of you undertakes to do any work, Allah loves to see him do it well and with efficiency." (*Musnad Abu Ya'laa:* 4386; *Al-Bayhaqee's Shu'ab Al-Eemaan:* 4312) Read more about moral character on page 225

Your Food and Drink

8

Permissible (*halaal*) food occupies a magnificent position in Islam, for it causes our supplications to be answered by Allah and makes Allah bless our wealth and children.

Halaal food is lawful food that is acquired by lawful means, without wronging anyone or encroaching upon anyone's rights.

Contents

The General Rule Regarding Food and Drink
Plants and Fruits
Intoxicants
Drugs
Seafood
Wild Animals
- Islamic Slaughter
- The Islamic Ruling Regarding Meat Sold in Restaurants and Shops Owned by Non-Muslims

Islamic Hunting
The Etiquette of Eating and Drinking

Your Food and Drink

The General Rule Regarding Food and Drink

The general rule in the *Sharee'ah*, or Islamic law, is that everything is allowed except what is expressly forbidden which is bound to harm people's health, character or religion. Allah reminds us that He has created everything on the earth so we can benefit from it, with the exception of things He has forbidden, as the Qur'an states, "It is He who created everything in and on the earth for you." (*Soorat Al-Baqarah*, 2:29)

Plants and Fruits

All types of plants that people plant or take off trees, herbs and mushrooms of all types are lawful and suitable for human consumption, with the exception of those ones that are hazardous to health or life or those that intoxicate and cloud the mind, such as alcoholic beverages and drugs, which are strictly forbidden due to the great harm they are bound to cause.

Intoxicants and Alcoholic Beverages

An intoxicant is an agent that clouds the mind and produces in a person a state ranging from elation to stupor, usually accompanied by loss of inhibitions and control. As the Prophet ﷺ said, "Every intoxicant is *khamr* (wine), and every *khamr* is forbidden." (*Saheeh Muslim:* 2003) Therefore, any alcoholic drink is unlawful, whether it is made from fruit, such as grapes, dates, figs and raisins, or from grains, such as wheat, barley, corn and rice, or from sweet substances such as honey. Thus, the definition of *khamr* extends to any substance that intoxicates, in whatever form and under whatever name it may appear, even if it is added to natural fruit juice, sweets and chocolate.

Islam protects the mind against anything that is bound to harm it in any way.

Preservation of the Mind

Islam seeks to realise people's benefits in this life and in the hereafter, and amongst these ultimate benefits are the five necessities, namely, religion, life, the mind, property and progeny.

The mind is the basis of legal responsibility (*manaat at-takleef*) and the main reason behind divine honour and favour on the human race. It is for this reason that Islam seeks to preserve it and protect it against anything that is bound to weaken it or derange it.

The Islamic Ruling on Alcoholic Drinks

Consuming alcoholic drinks, such as wine, is one of the major sins and its prohibition is confirmed by textual evidence from the Qur'an and the Prophet's traditions, including the following:

- The Qur'an says, "O you who believe, intoxicants, gambling, stone altars and divining arrows are abominations devised by Satan. Avoid them so that you may be successful." (*Soorat Al-Maa'idah,* 5:90) Allah ﷻ describes all types of intoxicants as a type of filth and abomination and commands the believers to avoid them in order to secure success in this life and in the hereafter.

- The Prophet ﷺ said, "Every intoxicant is wine (*khamr*), and every wine is unlawful. Whoever drinks wine in this world and dies addicted to it without repentance will not drink it in the hereafter." (*Saheeh Muslim:* 2003)

- Explaining once that drinking wine decreases faith and contradicts it altogether, he once declared, "When somebody takes an alcoholic drink, then he is not a believer at the time of drinking it." (*Saheeh Al-Bukhaaree:* 5256; *Saheeh Muslim:* 57)

Allah has imposed corporal punishment on drinkers, and so they lose their dignity and credibility in society.

He ﷺ warns those who persist in drinking wine, and all intoxicants for that matter, and die without ever repenting with a severe punishment in the hereafter. As the Prophet ﷺ said, "Allah, the Exalted and Glorious, made a covenant to those who drink intoxicants to make them drink *Teenat al-Khabaal.*" (*Saheeh Muslim:* 2002). *Teenat al-Khabaal* refers to the pus and other unpleasant fluids that ooze out of the bodies of those doomed to Hellfire.

In fact, this severe warning also extends to those who get involved in any way in any action related to the production and drinking of alcohol, for the Prophet ﷺ "cursed ten types of people in connection with alcoholic drinks: those who produce them, those for whom they are produced, those who drink them, those who carry them, those for whom they are carried, those who serve them, those who sell them, those who benefit from the price paid for them, those who buy them, and those for whom they are bought." (*Sunan At-Tirmidhee:* 1295).

Drugs

Taking drugs, whether such drugs are plant-based or manufactured and whether they are inhaled, swallowed or injected, is considered to be one of the major sins in Islam, for while they serve as intoxicants they destroy the nervous system and afflict those who take them with various psychological and neurological disorders and even lead to their death. Allah ﷻ, the Most Merciful, says in the Qur'an, "Do not kill yourselves. Allah is Most Merciful to you." (*Soorat An-Nisaa',* 4:29)

Seafood

Seafood comes from edible sea plants as well as aquatic animals which live only in water for most or all of their lives.

The term seafood also applies to any freshwater life eaten by humans; therefore, all edible aquatic life can be referred to as seafood.

All types of sea plants as well as aquatic animals are permissible to be used for food, whether they are caught or found dead, unless they are hazardous to life or health. As the Qur'an states, "Anything you catch in the sea is lawful for you, and so is all food from it." (*Soorat Al-Maa'idah,* 5:96)

The phrase 'anything you catch' in the above verse refers to aquatic animals that are caught alive, while the word 'food' refers to dead aquatic animals that are washed ashore.

Land Animals

For land animals to be lawful, two conditions must be met:

1. They must be considered lawful for their flesh to be used for food.
2. They must be hunted or slaughtered according to Islamic law (*Sharee'ah*).

What are the lawful animals?

The general rule in Islamic Law is that all animals are allowed to be used for food except for those that are expressly forbidden in the Qur'an or the Prophet's traditions.

Forbidden animals are as follows:

1. **Pigs:** Pigs, indeed any of their body parts and by-products, are considered 'filthy' in Islam and thus forbidden for human consumption. As the Qur'an states, "Forbidden to you for food are dead animals, blood and the flesh of swine." (*Soorat Al-Maa'idah*, 5:3)

2. **All meat eating animals,** whether they are large, such as lions and tigers, or small, such as cats. and dogs are also included in this category.

3. **All predatory birds,** such as falcons and eagles.

4. **Insects:** All land insects are not lawful because they cannot be slaughtered, with the exception of locusts, as the Prophet ﷺ said, "Made lawful for you is the flesh of two dead animals: locusts and fish." (*Sunan Ibn Maajah:* 3218)

5. **Snakes and Mice:** These are also considered unlawful and Islam even goes as far as to command us to kill them. The Prophet ﷺ said, "There are five animals for which there is no blame on the one who kills them even if he is in a state of consecration for the pilgrimage (*ihraam*): crows, kites (hawk-like birds), mice/rats, scorpions and mad dogs." (*Saheeh Al-Bukhaare:* 3136; *Saheeh Muslim:* 1198)

6. **Domestic donkeys,** which are generally used in the countryside for riding and carrying loads.

Any animal that is not specifically forbidden in the Qur'an and the Prophet's traditions is considered lawful for Muslims to eat.

Types of Lawful Animals

Animals which Allah has made lawful for Muslims are of two types:

- Wild animals, which live in natural conditions (that is, not kept in a house or on a farm), and which tend to run away from humans and cannot be easily caught in order to slaughter them: These can become lawful only by hunting them according to Islamic guidelines in this respect.

- Domesticated animals which can be easily caught: These can become lawful only by slaughtering them according to Islamic law.

Islamic Slaughter

This means slaughtering animals in a manner which satisfies the conditions of slaughtering stipulated by Islamic law.

Conditions for slaughtering animals in Islam

- The person undertaking the slaughtering process must be Muslim or a member of the People of the Book (that is, Jews or Christians). In addition, he must have reached the age of discretion and carries out this act for the intended purpose.

- The tool used for slaughtering the animal must be suitable for the intended purpose and sharp, such as a knife. It is forbidden to use anything that may kill the animal due to its heavy weight, hit its head to death or shock it and render it unconscious by resorting to electric stunning, for instance.

Allah ﷻ has made the food of the People of the Book (Jews and Christians) lawful for us as long as it is slaughtered in the legal method of slaughtering the animal.

- The name of Allah must be pronounced by saying *Bismillaah* (in the name of Allah) at the time of slaughtering the animal.

- The cut must sever at least three of the following: the trachea, the oesophagus and the two blood vessels on either side of the throat.

If these conditions are met, the meat of the slaughtered animal will be lawful; however, if one single condition is not met, its meat will not be lawful.

Types of Meat Served in Restaurants and Shops

1. Meat from animals that are slaughtered by other than a Muslim or a member of the People of the Book (a Christian or a Jew), such as a Buddhist or a Hindu, is strictly forbidden. This includes meat served in restaurants in countries where Muslims or People of the Book constitute a minority.

2. Meat from animals killed by a Muslim or a member of the People of the Book is lawful. **Muslim scholars' opinions on this point is unanimous.**

3 Meat from animals killed by a Muslim or a member of the People of the Book but not according to Islamic law, such as by electric stunning or drowning, is strictly forbidden.

4 Meat from animals killed by a member of the People of the Book while the manner of such slaughter is not known, or meat of animals generally found in their restaurants and shops: The preponderant view is that it is permissible to eat such meat, making sure, however, to invoke Allah's name at the time of eating (that is, saying *Bismillaah*), but it is better to look for *halaal* meat elsewhere.

Hunting according to Islamic Law

Muslims are permitted to hunt lawful animals and birds which cannot be easily caught and slaughtered, including non-meat eating animals such as deer and wild rabbits.

A number of conditions must be met for hunting wild animals, including the following:

1. The hunter must be sane and intends to carry out this act for the intended purpose. Therefore, game hunted by a pagan or an insane person is not lawful (*halaal*).

2. The game must belong to the category of animals that cannot be easily slaughtered, as they tend to run away from humans. If, however, it can be slaughtered, such as sheep and chicken, then it is not permissible to hunt them.

3. The hunting weapon must kill by reason of its sharpness, like an arrow or a bullet. Meat from animals that are killed by anything else by reason of its weight, such as a rock, is not lawful for eating, unless one manages to slaughter the game before it dies.

4. The name of Allah must be pronounced when the hunting weapon is discharged.

5. If the hunted game is still alive, it must be slaughtered straightaway.

6. Hunting is permitted in Islam only when necessary for food. Taking the life of an animal for sport, without intending to eat from it or otherwise benefit from it, is prohibited.

The Etiquette of Eating and Drinking

Allah has laid down a number of rules relating to eating and drinking, which generally serve to realise certain divine purposes, such as reminding people of Allah's bounty upon them, protecting them against diseases and avoiding extravagance and pride.

These rules include the following:

- Avoidance of eating or drinking in gold and silver dishes or gold-plated dishes, as this is a form of extravagance which also breaks poor people's hearts. The Prophet 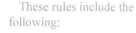 once advised, "Do not drink out of gold and silver vessels, nor eat from gold or silver plates, for they are for the unbelievers in this world and for us in the hereafter." (*Saheeh Al-Bukhaare:* 5110; *Saheeh Muslim:* 2067)

- Washing one's hands before and after eating: Doing so becomes all the more emphasised if the hands are dirty or there are some food residue on them.

- Pronouncing the name of Allah (that is, saying *Bismillaah*) before eating or drinking: If, however, a person forgets to mention Allah's name at the beginning of the meal and remembers that he has not said so only after he has already started eating, he must say upon remembering, *Bismillaahi awwalihi wa aakhirihi* (I begin with the Name of Allah at the beginning and at the end)".

Perceiving once that a young boy was not observing the Islamic etiquette of eating, the Prophet advised him, "Young man, mention the name of Allah, eat with your right hand and eat from what is directly in front of you." (*Saheeh Al-Bukhaaree:* 5061; *Saheeh Muslim:* 2022)

- Eating and drinking with the right hand: The Prophet said, "Do not eat with your left hand, for Satan eats with his left hand." (*Saheeh Muslim:* 2019)

- It is recommended not to eat or drink while standing.

- Eating from the side of the dish nearer to oneself, for it is not polite to eat from other sides of the dish that are nearer to other people. Advising the young boy, the Prophet ﷺ said to him, "Eat from what is directly in front of you."

- It is recommended to pick up a morsel that has fallen down, clean it, wipe off any dirt on it and eat it, so as not to be wasteful.

- Not to criticise food for any reason. One must either praise it or leave it without saying anything. The Prophet ﷺ never criticised any food presented to him; he would eat it if he liked it; otherwise, he would leave it without expressing his dislike. (Saheeh Al-Bukhaaree: 5093; Saheeh Muslim: 2064)

- Avoiding excessive eating, for doing so generally causes diseases and laziness, while moderation is the best course of action in this respect. As the Prophet ﷺ once observed, "No man fills a vessel worse than his stomach. A few mouthfuls would suffice to give him the strength he needs. But if he must eat more, then he should fill one third [of his stomach] with food, one third with drink and leave one third for easy breathing." (Sunan At-Tirmdhee: 2380; Sunan Ibn Maajah: 3349)

- Expressing thanks to Allah by saying Al-hamdu lillaah (All praise is due to Allah). One may, however, add the following words: Al-hamdu lillaah-illadhee at'amanee haadhaa wa razaqaneehi min ghayri hawlin minnee walaa quwwah (Praise be to Allah who has fed me this food and provided it for me, without any strength or power on my part).

> The Prophet ﷺ said, "Allah is pleased with a slave of His who eats something and praises Him for it and drinks something and praises Him for it." (Saheeh Muslim: 2734)

Your Dress Code

9

Clothing is one of the countless blessings Allah ﷻ has bestowed on mankind, as the Qur'an states, "Children of Adam, We have sent down clothing to you to conceal your private parts and as adornment for you; the garment of piety is the best of all garments. This is one of Allah's signs, so that people may take heed." (*Soorat Al-A'raaf,* 7:26)

Contents

Dress in Islam

Forbidden Types of Clothing

- Clothing that reveals the private parts
- Clothing that involves dressing like or imitating the opposite sex
- Clothing that involves imitation of the dress traditionally worn by non-Muslims
- Clothing that is worn with pride and conceit
- Silk clothing or clothing adorned with gold or silk for men
- Extravagant clothing

Clothing from an Islamic Perspective

Muslims are required to pay attention to their appearance, making sure that their clothing is beautiful and clean, especially when dealing with others and when performing the prayers, as the Qur'an states, "Children of Adam, wear your best clothes to every mosque." (*Soorat Al-A'raaf,* 7:31)

Allah ﷻ has permitted people to wear nice clothes and put on a good appearance, as doing so is one aspect of remembering Allah's blessings upon them. As the Qur'an states, "Say, 'Who has forbidden the adornment of Allah, which He has brought forth for His servants and the good things, clean and pure, which Allah has provided for them?' Say, 'They are [lawful] for the believers in the present life but they shall be exclusively for them on the Day of Resurrection.' Thus We explain Our signs for a people who understand." (*Soorat Al-A'raaf,* 7:32)

Clothing Serves a Number of Purposes

1. It covers the parts of the body that must be covered in public, following the standards of modesty which are innate in all human beings: "Children of Adam, We have sent down clothing to you to conceal your private parts." (*Soorat Al-A'raaf,* 7:26)

2. It covers the body against heat, cold and harm in general. Heat and cold are weather phenomena which can harm people. Describing the benefits of clothing which He has provided for His servants, Allah states, "He has made shelters for you in the mountains and He has made garments for you to protect you from the heat and garments to protect you from each other's violence. In that way He perfects His blessing on you so that hopefully you may devote yourselves to Him." (*Soorat An-Nahl,* 16:81)

> Clothing provides mankind with countless benefits

> The General Rule Regarding Clothing

> While Islam outlines a code of modesty, it has no fixed standard as to a type of clothing that Muslims must wear. However, Muslims may use the same type of clothes commonly used in their respective countries, with the exception of those that Islam has declared forbidden.

Islam is a religion which lays down rules based on the dictates of the pure nature innate in all humans *(fitrah)*, straightforward reasoning and sound logic.

The general rule in the *Sharee'ah* is that all types of clothing and adornment are allowed.

Indeed, Islam does not require Muslims to wear a certain type of clothing. It considers all types of clothing lawful as long as such clothing serves the required purposes without exceeding the bounds set by Islam in this respect.

The Prophet ﷺ wore the same type of clothes prevalent in his time and did not order people to wear a particular type of clothing. He only warned them against certain qualities relating to clothing, for the general rule in Islamic law regarding dealings in general, including clothing, is that everything is allowed unless there is evidence which states otherwise; this means nothing is considered forbidden except with evidence, as opposed to acts of worship, such as the prayer and fasting, which are governed by the principle of restriction, in that legally responsible people must not perform any act of worship unless it becomes clear to them that it is prescribed and approved by Allah Himself, and thus no act of worship may be performed without textual evidence from the Qur'an and the Prophet's *Sunnah*.

The Prophet ﷺ said, "Eat, drink, dress and give charity, but without extravagance or arrogance." (*Sunan An-Nasaa'ee:* 2559)

Forbidden Types of Clothing

1. **Clothing that reveals the private parts:** Muslims are required to cover their private parts with appropriate clothing, as the Qur'an states, "Children of Adam! We have sent down clothing to you to conceal your private parts." (*Soorat Al-A'raaf,* 7:26)

Islam has fixed the standards of modesty for both men and women. For men, the minimum amount to be covered is between the navel and the knee. For women who are in the presence of men not related to them, they must cover their bodies except for their face and hands.

Islam requires that clothing must also be loose enough to cover the body properly. Therefore, skin-tight and see-through clothes are not allowed in Islam. In fact, the Prophet ﷺ warned those people who do not observe modesty in dress, calling them "types among the people of Hellfire", one of them being "women who are clothed yet naked".

② **Clothing that involves dressing like or imitating the opposite sex:** This type of clothing is strictly forbidden in Islam and wearing it is considered one of the major sins. This imitation may be extended to include imitation in the manner of speaking, gait and movement, for Allah's Messenger ﷺ cursed men who wear women's clothes and women who wear men's clothes. (*Sunan Abu Daawood:* 4098) He also cursed men who make themselves look like women and women who make themselves look like men. (*Saheeh Al-Bukhaaree:* 5546) By directing men and women to observe different modes of dress, Islam takes into account the biological differences between them and encourages them to act in accordance with the dictates of sound reason and the pure inner nature innate in all humans (*fitrah*).

③ **Clothing that involves imitation of the dress traditionally worn by non-Muslims,** such as the type of clothing worn by monks and priests and wearing a cross. This also includes clothing that is specific to a certain religion, for the Prophet ﷺ said, "Whoever imitates a people is one of them." (*Sunan Abu Daawood:* 4031) This imitation extends to wearing clothing of religious significance. Imitation of this type is a sign of weakness and lack of confidence in the truth one adopts.

Imitation here does not include wearing clothing that is predominant in one's country even if such dress is worn by the majority of non-Muslims, for the Prophet ﷺ used to wear clothing that was common amongst the Quraysh pagans with the exception of those clothing items that are expressly forbidden.

④ **Clothing that is worn with pride and conceit:** The Prophet ﷺ said, "No one who has an atom's weight of pride in his heart will enter Paradise." (*Saheeh Muslim:* 91)

It is for this reason that Islam warns against trailing one's lower garments on the ground out of pride. The Prophet ﷺ said, "On the Day of Resurrection, Allah will not even look at those who drag their garments on the ground out of pride." (*Saheeh Al-Bukhaare:* 3465; *Saheeh Muslim:* 2085)

> It is prohibited to wear clothing which involves imitation of the dress traditionally worn by non-Muslims or clothing of religious significance.

Islam also warns against wearing the so-called *libaas ash-shuhrah* (flamboyant, flashy clothing). In fact, this term refers to a number of things including any type of weird clothing which has certain qualities that attract the attention of the general public, making its wearer known for it; 'notorious clothing' due to its type or loud and repulsive colour; any type of clothing that makes its wearer an object of pride and fame, attracting too much attention to himself. The Prophet ﷺ said, "Whoever wears clothes of *shuhrah* in this world, Allah will make him wear clothes of humiliation on the Day of Judgement." (*Musnad Ahmad:* 5664; *Sunan Ibn Maajah:* 3607)

5. **Silk clothing or clothing adorned with gold or silk for men**: Referring to gold and silk once, the Prophet ﷺ said, "These are forbidden for men among my followers but permissible for women." (*Sunan Ibn Maajah:* 3595; *Sunan Abu Daawood:* 4057)

By silk is meant pure silk obtained from the cocoon of the silkworm.

6. **Extravagant clothing:** The Prophet ﷺ once said, "Eat, give charity and wear clothes. Let no extravagance or pride be mixed with what you do." (*Sunan An-Nasaa'ee:* 2559)

The manner of dressing, however, varies from one person to another depending on one's social position. If a person is rich, he may purchase clothing that a poor person cannot afford, given his monthly outcome, economic position and other financial obligations he has to fulfil. While a piece of clothing may be considered a form of extravagance for a poor person, it may not be considered as such for a rich person.

> Extravagant clothing is forbidden, but this varies from one person to another depending on one's income and the financial obligations one has to fulfil.

Your Family

Islam attaches great importance to the family, encourages its adherents to lay its foundations and protect it against anything that may harm or destroy it, for a good family paves the way for its members to be good and, by extension, society at large.

Contents

The Position of the Family in Islam

The Position of Women in Islam

- Women That Islam Enjoins Muslims to Look after
- No Place for a Struggle between the Sexes
- Categories of Women in Relation to a Man
- Rules Governing the Relationship between a Man and Women he Is Allowed to Marry
- What Must the *Hijaab* Cover?

Marriage in Islam

The Rights of Husband and Wife

Divorce

Parents' Rights

Children's Rights

The Position of the Family in Islam

Islam's concern about the welfare of the family may be summarised in the following points:

1. Islam stresses the principle of marriage to form a family and considers it one of the most meritorious acts as well as one of the practices of Allah's prophets and messengers. The Prophet ﷺ said in this regard, "Sometimes I fast and sometimes I don't; I engage in night prayer and I also sleep, and I marry women. Therefore, whoever does not follow my practice is not one of my true followers." (_Saheeh Al-Bukhaaree:_ 4776; _Saheeh Muslim:_ 1401)

> The Qur'an considers tranquillity, affection and compassion between spouses amongst the countless and greatest blessings of Allah.

- Amongst the countless and greatest blessings that Allah ﷻ has bestowed upon us, the Qur'an mentions, are love and tenderness which He has placed between spouses: "Among His signs is that He created spouses for you of your own kind so that you might find tranquillity in them, and He has placed affection and compassion between you." (_Soorat Ar-Room,_ 30:21)

- Islam commands its followers to get married and to make marriage easy for those who seek it to guard their chastity, as the Prophet ﷺ said, "There are three people whom Allah will surely help." Amongst these three he mentioned "a person who wants to get married in order to preserve his chastity." (_Sunan At-Tirmidhee:_ 1655)

- It also commands young men to get married, for marriage is the right course of action to help them control their intense sexual impulses and to find tranquillity in their spouses.

 It has shown respect to every member of the family, males and females alike.

It has charged the parents with the great responsibility of bringing up their children. 'Abdullaah ibn 'Umar ؓ narrated that he heard Allah's Messenger ﷺ say, "Every one of you is a guardian and is responsible for those in his custody. The ruler is a guardian of his subjects and responsible for them; a husband is a guardian of his family and is responsible for it; a woman is a guardian of her husband's home and is responsible for it, and a servant is a guardian of his master's property and is responsible for it." (_Saheeh Al-Bukhaaree:_ 853; _Saheeh Muslim:_ 1829)

3 It encourages children to honour their parents and commands them to express respect and appreciation to them, look after them and show them due obedience until their death.

No matter how old children may be, they are duty-bound to obey their parents and show kindness to them. Indeed, the Qur'an regards obedience to one's parents a meritorious act of worship and warns the believers against being rude to their parents, even by saying a word of disrespect to them: "Your Lord has decreed that you should worship none but Him, and that you should show kindness to your parents. Whether one or both of them reach old age with you, do not say 'Ugh!' to them out of irritation and do not be harsh with them but speak to them with gentleness and generosity." (*Soorat Al-Israa'*, 17:23)

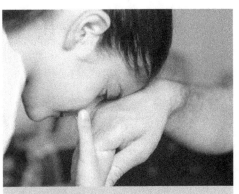

Islam inculcates in children the principle of expressing respect and appreciation to the parents.

4 It commands parents to safeguard their children's rights and urges them to spend on them equally and treat them justly in all apparent matters.

5 It directs its adherents to maintain the ties of kinship by keeping in touch with their relatives from both parents' sides and showing kindness to them.

These relatives include paternal and maternal aunts and uncles and their children. Indeed, Islam regards maintaining the ties of kinship as one of the most commendable acts, warns against severing such ties and considers doing so a major sin. The Prophet ﷺ said, "The person who severs the bonds of kinship will not enter Paradise." (*Saheeh Al-Bukhaaree:* 5638; *Saheeh Muslim:* 2556)

>The Position of Women in Islam

Islam has honoured women and freed them from servitude and subordination to men. It has also liberated them from being a cheap commodity with no respect or honour whatsoever. Examples of forms of respect Islam shows to women include the following:

- Islam grants them the right to inheritance, allocating them equitable shares with men, which sometimes differ under certain circumstances depending on their relationship with others and the financial obligations they have to discharge. While men support the family as a matter of religious obligation, women are not obliged to spend a penny.

- It establishes total equity between men and women in numerous matters including financial transactions. As the prophet ﷺ said, "Women are the twin halves of men." (*Sunan Abu Daawood:* 236)

- It grants them the right to choose their husbands and places a large amount of the responsibility of bringing up children upon them, as the Prophet ﷺ said, "A woman is a guardian of her husband's home and is responsible for it." (*Saheeh Al-Bukhaaree:* 853; *Saheeh Muslim:* 1829)

- It grants them the right to keep their maiden names. In Islam, a woman does not change her surname to that of her husband upon marriage, as is common in many parts of the world; rather, she retains her maiden name, and thus her independent personality.

- It makes it the husband's duty to spend on those women entitled to his support, such as his wife, mother and daughters, without attempting in the least to remind them of his favours.

- It stresses the importance of helping weak women who are in need of support, even if they are not one's relatives, and urges its followers to engage in such a noble act, regarding it one of the meritorious deeds in the sight of Allah. The Prophet ﷺ said, "The person who looks after a widow or a poor person is like a warrior who fights for Allah's cause, or like one who performs prayers all night without slackness and fasts continuously and never breaks his fast." (*Saheeh Al-Bukhaaree:* 5661; *Saheeh Muslim:* 2982).

Women That Islam Enjoins Muslims to Look after

The Mother: Abu Hurayrah ؓ narrated that a man once asked the Prophet ﷺ, "To whom should I show kindness most?" "Your mother," he replied. The man said, "Then who?" The Prophet [again] said, "Your mother." The man further asked, "Then who?" The Prophet ﷺ replied, "Your mother." The man asked again, "Then who?" The Prophet ﷺ said, "Then your father." (*Saheeh Al-Bukhaaree:* 5626; *Saheeh Muslim:* 2548)

The Daughter: 'Uqbah ibn 'Aamir ؓ narrated that he heard Allah's Messenger ﷺ say, "Whoever has three daughters and he remains patient with them, provides for them and clothes them from his money, they will be a shield for him from the Hellfire on the Day of Resurrection." (*Sunan Ibn Maajah:* 3669)

The Wife: 'Aa'ishah ؓ narrated that Allah's Messenger ﷺ said, "The best among you are those who are best to their wives, and I am the best amongst you to my wives." (*Sunan At-Tirmidhee:* 3895)

> Islam considers the relationship between husband and wife to be complimentary, each of which remedies the deficiency of each other in building the Muslim society.

No Place for a Struggle between the Sexes

The struggle between men and women ended with either men gaining power over women, as in some pre-Islamic societies, or with women rebelling against their innate natural predisposition, as in some other non-Muslim societies which have rejected Allah's laws.

This only happened as a result of rejecting Allah's guidance. As the Qur'an states, "Do not covet what Allah has given to some of you in preference to others — men have a portion of what they acquire and women have a portion of what they acquire; but ask Allah for His bounty. (*Soorat An-Nisaa',* 4:32) Indeed,

Islam has honoured both men and women, and allocated each of them distinctive characteristics and roles whereby they may strive to gain Allah's rewards and attain His pleasure. It does not give preference to any of the two sexes; rather, it aims to promote the welfare of the individual in general and that of society at large.

Therefore, there is no such thing in Islam as truggle between the sexes; there is no need for a fierce rivalry for worldly pursuits between them; nor is there a necessity to launch an attack against either of them in an attempt to disparage, harm, criticise or find fault with any one of them.

All this is vain in Islam and constitutes a misunderstanding of Islam's view of the roles it has assigned to each one of them. In Islam, each one of them has a share according to what they have earned in both material and spiritual terms. Instead of envying each other, they are required to ask Allah to give them more of His bounty through lawful labour and through prayer.

Categories of Women in Relation to a Man

Women in relation to a man fall into three categories:

 She could be his wife:

In this case, he is allowed to enjoy her company in any way he likes, just as she is allowed to enjoy his company. In fact, Allah describes each one of them to be a 'garment' for the other, revealing an excellent image of a perfect physical, emotional and mental union: "They are clothing for you and you are clothing for them." (*Soorat Al-Baqarah,* 2:187) (See page 213)

She could be a relative whom he is never permitted to marry at any time in his life whatsoever (*maḥram*):

This category consists of the following:

The mother and above (the maternal grandmother, the paternal grandmother, etc.)

The daughter and below (granddaughter, great-granddaughter, etc.)

The full sister, consaguine or uterinesister.

The paternal aunt, (that is, the father's full sister) or his consaguibe or uterine sister. This includes the paternal aunt of one's father and the paternal aunt of one's mother.

The maternal aunt, (that is, the mother's full sister) or her consanguine or uterine sister. This includes the maternal aunt of one's father and the maternal aunt of one's mother.

The full brother's daughters or the daughters of the sanguine or uterine brother and below (brother's son's daughters, for instance).

The full sister's daughters or the daughters of the consanguine or uterine sister and below (sister's daughter's daughters, for instance).

The mother-in-law, whether he is still married to her daughter or has divorced her, and grandmother-in-law

The stepdaughter (the daughter one's wife has from an earlier marriage to another man).

The son's wife and below (such as the grandson's wife).

stepmother and above, e.g. the stepbrother's wife (from the step father's side).

The foster mother: A foster mother is a woman who breastfeeds a child during his first two years at least five times to his satisfaction. Islam grants her such a right by reason of such breastfeeding (*raḍaa'ah*).

The foster sister: a foster sister is the daughter of the foster mother. Indeed, a man is not allowed to marry any of the relations through breastfeeding, just as he is not permitted to marry any of the relations through blood relationship. Relations through breastfeeding include foster aunts (foster mother's sisters) and foster nieces (foster sister's daughters).

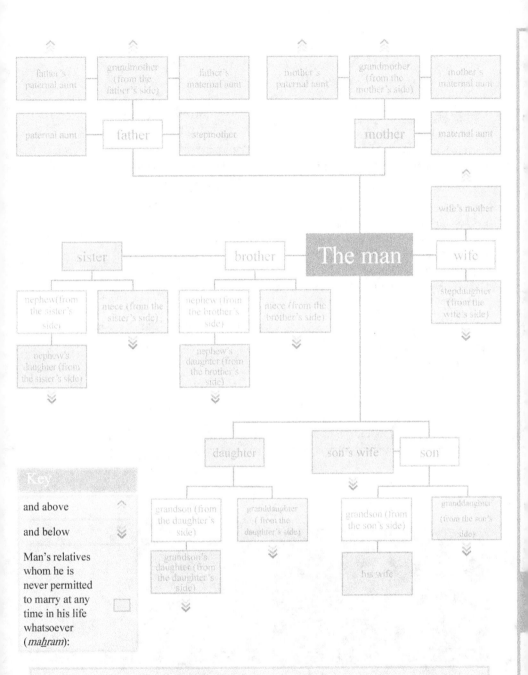

These female relatives may appear before him without covering the body parts that are not customarily covered, such as the arms, neck and hair, but without going to extremes.

She could be one he is allowed to marry (*ajnabiyah*, literally, foreigner, not related to him):

Such a woman is one who does not belong to the category of women known as *mahram* stated above, whether she is one of his relatives, such as his maternal or paternal cousin or sister-in-law, or she is not one of his relatives at all.

Regarding this category of women, Islam has laid down a number of rules and criteria which govern a Muslim man's relationship with such women. By doing this, Islam aims to protect people's honour and block all the means that are bound to lead to evil. Allah who has created man knows exactly what is best for him, as the Qur'an states, "Does He who created not then know while He is the All-Pervading, the All-Aware?" (*Soorat Al-Mulk*, 67:14)

> Every day, we read new reports and statistics of cases of rape and illicit sexual relationships that have ruined countless families and societies that do not implement Allah's laws.

Rules Governing the Relationship between a Man and Women he Is Allowed to Marry

Lowering the Gaze

A Muslim man must not look at other women or at anything for that matter which is bound to sexually arouse him, nor should he unnecessarily look at women.

Allah commands both men and women to lower their gaze, for doing so leads to modesty and serves to safeguard one's honour, while lustful looks generally pave the way to sins, as the Qur'an states, "Say to the believing men that they should lower their gaze and guard their modesty. That will make for greater purity for them. Allah is aware of what they do. Say to believing women that they should lower their gaze and remain chaste." (*Soorat An-Noor*, 24:30-31)

However, if a Muslim accidentally sees a woman, he must divert his eyes from her. In fact, the order to lower the gaze applies to anything that is bound to lead to sexual arousal, including those scenes that are presented in the media and on the Internet.

Islam has laid down rules which govern the relationship between men and women.

Lowering the gaze to avoid looking at things Allah has forbidden leads to modesty and protects one's honour.

2. Observing Modesty in Speech

When talking to a woman who is not related to him, he must observe politeness and modesty and avoid any words or gestures which may lead to sexual stimulation. It is for this reason that:

- Allah ﷻ warns women against speaking in a coquettish and too soft a manner when addressing men, as the Qur'an states, "Do not be too soft-spoken in your speech lest someone with sickness in his heart becomes desirous. Speak correct and courteous words." (*Soorat Al-Ahzaab,* 33:32)

- Allah ﷻ warns them against using suggestive gestures and manner of walking or displaying their charms and some of their ornaments: "They should not strike their feet in order to draw attention to their hidden ornaments ." (*Soorat An-Noor,* 24:31)

3. Avoiding Private Seclusion with Non-*Mahram* Women Altogether (*Khalwah*)

The Arabic word *khalwah* means the state of being alone with a non-*mahram* woman in a place where no one can see them. Islam strictly prohibits this as it could, through Satan's temptations, lead to illicit sexual relationships. The Prophet ﷺ once said, "Never is a man alone with a woman except that Satan is the third." (*Sunan At-Tirmidhee:* 2165)

4. Wearing the *Hijaab* (the Modest Muslim Style of Dress)

Allah ﷻ commands women, but not men, to wear the *hijaab* because women in particular enjoy a natural beauty and attraction that could easily tempt men into sinful acts.

Islam commands women to wear the *hijaab* for a number of reasons, including the following:

- So that they could carry out their mission in life and society in scientific and academic fields in the best possible manner while at the same time guarding their modesty.

- So that they would reduce chances of temptation in order to purify society, on the one hand, and safeguard women's honour, on the other.

- So that they would help male onlookers control themselves even more and thus treat them as civilised and educated human beings and not as sex objects that only serve to tempt men and stimulate them.

What Must the *Hijaab* Cover?

Allah commands women to cover all their bodies except the face and the hands, as the Qur'an states, "They should not display their beauty and ornaments except what must ordinarily appear thereof." (*Soorat An-Noor,* 24:31) However, in cases of likely temptation due to their striking beauty, they may have to cover their faces and hands as well.

Criteria of Proper *Hijaab*

A woman may choose any design or colour she likes for her *hijaab* as long as the following conditions are met:

- It must appropriately cover the parts of the body which must be covered in public.

- It must hang loose and must not fit very closely to the body, so that the shape of the body is not revealed.

- It must not allow the wearer's body to be seen through its fabric.

The *hijaab* safeguards women's honour and affords them the chance to carry out their mission in society in the most modest manner mankind has ever witnessed.

> Marriage in Islam

> Marriage is one of the strongest relationships Islam has stressed.

Marriage is one of the strongest relationships which Islam stresses, encourages and considers as one of the prophets' practices. (See page 202)

Indeed, Islam attaches much importance to marriage rulings, etiquette and the spouses' rights in such a way as to guarantee marital stability and permanence and create a successful family in which children are brought up enjoying psychological stability, observing devoutness and moral integrity, and displaying excellence in various aspects of life.

These rulings include the following:

Islam has laid down several conditions for the validity of the marriage contract. They are as follows:

The Conditions Islam Stipulates Regarding the Wife

The wife must be Muslim, Jewish or Christian, believing in her religion. However, Islam encourages Muslim men to choose devout Muslim women for this purpose because a practising Muslim will be a good mother who will give her children the best possible upbringing and help her husband adhere to the teachings of Islam. As the Prophet ﷺ said, "Marry a devout Muslim woman and you will prosper." (Saheeh Al-Bukhaaree: 4802; Saheeh Muslim: 1466)

- She must be a chaste woman, as it is forbidden to marry a woman known for her lewdness and immorality. As the Qur'an states, "It is lawful for you to marry the chaste believing women and the chaste women of the people who were given the Book before you." (*Soorat Al-Maa'idah*, 5:5)

- She must not be one of those women whom he is never permitted to marry at any time in his life whatsoever (*mahram*) (See page 206), nor must he marry two sisters at the same time or a woman and her aunt at the same time.

The Conditions Islam Stipulates Regarding the Husband

The husband must be Muslim, and a Muslim woman is forbidden from marrying a non-Muslim man, no matter what his religion may be and whether he is a member of the People of the Book (i.e. Jewish or Christian) or not. Islam stresses that a man must be accepted as a husband as long as he meets the following two conditions:

- Adherence to religion

- Good character

The Prophet ﷺ said, "If a man with whose religion and character you are satisfied asks your daughter's hand in marriage, comply with his request." (*Sunan At-Tirmidhee:* 1084; *Sunan Ibn Maajah:* 1967)

> The Spouses' Rights and Obligations

Allah ﷻ has entitled husband and wife to certain rights, made it incumbent upon both of them to discharge their duties and encourages them to engage in anything that is bound to promote marital life and preserve it. Indeed, they are both responsible for the welfare of the family and neither of them should demand the other to do something beyond their capacity, as the Qur'an states, "And women have rights similar to those of men over them in kindness." (*Soorat Al-Baqarah*, 2:228) Therefore, tolerance and kindness are required to create a prosperous life and help build a strong family.

The Wife's Rights

 Maintenance and Residence

- The wife's maintenance entails her incontestable right to food, drink, clothing, general care and a suitable home, even if she is wealthy.

- How is the amount of maintenance calculated? The husband ought to spend on his wife in accordance with his means without extravagance or miserliness, as the Qur'an states, "Let the man of means spend according to his means: and the man whose resources are restricted, let him spend according to what Allah has given him. Allah puts no burden on any person beyond what He has given him."(*Soorat At-Talaaq*, 65:7)

> A Muslim man is duty-bound to support his wife and children in kindness.

- He must spend on her in kindness, without ever implying that he is doing her favours or humiliating her in any way whatsoever. Indeed, such maintenance is not a favour but a duty he ought to discharge towards his wife in kindness, as the Qur'an clearly exhorts him.

- When a Muslim man fulfils his duty of supporting his wife and children, he will be rewarded abundantly by Allah, as the Prophet ﷺ said, "When a man spends on his family, anticipating Allah's reward in the hereafter, this act of his will be counted as an act of charity." (*Saheeh Al-Bukhaaree:* 4776; *Saheeh Muslim:* 1401) He also said, "You will be rewarded for whatever you spend for Allah's sake even if it were a morsel of food which you put in your wife's mouth." (*Saheeh Al-Bukhaaree:* 56; *Saheeh Muslim:* 1628) Those who refuse or neglect their duty to spend on their families despite their ability to do so are committing a terrible sin for their negligence, as the Prophet ﷺ said, "A man who neglects those who are under his care would surely be committing a sin." (*Sunan Abu Daawood:* 1692)

Living with Her in Kindness

This means showing good character, kindness, gentleness in word and deed and putting up with the occasional faults and negligence. As the Qur'an states, "Live together with them courteously and in kindness. If you dislike them, it may well be that you dislike something in which Allah has placed a lot of good." (*Soorat An-Nisaa', 4:19*)

The Prophet ﷺ said, "The believers who have perfect faith are those with the best character, and the best of them are those who treat their women the best." (*Sunan At-Tirmidhee:* 1162)

"The believers who have perfect faith are those with the best character, and the best among you are those who treat their wives the best." (*Sunan At-Tirmidhee:* 2612; *Musnad Ahmad:* 24677)

"The best of you are the kindest towards their wives, and I am the kindest amongst you to my wives." (*Sunan At-Tirmidhee:* 3895)

One of the Prophet's companions once asked him, "Messenger of Allah, what is the right the wife of one of us has on him?" he said, "To feed her whenever you feed yourself and to clothe her whenever you clothe yourself; do not slap her across the face, revile her or separate yourself from her except in the house."(*Sunan Abu Daawood:* 2142)

Patience and Tolerance

A man must make allowances for women's nature, which is obviously different from that of men; he must also try to look at life from all sides, considering the advantages and disadvantages of his wife, for no one is free from faults. Both spouses must exercise

patience and take into account the positive aspects of each other's personality, as the Qur'an states, "Do not forget to show kindness to each other." (*Soorat Al-Baqarah*, 2:237) The Prophet ﷺ also said in this respect, "A believer must not harbour any rancour against a believing woman; if he dislikes one of her characteristics, he will certainly be pleased with another." (*Saheeh Muslim:* 1469)

The Prophet ﷺ urges men to treat women with kindness, pointing their attention to the fact that women's emotional and psychological nature is different from that of men, that such differences between men and women are in actual fact complementary and must in no way give rise to discord and eventual divorce. The Prophet ﷺ said, "Treat women well and with kindness, for a woman was created from the rib and thus she will not be straightened according to your way. If you want to enjoy her, you will have to enjoy her with her twist. If you try to straighten her, you will break her, and breaking her is divorcing her." (*Saheeh Al-Bukhaaree:* 3153; *Saheeh Muslim:* 1468)

 Spending the Night with the Wife

The husband is recommended to spend the night with his wife and must do so at least once every four days. He must also observe equal division of nights between co-wives in cases of polygamy.

 Defending Her, Representing His Honour

When a man marries a woman, she becomes his 'honour' which he must stubbornly defend even if he gets killed in the process, as the Prophet ﷺ said, "Whoever is killed defending his wife is a martyr." (*Sunan At-Tirmidhee:* 1421; *Sunan Abu Daawood:* 4772)

 Not Revealing Bedroom Secrets

The husband must not talk to others about his wife's particularities and bedroom secrets to other people. The Prophet ﷺ said, "The worst person in the eyes of Allah on the Day of Judgement is that one who has an intimate relationship with his wife and the man then he reveals their bedroom secrets to others." (*Saheeh Muslim:* 1437)

 Not Engaging in Aggressive or Hostile Actions against her

To solve marital problems, Islam has laid down a number of rules, including the following:

- Problems may be solved through constructive dialogue and wisdom in order to correct mistakes.

- In cases of rebellion, disloyalty and ill-conduct, the husband may stop talking to her, but without exceeding three days; if this course of action does not seem to work, then he may temporarily abandon her in bed or abstain from the usual sexual intimacy, but without leaving the house.

- 'Aa'ishah ؓ narrated, "Allah's Messenger ﷺ never hit anything with his hand ever, except when fighting in the path of Allah. Nor did he ever hit a servant or a woman." (*Saheeh Muslim:* 2328)

 Teaching and Advising Her

The husband must enjoin his family members to act rightly and forbid them to act inappropriately. He ought to strive hard to help them follow the path that leads to Paradise and avoid those paths that lead to Hellfire. Teaching them by precept and example, he can

215

do so by acting on obeying Allah's commands and avoiding things He has prohibited. The wife must also advise her husband, guide him to the right path and discuss with him ways of giving the best possible upbringing to their children. As the Qur'an states, "O you who believe, safeguard yourselves and your families from a Fire whose fuel is people and stones." (*Soorat At-Tahreem*, 66:6) The Prophet ﷺ also said in this regard, "Every one of you is a guardian and is responsible for those in his custody." (*Saheeh Al-Bukhaaree:* 2416; *Saheeh Muslim:* 1829)

9. Honouring the Conditions Stipulated by the Wife

If the wife makes a stipulation at the time of concluding the marriage contract, such as having a particular kind of accommodation or expenses and the husband agrees to such a condition, he must fulfil such an obligation, for a marriage contract is one of the most solemn agreements and obligations. The Prophet ﷺ said, "Of all the conditions which you have to fulfil, the conditions which make it legal for you to have sexual relations (i.e. the marriage contract) have the greatest right to be fulfilled." (*Saheeh Al-Bukhaaree:* 4856; *Saheeh Muslim:* 1418)

> The husband must honour the marriage contract and fulfil the conditions stipulated in it.

The Husband's Rights

Obedience in Kindness

Allah ﷻ has placed men in charge of women, being responsible for their maintenance, guidance and general care, due to the characteristics with which He has endowed them, in addition to the money they spend to support them. As the Qur'an states, "Men have charge of women because Allah has given the one more [strength] than the other and because they spend their wealth on them." (*Soorat An-Nisaa'*, 4:34)

Attentiveness to His Sexual Needs

A Muslim woman must be attentive to her husband's sexual needs and is recommended to beautify herself for him. If she refuses to respond to his legitimate sexual advances, she would be committing a monstrous sin, unless there is a legitimate excuse, such as being on her menses, making up an obligatory fast she has previously missed or being sick.

The Prophet ﷺ said, "If a man calls his wife to bed and she refuses, and then he spends the night angry with her, the angels will continue to curse her until the morning." (*Saheeh Al-Bukhaaree:* 3065; *Saheeh Muslim:* 1436)

Not Allowing Anyone He Does not Like in His House

This is his right which she must respect. The Prophet ﷺ said, "It is not lawful for a woman to observe a voluntary fast without the permission of her husband, nor is it lawful for her to allow anyone to enter his house without his permission." (*Saheeh Al-Bukhaaree:* 4899)

Not Leaving the House without His Permission

One of the husband's rights is that she is not allowed to leave the house without his permission, whether she wants to go out for a personal or general need.

Service

A woman is recommended to serve her husband in kindness by preparing meals for him and undertaking other household chores.

> Divorce

> Islam requires spouses to preserve their marital relationship and urges them to do their utmost to keep it going. However, should there be a genuine need for divorce, Islam requires them to follow certain rules it has laid down in this respect.

Islam urges that the marriage contract be permanent and that the marriage relationship be characterised by continuity so much so that husband and wife remain together until death separates them. Islam goes as far as to call marriage a "solemn pledge". Specifying a date for terminating the marriage contract is strictly prohibited.

While Islam stresses all this, it does, however, take into account the fact that it lays down rules and regulations for human beings with frailties that characterise human nature, and so it lays down rules and regulations as to how a divorce may be negotiated after all efforts of reconciliation have been exhausted and there is no other recourse. In this way, it deals fairly and in a practical manner with both spouses. When aversion and conflicts between spouses persistently become intolerable, divorce becomes a necessity for the prosperity and familial and social stability for each one of them. The reason for such an inevitable course of action explains the failure of marriage to realize its purpose, hence dissolution of marriage becomes the lesser of two evils.

It is for this reason that Islam allows marriage dissolution through divorce as a means to end an unsuccessful marriage and to give each spouse the chance to find another spouse for a better relationship. As the Qur'an states, "If a couple do separate, Allah will enrich each of them from His boundless wealth. Allah is All-Encompassing, All-Wise." (*Soorat An-Nisaa'*, 4:130)

However, it has laid down a number of rules and criteria concerning divorce, including the following:

* As a general rule, divorce rests with the husband except under certain circumstances.

* The wife may request a divorce from the judge if she cannot bear to live with her husband any longer for legitimate reasons and the latter refuses to divorce her. The judge then undertakes to dissolve the marriage contract if the reason for requesting a divorce is acceptable.

* A husband can remarry his wife after a second divorce; however, if he divorces her a third time, he cannot possibly remarry her unless she marries another man who has genuinely divorced her.

> Parents' Rights

Showing kindness to parents is one of the most meritorious acts and the best of rewarded in the sight of Allah. In fact, Allah ﷻ mentions it alongside the act of worshipping Him in many places in the Qur'an.

Islam considers dutifulness to parents one of the deeds that lead to Paradise. The Prophet ﷺ said, "A parent is the middle gate of all the gates of Paradise. (That is, obeying parents leads to entering Paradise from its middle gate, which is the best of them all) Now, if you like, you may lose it or keep it." (*Sunan At-Tirmidhee:* 1900)

- **Seriousness of disobedience to parents**

All revealed religions consider disobedience to parents one of the greatest of all major sins and warned against such a monstrous act. The Prophet ﷺ once asked his companions, "Shall I not inform you of the greatest of the major sins?" "Yes, please do, Messenger of Allah," they replied. He said, "Associating partners with Allah in worship and being disobedient to parents." (*Saheeh Al-Bukhaaree:* 5918)

- **Dutifulness to parents but without disobeying Allah**

A Muslim must obey his parents in everything unless they ask him to do something which Allah has forbidden. In this case, he must not obey them but must still be kind to them, as the Qur'an states, "We have instructed man to honour his parents, but if they endeavour to make you associate with Me something about which you have no knowledge, do not obey them." (*Soorat Al-'Ankaboot*, 29:8)

- **Showing kindness to them in their old age**

Allah ﷻ says, "Your Lord has decreed that you should worship none but Him, and that you should show kindness to your parents. Whether one or both of them reach old age with you, do not utter the slightest harsh word to them out of irritation and do not be harsh with them but speak to them with gentleness and generosity." (*Soorat Al-Israa'*, 17:23)

This verse informs us that a Muslim must honour his parents and obey them and that he must not repel them especially if they have attained old age, even by muttering sounds to express annoyance, let alone saying a word of contempt.

- **Non-Muslim parents**

A Muslim is required to obey his parents and show kindness to them even if they are not Muslim, as the Qur'an states, "But if they strive with you to make you associate with Me something of which you certainly have no knowledge do not obey them. Even then, treat them with kindness and due consideration in respect of [the life of] this world." (*Soorat Luqmaan*, 31:15)

> Children's Rights

- Marrying a good devout woman to provide the best possible upbringing to her children. Indeed. This is the best gift a man can give his children.

- Giving them good names, as a person's name conveys meaning and becomes a symbol of that person.

- Teaching them the principles of Islam: "Every one of you is a guardian and is responsible for those is in his custody. The ruler is a guardian of his subjects and responsible for them; a man is a guardian of his family and is responsible for it; a woman is a guardian of her husband's home and children and is responsible for them, and a servant is a guardian of his master's property and is responsible for it. Therefore, all of you are guardians and all of you are responsible for those under your care." (*Saheeh Al-Bukhaaree:* 2416; *Saheeh Muslim:* 1829)

- Maintenance

The father must support all his children without exception and must not neglect this duty. Rather, he must carry it out to the best of his ability and according to his means, as the Prophet ﷺ said, "A man who neglects those who are under his care would surely be committing a sin" (*Sunan Abu Daawood:* 1692)

Regarding spending and caring for girls in particular, he also said, "Whoever is in charge of any of these girls and treats them well, they will be a shield for him against the Fire." (*Saheeh Al-Bukhaaree:* 5649; *Saheeh Muslim:* 2629)

- Justice

All children must be treated equally, as the Prophet ﷺ said, "Fear Allah and treat your children justly." (*Saheeh Al-Bukhaaree:* 2447; *Saheeh Muslim:* 1623)

Your Moral Character

11

Far from being superfluous or trivial, noble character and good manners are part and parcel of Islam and are related to it in all its aspects. Indeed, noble character occupies a lofty position, which is obvious in all its rules and regulations, and the Prophet ﷺ was chosen as a messenger to perfect high moral standards.

Contents

The Position of Good Character in Islam
- Perfecting noble character was one of the most important reasons behind the Prophet's mission
- Noble character is part and parcel of faith and belief
- Noble character permeates all acts of worship without exception
- The immense rewards Allah ﷻ has in store for those who observe good character

Distinguishing Features of Noble Character in Islam
- Noble character is not confined to a particular type of people
- Noble character is not confined only to human beings
- Noble character in all aspects of life
- Noble character under all circumstances

Some Aspects of the Prophet's Life
- Humility
- Justice
- Mercy
- Kindness and Generosity

The Position of Good Character in Islam

1 Perfection of noble character was one of the most important objectives of the Prophet's mission

Allah ﷻ says, "It is He who raised up among the unlettered [Arabs] a Messenger from them to recite His verses to them and purify them and teach them the Book and Wisdom, even though before that they were clearly misguided." (*Soorat Al-Jumu'ah*, 62:2) This verse reveals one of the favours Allah ﷻ has bestowed on the believers, stating that He has sent them His Messenger, Muḥammad ﷺ, to teach them the Qur'an and to purify them. Purification can only be attained by purging one's heart from such imperfections as associating others with Allah in worship, having bad moral character like hatred and jealousy and ridding one's speech and deeds of all forms of evil practices. The Prophet ﷺ once declared, "I have been sent to perfect noble character." (*Sunan Al-Bayhaqee:* 21301) This statement makes it clear that one of the reasons behind the Prophet's mission was to elevate and perfect the moral character of the individual and society at large.

2 Noble character is part and parcel of faith and belief

When asked about the best of the believers, the Prophet ﷺ replied, "They are those who have the best character and manners." (*Sunan At-Tirmidhee:* 1162; *Sunan Abu Daawood:* 4682)

In fact, the Qur'an uses the comprehensive Arabic word *birr* to refer to faith. As the Qur'an states, "Righteousness (*birr*) does not lie in turning your faces [during prayer] to the East or to the West. Rather, those with true devoutness are the ones who believe in Allah, the Last Day, the angels, the Book and the Prophets…" (*Soorat Al-Baqarah*, 2:177) The word *birr* is a rather comprehensive term which includes all forms of righteousness, in

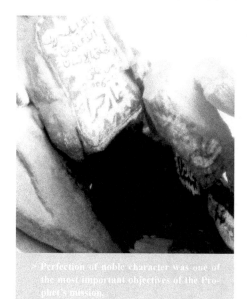

> Perfection of noble character was one of the most important objectives of the Prophet's mission.

word and deed. It is for this reason that the Prophet ﷺ said, "Righteousness (*birr*) is good character." (*Saheeh Muslim:* 2553)

This becomes clear in the Prophet's declaration: "Faith (*eemaan*) has sixty odd branches. The uppermost of all these is the Testimony of Faith: *Laa ilaaha illallaah* (There is no god worthy of worship except Allah), while the least of them is the removal of a harmful object from the road. Shyness is a branch of faith." (*Saheeh Muslim:* 35)

3 Noble character permeates all acts of worship

Every time Allah commands the believers to perform an act of worship, He draws their attention to its moral significance or its positive effect on the individual and society. Examples of this are numerous and include the following:

The Prayer: "Establish the prayer, for the prayer restrains from shameful and unjust deeds." (*Soorat Al-'Ankaboot*, 29:45).

The Obligatory Charity (*Zakaat*): "Take *zakaat* from their wealth to purify and cleanse them with it." (*Soorat At-Tawbah:* 9:103) Besides showing kindness and giving comfort to people, *zakaat* refines the the benefactor's "character and purges it from evil practices".

Fasting: O You who believe, fasting has been prescribed for you just as it was prescribed for those before you, so that you may remain conscious of Allah." (*Soorat Al-Baqarah:* 183) This verse makes it abundantly clear that the foremost objective of fasting is to realise consciousness of Allah by obeying His commands and avoiding all words and deeds He has prohibited. As the Prophet ﷺ said, " Whoever does not abandon false speech and false conduct, then Allah has no need of his abandoning of food and drink." (*Saheeh Al-Bukhaaree:* 1804) Therefore, if fasting fails to effect a change in one's character and dealings with others, it will by no means serve its real purpose.

4 The immense rewards Allah ﷺ has in store for those who observe good character Textual proofs from the Qur'an and the *Sunnah* to this effect are numerous, including the following:

- Good character will be the heaviest righteous deed to be placed on a person's scale of deeds on the Day of Judgement:

The Prophet ﷺ said, "No deed that will be placed on the scale of deeds [on the Day of Judgement] will be heavier than good character. Indeed, a person with good character will attain the rank of those with a good record of voluntary fasts and prayers." (*Sunan At-Tirmidhee:* 2003)

- It is the very deed that will lead people to enter Paradise the most:

When the Prophet ﷺ was asked about which act leads people to enter Paradise the most, he replied, "Piety and good character." (*Sunan At-Tirmidhee:* 2004; *Sunan Ibn Maajah:* 4246)

- Of all people, those who have good character will be the closest to the Prophet ﷺ on the Day of Judgement:

The Prophet ﷺ said, "The dearest to me among you and the nearest to me on the Day of Judgement are those who have the best character." (*Sunan At-Tirmidhee:* 2018)

- The Prophet ﷺ guarantees a house in the highest part of Paradise to those who have good character:

"I guarantee a house in the surroundings of Paradise for those who give up arguing, even if they are in the right; and I guarantee a house in the middle of Paradise for those who abandon lying even when joking; and I guarantee a house in the highest part of Paradise for those who have good character and manners." (*Sunan Abu Daawood:* 4800)

Good character is one of the meritorious deeds in the sight of Allah and serves to give us a sense of inner fulfilment and happiness.

Distinguishing Features of Noble Character in Islam

Noble character in Islam is characterised by unique qualities which distinguish it from all other faiths, including the following

1. Noble character is not confined to a particular type of people

Almighty Allah has made people into different shapes, colours and languages. They are all equal in His sight, and no one has an advantage over another except in piety and noble conduct, as the Qur'an states, "O mankind, We have created you of a male and a female, and made you into nations and tribes that you may know one another; verily, the most honourable of you, in the sight of Allah, are the most pious of you." (*Soorat Al-Hujuraat*, 49:13)

Indeed, noble character characterises Muslims' relationship with all members of society: There is no difference whatsoever between rich and poor, black and white, Arab and non-Arab, or a prince and a pauper.

How to Treat Non-Muslims

Allah commands us to show kindness and courtesy to everyone without exception, for justice, kindness and mercy are aspects of good character which a Muslim observes in his words and deeds with Muslims and non-Muslims alike. A Muslim ought to embody good character traits as a means to call others to this great religion of Islam.

The Qur'an says, "Allah does not forbid you from being good to those who have not fought you on account of your religion or driven you from your homes, or from being just towards them. Allah loves those who are just." (*Soorat Al-Mumtahinah*, 60:8)

Allah only forbids us to make friends with those belligerent non-Muslims who fight us because of our religion. He also forbids us to admire their way of life which clearly upholds unbelief and polytheist practices, as the Qur'an states, "Allah only forbids you respecting those who made war upon you on account of [your] religion, and drove you forth from your homes and backed up [others] in your expulsion, that you make friends with them. Whoever takes them for friends are wrongdoers." (*Soorat Al-Mumtahinah*, 60:9)

A Muslim always maintains high moral standards when dealing with people regardless of their religion or race.

2. Noble character is not confined only to human beings

Good treatment of animals

The Prophet ﷺ once mentioned that a woman deserved punishment in Hellfire because of a cat that she had restrained and left it to starve to death. He also mentioned the story of a man whom Allah had forgiven after giving a thirsty dog some water to drink: "A woman entered Hellfire because of a cat which she had tied, neither giving it food nor setting it free to eat from the vermin of the earth."(*Saheeh Al-Bukhaaree:* 3140; *Saheeh Muslim:* 2619)

He also said, "While a man was walking along a road, he became very thirsty and he found a well. He lowered himself into the well, drank and came out. Then he saw a dog panting and eating mud because of excessive thirst. The man said,'This dog has become exhausted from thirst in the same way as I.' He lowered himself into the well again and filled his shoe with water and gave the dog some water to drink. Allah thanked him for his good deed and forgave him." The people asked, "Messenger of Allah! Is there a reward for us in serving these animals?" "Yes," he replied, "There is a reward for serving every living thing." (*Saheeh Al-Bukhaaree:* 5663; *Saheeh Muslim:* 2244).

Preservation of the environment

Islam instructs us to make the world a better place by utilising the earth's natural resources to build a civilization and engage in development and production for the general welfare of mankind, while at the same time trying to preserve such resources and prevent others from abusing or unnecessarily wasting them. Corruption in all its forms and by whatever means it may be caused is frowned upon in Islam and abhorred by the Creator Himself, as the Qur'an states, "Allah does not like corruption." (*Soorat Al-Baqarah,* 2:205)

In fact, Islam is so concerned about this issue that it goes as far as to direct its adherents to do righteous deeds and engage in such things as cultivating the land even in times of great turmoil and under terrifying circumstances, such as the Day of Judgement. As the Prophet ﷺ once instructed, "If the Day of Judgement takes place [and you recognise the Event], while a man is holding a palm-tree seedling [to plant in the soil], let him, if he can, plant it." (*Musnad Ahmad:* 12981)

Islam urges its adherents to safeguard the environment.

3. Noble character in all aspects of life

The Family

Islam stresses the importance of noble character among all members of the family, as the Prophet ﷺ said, "The best of you are those who treat their wives the best, and I am the best of you in this respect." (*Sunan At-Tirmidhee:* 3895)

- Despite being the best human being of all time, Prophet Muḥammad ﷺ shared household chores with his wives and helped around the house, as 'Aa'ishah ؓ, one of his wives, once said about him, "He used to help his wives with the housework."(*Saḥeeḥ Al-Bukhaaree:* 5048)

- He also used to joke with his family members. 'Aa'ishah ؓ said, "I accompanied the Prophet ﷺ on a certain journey when I was young and thin. The Prophet ﷺ asked the people to move on, and they marched ahead. Then he turned to me and said, 'Come on, let us have a race'. I raced him and I won the race. He did not mention this incident again. However, when I later put on more weight and I forgot all about this incident, I accompanied him again on some other journey. He asked the people to march ahead, and they did. Then he asked me to race him. I raced him, but he won. The Prophet laughed and said, 'This was to make up for my previous defeat.'"(*Musnad Aḥmad:* 26277)

Trade

Because people's love of wealth may get the better of them and prompt them to engage in forbidden practices, Islam stresses the importance of observing noble character which serves to put an end to such practices. The following are some examples of the points Islam stresses in this respect:

- It warns traders who deal with fraud against a severe punishment on the Day of Judgement, as the Qur'an states, "Woe to those who give short measure or weight; those who, when they take a measure from people, exact full measure, but when they give them a measure or weight, hand over less than is due." (*Soorat Al-Muṭaffifeen,* 83:3).

- It urges traders to show kindness and leniency, as the Prophet ﷺ said, "May Allah have mercy on a man who is kind when he buys, when he sells and when he demands his due."(*Saḥeeḥ Al-Bukhaaree:* 1970)

Industry

Islam advises workers to observe a number of ethical principles and standards, including the following:

- To be as highly proficient at their jobs as they possibly can. The Prophet ﷺ said, "Allah likes to see that when you do something that you do it well." (*Musnad Abu Ya'laa:* 4386, *Al-Bayhaqee's Shu'ab Al-Eemaan:* 5313)

- To honour their obligations, as the Prophet ﷺ said, "The signs of the hypocrite are three: when he speaks he lies, when he promises he breaks his promise and when he is entrusted he betrays the trust." (*Saheeh Al-Bukhaaree:* 33)

4. Noble character under all circumstances

There are no exceptions whatsoever when it comes to talking about good moral character in Islam. A Muslim is required to follow the dictates of Islamic law and observe noble character even in times of war and in difficult times, for there is no such thing in Islam as the end justifies the means. In other words, bad or unfair methods of doing something are by no means acceptable even if the result of that action is good or positive.

It is for this reason that Islam has laid down rules and criteria which govern Muslims' behaviour even in times of war so that they would not succumb to fits of rage, driven by intolerance which feeds their anger and satisfies hatred and malicious and selfish tendencies.

Some War Ethics in Islam

1. Islam commands justice even with non-Muslims and warns against wronging them in any way

The Qur'an says, "Do not let the hatred of others to you make you swerve to wrong and depart from justice. Be just: that is next to piety." (*Soorat Al-Maa'idah,* 5:8) That is, do not let your enmity for your enemies exceed the limits and turn you away from justice in either words or actions.

2. It strictly forbids treachery and betrayal when dealing with the enemy

Islam forbids treachery and betrayal even against the enemy, as the Qur'an states, "Allah does not love treacherous people." (*Soorat Al-Anfaal,* 8:58)

3. It strictly forbids mutilation of dead bodies of enemies

It declares mutilation of corpses strictly impermissible, as the Prophet ﷺ once ordered, "Do not mutilate people." (*Saheeh Muslim:* 1731)

4. It prohibits the killing of non-combatants, destroying the environment and causing corruption in the land

Upon despatching a military expedition to the northern borders of the Roman territory, Abu Bakr As-Siddeeq ؓ, the first Rightly-Guided Caliph and the best of all the Prophet's companions, addressed its leader, Usaamah ibn Zayd ؓ, saying, "Do not let your army kill young children, old people or women. Do not uproot or burn palms or cut down fruitful trees. Do not slaughter sheep, cows or camels, except for food. You will come across some people who have set themselves apart in hermitages; leave them to accomplish the purpose for which they have done this."(*Taareekh Ibn 'Asaakir, vol.* 2, p. 50)

Some Aspects of the Prophet's Life and High Moral Standards

The Prophet ﷺ was the epitome of good character and personal integrity. When 'Aa'ishah ؓ, one of the Prophet's wives, was asked about the character of the Prophet ﷺ, she replied, "His character was the Qur'an." (*Musnad Ahmad:* 24601; *Saheeh Muslim:* 746) This means he translated the noble teachings of the Qur'an into reality.

The Prophet ﷺ was the epitome of good moral character.

Humility

The Prophet ﷺ was so humble that he did not like people to rise to their feet upon his arrival and he even forbade them from doing so. Although no one was dearer to his noble companions than the Messenger of Allah ﷺ, they would not stand up for him when they saw him coming, for they knew that he disliked that. (*Musnad Ahmad:* 12345; *Musnad Al-Bazzaar:* 6637)

Before 'Adiyy ibn Haatim ؓ, an Arab notable, embraced Islam, he came to Madeenah to find out about the new faith. "As we were making for [the Prophet's] house," he later recalled, "there met him an old feeble lady with some children who asked him to stop and he stopped for a long time while she was telling him of her needs. I said to myself, 'This is certainly no king; he does not behave like Chosroes or Caesar.'" (*Musnad Ahmad:* 19381)

His actions and movements while in the company of his companions were characterised by homely simplicity and utter humility, so much so that a stranger would not be able to tell who he was. Once, a man came and said, "who amongst you is Muhammad?" (*Saheeh Al-Bukhaaree:* 63)

Anas ibn Maalik ؓ said, "Any of the female slaves of Madeenah could take hold of the hand of Allah's Messenger and take him wherever she wished." (*Saheeh Al-Bukhaaree:* 5724) The expression "take hold of the hand of Allah's Messenger" is an indication of his extreme kindness and prompt response to the young and the weak. This report reveals the Prophet's utter humility, in that it mentions his readiness to attend to the needs of some of the most vulnerable members of society, women and female slaves.

Once he declared, "A person who has an atom's weight of pride in his heart will not enter Paradise." (*Saheeh Muslim:* 91)

Mercy

The Prophet ﷺ said, "Those who are merciful will be given mercy by the Most Merciful. Be merciful to those on the earth and the One above the heavens will have mercy on you." (*Sunan At-Tirmidhee:* 1924; *Sunan Abu Daawood:* 4941)

His mercy embraced countless aspects, including the following:

Mercy towards children

A Bedouin once came to the Prophet ﷺ and said, "Do you kiss your children? We do not kiss them." The Prophet ﷺ said, "Can I put mercy in your heart after Allah has removed it?" (*Saheeh Al-Bukhaaree:* 5652; *Saheeh Muslim:* 2317)

On another occasion, a man saw the Prophet ﷺ kissing his grandson, Al-Hasan ibn 'Ali, and said to him, "I have ten children, but I have never kissed any of them." The Prophet ﷺ looked disapprovingly at him and said, "He who does not show mercy to others will not be shown mercy." (*Saheeh Muslim:* 2318)

Once he carried his granddaughter Zaynab while standing in prayer, and he put her down gently when he prostrated. (*Saheeh Al-Bukhaaree:* 494, *Saheeh Muslim:* 543)

If he heard a baby crying while the mother was praying behind him, he would shorten the prayer so that the mother could attend to the baby's needs. Abu Qataadah narrated that the Prophet ﷺ said, "When I begin the prayer, I always intend to make it long; however, if I hear a baby crying, I shorten it, as I do not wish to cause his mother any distress." (*Saheeh Al-Bukhaaree:* 675; *Saheeh Muslim:* 470)

Mercy towards Women

The Prophet ﷺ urged his companions to look after girls and show kindness to them; he used to say, "Whoever is in charge of any of these girls and treats them well, they will be a shield for him against the Fire." (*Saheeh Al-Bukhaaree:* 5649; *Saheeh Muslim:* 2629)

He even stressed that women must be given their rights and be well cared for and commanded Muslims to make this issue their concern and to advise one another to do so: "Take good care of women." (*Saheeh Al-Bukhaaree:* 4890)

He was a shining example of kindness to family members. He once sat beside his camel and put his knee for Safiyyah, one of his wives, to put her foot on, in order to get onto it. (*Saheeh Al-Bukhaaree:* 2120)

Whenever his daughter Faatimah came to visit him, he would get up to welcome her, take her by the hand, kiss her and make her sit where he was sitting. (*Sunan Abu Daawood:* 5217)

Mercy to the weak members of society

The Prophet ﷺ commanded people to sponsor orphans and look after them. "A person who takes care of an orphan and I will be like this in Paradise," he once said, joining his forefinger and middle finger together by way of illustration. (*Saheeh Al-Bukhaaree:* 4998)

He considered a person who looks after a widow or a poor person just like a war-

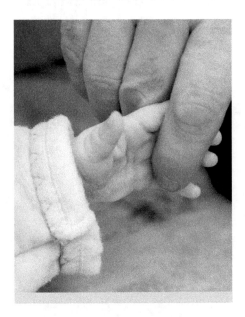

rior who fights for Allah's cause, or like one who performs prayers all night without slackness and fasts continuously and never breaks his fast. (*Saheeh Al-Bukhaaree:* 5661; *Saheeh Muslim:* 2982)

- He regarded showing kindness to the weak members of society and giving them their rights a strong reason to gain Allah's victory over the enemy as well as gaining more means of sustenance: "Seek help among your weak ones, for you are given provision and help only because of the weak amongst you."(*Sunan Abu Daawood:* 2594)

Mercy towards animals

- The Prophet's comprehensive sense of mercy extends even to animals and insects. He urged people to show kindness to animals and warned them against harming them or laying loads on them which are more than they can bear. He said, "Allah has prescribed proficiency in all things. Thus, if you kill, kill well; and if you slaughter, slaughter well. Let each one of you sharpen his blade and

Allah's messenger ﷺ likened a person who looks after a widow or a poor person to a warrior who fights for Allah's cause, which is a highly meritorious deed in the sight of Allah.

let him spare suffering to the animal he slaughters." (*Saheeh Muslim:* 1955)

- Once he noticed a mound of ants which had been burned up. "Who has set fire to this?" he asked. One of his companions replied, "We have." "No one should punish with fire except the Lord of the fire," he disapprovingly said. (*Sunan Abu Daawood:* 2675)

Justice

- The Prophet ﷺ upheld justice under all circumstances and judged by Allah's rule even if that was against one of his closest family members, in compliance with Allah's command, "O you who believe, be upholders of justice, bearing witness for Allah alone, even against yourselves or your parents and relatives." (*Soorat An-Nisaa',* 4:135)

- When some of his companions came to intercede with him on behalf of a noblewoman who had committed a theft so that she would be spared the punishment, he said, "By Him in whose hand is Muhammad's soul, even if Faatimah, the daughter of Muhammad, committed a

Once, seeing a mother bird flapping its wings in desperation after some of his companions had taken some of its chicks away, the Prophet ﷺ disapprovingly said to them, "Who has distressed this bird by taking her young? Give her chicks back to her at once."

theft, I would cut off her hand." (*Saheeh Al-Bukhaaree:* 4053; *Saheeh Muslim:* 1688)

When he declared all forms of usury (*ribaa*) forbidden, he stated that the first usury he declared entirely remitted was that of Al-'Abbaas ibn 'Abd Al-Muttalib, his own uncle: "The person whose usury I claim authority over is Al-'Abbaas ibn 'Abd Al-Muttalib; it will be abolished, all of it." (*Saheeh Muslim:* 1218)

A civilized and cultivated society in his estimation is one in which the weak can claim their rights without fear or hesitation: "Woe to the nation whose individuals do not give the weak his due in full." (*Sunan Ibn Maajah:* 2426)

Benevolence and Generosity

The Prophet ﷺ was the most generous of all people, and he was most generous of all in the month of *Ramadaan* when Jibreel met him; Jibreel used to meet him every night in *Ramadaan* until the end of the month and teach him the Qur'an. When Jibreel met him, he would be more generous in doing good than a blowing wind [which comes with rain and prosperity]. (*Saheeh Al-Bukhaaree:* 1803; *Saheeh Muslim:* 2308)

He never denied the request of anyone who asked him anything. Once a man came to him and asked him for something. The Prophet ﷺ gave him a flock of sheep filling the area between two mountains. The man was so happy that he returned to his people and called them to Islam, saying, "Embrace Islam, for Muhammad is so generous that he gives in charity without fearing poverty." (*Saheeh Muslim:* 5423)

Once he received eighty thousand dirhams, so he placed the amount on a mat and gave it in charity, not turning away anyone who asked him for something until the full amount was distributed. (*Mustadrak Al-Haakim:* 5423)

On another occasion, a man approached him and made a request for something, and the Prophet ﷺ said to him, "I do not have anything right now, but you can buy something in my name, and I will certainly pay for it when I get the money." 'Umar ؓ turned to him and said, "Allah has not made it compulsory for you to do something beyond your capacity." This comment offended the Prophet ﷺ a great deal. The man then said to him, "Spend in charity without fearing poverty, for the Lord of the Mighty Throne will not decrease your wealth." The Prophet ﷺ smiled and his face was radiant with happiness. (*Al-Ahaadeeth Al-Mukhtaarah:* 88)

When the Prophet ﷺ returned from the Battle of Hunayn, some new converts from the Bedouin tribes who were eager to get their share of the spoils of war followed him. They drove him to a tree where one of the uncouth Bedouins snatched his mantle off his shoulders, thinking it was part of the spoils of war. "Give me back my mantle," he said, "for if I had as many camels as the trees [around here], I would divide them all among you. You know very well that I am neither miserly, nor deceitful, nor cowardly." (*Saheeh Al-Bukhaaree:* 2979)

May Allah's peace and blessings be upon Prophet Muhammad ﷺ, for he is indeed the epitome of excellent moral character in all aspects of life.

Your New Life

12

The very moment a person embraces Islam is doubtless the greatest moment in his life, for it signifies his real birth through which he has come to understand the real reason behind his existence in this life and the manner of conducting his life according to the dictates of this great religion of Islam.

Contents

How to Convert to Islam

Sincere Repentance

Showing Gratefulness to Allah for His Guidance

Inviting Others to Islam

- Virtues of Calling Others to Islam
- Requirements of the Correct Manner of Inviting Others to Islam
- Inviting Family Members and Relatives to Islam

Your Environment and Family

Children's Religion

Changing One's Name after Embracing Islam

Sunan Al-Fitrah (Practices dictated by Man's Pure Nature)

>How to Convert to Islam

To enter the fold of Islam, all one needs to do is to pronounce the testimony of faith (*shahaadah*) with sincere conviction, being fully aware of its meaning. The *shahaadah* is the first and most important of the five pillars of Islam and consists of two parts, namely:

1. ***Ashhadu an laailaaha illallaah:*** This means: I bear witness that there is no god worthy of worship except Allah; I worship Him alone without associating any partners with Him in worship.

2. ***Wa ash hadu anna Muhammadan rasool-ullaah:*** **This means:** And I bear witness that Muhammad is the Messenger of Allah whom Allah has sent to all mankind; I will obey his commands and avoid anything he has forbidden and worship Allah according to His law and the teachings of His Messenger ﷺ. (See page 42-50)

Taking a Bath

The very moment a person embraces Islam is doubtless the greatest moment in his life, for it signifies his real birth through which he has come to understand the real reason behind his existence in this life. Now that he has entered the fold of Islam, he is recommended to take a bath (*ghusl*), washing his entire body with water. Just as he has cleansed his soul of such things as associating partners with Allah in worship (*shirk*) and committing sins, he is recommended to cleanse his body by taking a bath.

When one of the Arab notables embraced Islam, the Prophet ﷺ directed him to take a bath. (*Al-Bayhaqee's As-Sunan As-Sughraa:* 837)

> Sincere Repentance

Repentance (*tawbah*) means "sincerely turning to Allah", and a repentant person is one who gives up sins and unbelief and turns to Allah in repentance.

A Muslim needs to repent and seek Allah's forgiveness at practically all stages of his life; because it is only human to err, a Muslim is required to repent and beg Allah's pardon every time he commits a sin.

What Are the Conditions of Sincere Repentance?

For repentance of all sins, including the sin of unbelief and *shirk*, to be valid and acceptable to Allah, a number of conditions must be met, including the following:

1 To give up the sin immediately

Sincere repentance from sin with the deliberate desire to continue to commit it is not valid and will not possibly take place; if, however, a person commits the sin again after sincerely repenting from it, his earlier repentance will still be valid but he will need fresh repentance, and so on.

2 To feel deep sorrow and regret for having committed it

True repentance cannot possibly take place without feeling deep remorse for having committed the sin. A person who talks about his past sins and brags about committing them is in no way considered penitent. As the Prophet ﷺ once stated, "Remorse is repentance." (*Sunan Ibn Maajah:* 4252)

3 To sincerely resolve not to commit it again

Sincere repentance cannot possibly take place if a penitent person intends to repeat the sin.

Steps towards Acquiring Determination

* Pledging oneself not to repeat the sin under any circumstances and obstacles, not even for an instant, for the Prophet ﷺ said, "Whoever possesses the following three qualities will relish the sweetness of faith." Of these three characteristics, he mentioned "to hate to return to unbelief (*kufr*) after Allah has saved him from it, as much as he would hate to be thrown into the Fire." (*Saheeh Al-Bukhaaree:* 21; *Saheeh Muslim:* 43)

* Keeping away from people and places that are bound to decrease his faith and tempt him to commit sins.

- Repeatedly begging Allah ﷻ to keep him on the right path and adhere firmly to Islam until death, in any language or form. Examples from the Qur'an and the Prophet's *Sunnah* include the following:

    - *"Rabbanaa laa tuzigh quloobanaa ba'da idh hadaytanaa"* (Our Lord, do not make our hearts deviate after You have guided us) (*Soorat Aal-'Imraan*, 3:8)

    - *"Yaa muqallibal-quloob, Thabbit qalbee 'alaa deenik"* (O Allah, Controller of hearts, make my heart adhere firmly to Your religion) (*Sunan At-Tirmidhee:* 2140)

What Happens after Repentance?

If a person turns to Allah in repentance, Allah ﷻ will definitely forgive his sins, no matter how serious they may be, for His mercy "extends to all things" (*Soorat Al-A'raaf,* 7:156). The Qur'an says, "Say: 'My slaves, you who have transgressed against yourselves, do not despair of the mercy of Allah. Truly Allah forgives all wrong actions. He is the Ever-Forgiving, the Most Merciful.'" (*Soorat Az-Zumar,* 39:53)

After a person sincerely repents to Allah, Allah ﷻ will definitely pardon him and forgive his sins; in addition, He will reward him; immensely: He will change his bad deeds into good ones, as the Qur'an states, "Except for those who repent, believe and act rightly: Allah will transform the wrong actions of such people into good — Allah is Ever-Forgiving, Most Merciful." (*Soorat Al-Furqaan*,25:70)

As this a reward is immense indeed, a sensible person ought to maintain such repentance and spare no effort to avoid falling into Satan's trap which will negatively affect his faith.

Sweetness of Faith

Those who will most certainly taste the sweetness of faith, experience deep tranquillity and take great delight in experiencing closeness to Allah are those who love Allah ﷻ and His Messenger ﷺ more than anyone or anything else, love others, commensurate with their closeness to Allah and dedication to Islam, and hate to convert to unbelief just as they hate to be punished in Hellfire. The Prophet ﷺ said, "Any person who combines these three qualities will certainly experience the sweetness of faith: (1) that Allah and His Messenger are dearer to him than anything else; (2) that his love of others is purely for Allah's sake; and (3) that he hates to relapse into unbelief as much as he hates to be cast into the Fire." (*Saheeh Al-Bukhaaree:* 21; *Saheeh Muslim:* 43)

> A Muslim relishes the sweetness of faith when he hates to relapse into unbelief just as much as he hates to be thrown into the Fire.

Showing Gratefulness to Allah for His Guidance

A Muslim owes Allah the Almighty a great debt of gratitude for helping him repent of the sins he has committed and for guiding him to the truth. The following are the best things a Muslim can possibly do to express gratitude to Allah for such blessings:

1. Holding Fast to Islam and Patiently Enduring Hardships that Come One's Way

It goes without saying that if a person has a priceless treasure, he will undoubtedly do his best to protect it. Islam is undeniably the best gift to mankind, for it is not a mere set of abstract ideology, nor is it a hobby which a person may practise whenever he feels like it; rather, it is a religion and a way of life which governs a Muslim's life in all its aspects without exception. Commanding His Messenger ﷺ to stubbornly hold fast to Islam and the teachings of the Qur'an, being on the right path, Allah ﷻ says in the Qur'an, "So hold fast to what has been revealed to you. You are on a straight path." (*Soorat Az-Zukhruf,* 43:43)

A Muslim must not feel sad if he experiences any form of hardship, for it is part of Allah's wise plan to test His servants. Allah ﷻ even tested His prophets and messengers, who are far better than us, and the Qur'an tells us how they encountered untold suffering at the hands of relatives and enemies alike, without losing heart, weakening in their faith or wavering under adversity. The great hardship a Muslim faces due to his dedication to the truth is one of the ways Allah ﷻ tests His servants' faith. Therefore, live up to your lofty principles, try your best to pass the test, adhere to the truth under all circumstances and constantly pray to Allah to keep you on the right path, just as the Prophet ﷺ himself did. Repeat the supplication: *"Yaa muqallibal-quloob, Thabbit qalbee 'alaa deenik"* (O Allah, Controller of hearts, make my heart adhere firmly to Your religion). (*Sunan At-Tirmidhee:* 2140)

Allah ﷻ says in this context, "Do people think that once they say, 'We believe,' they will be left alone and not be put to the test? We certainly tried those who have gone before them, so Allah will certainly distinguish between those who are truthful and those who are lying." (*Soorat Al-'Ankaboot,* 29:2-3)

2. Doing One's Best to Call to Islam with Wisdom and Fair Admonition

Engaging in *da'wah* work (calling others to Islam) is undoubtedly one of the best ways of expressing gratitude to Allah as well as one of the most effective means to remain constant in faith. If a person recovers from a life-threatening disease which has caused him a great deal of suffering and misery after discovering the right cure for his disease, he will certainly spread such a remedy amongst people, particularly amongst his relatives and closest friends. This point is elucidated as follows:

Calling Others to Islam (da'wah)

Virtues of Calling Others to Islam

Engaging in *da'wah* work is indisputably one of the best deeds in the sight of Allah and is highly commended in the Qur'an and the Prophet's *Sunnah*. Evidence to this effect includes the following:

1. *Da'wah is the means to success in this life and in the hereafter,* as the Qur'an states, "Let there be a group among you who call others to good, and enjoin what is right, and forbid what is wrong: those who do this shall be successful." (*Soorat Aal 'Imraan,*3:104)

2. *No one has a better speech than that of those who engage in da'wah activities.* Commending such people, the Qur'an says, "Who speaks better than one who calls to Allah, does good works and says, 'I am surely one of the Muslims.'?" (*Soorat Fussilat,* 41:33) It is clear, therefore, that there is no one whose speech is better than that of a person who calls people to the truth, for he is their guide to their Creator and Lord and the one who takes them out of the darkness of misguidance into the light of faith.

3. *Engaging in da'wah work testifies to one's compliance with Allah's command:* "Call to the way of your Lord with wisdom and fair admonition, and argue with them in the best manner possible." (*Soorat An-Nahl,* 16:125) A person who dedicates himself to such a noble task must invite others to Islam with wisdom, making sure that he knows the personality of the people he wants to call to Islam so as to choose the best possible method to carry out the task, all the while arguing with them in the kindest, most gracious manner which appeals to them.

4. *Engaging in da'wah work was the very task carried out by all of Allah's messengers without exception,* foremost of whom was Prophet Muhammad ﷺ, whom Allah sent to all mankind as a witness over people, giving news to the believers of immense reward in the hereafter, warning the unbelievers against severe punishment and spreading his light to all mankind. The Qur'an says, "Prophet, We have sent you as a witness, as a bearer of good news and a warner, and a caller to Allah by His permission and a light-giving lamp. Convey to the believers the good news that they will receive immense favour from Allah." (*Soorat Al-Ahzaab,*33:45-47)

5. *Inviting people to Islam is the source of unlimited goodness* for each person you invite to Islam, you will get the same rewards for his prayer, worship and teaching others. What a great blessing Allah bestows on those who engage in *da'wah* work! The Prophet ﷺ said, "Whoever calls to guidance will have a reward similar to that of those who follow it, without the reward of either of them being lessened at all." (*Saheeh Muslim:* 2674)

6. *The reward Allah has in store for those who invite others to Islam is far better than all the enjoyments of the present world,* for such a reward is from Allah Himself, the Most Generous, who will recompense them abundantly

for such a noble endeavour: "If you turn away from me, remember I ask no reward from you. Only Allah will reward me, and I have been commanded to submit completely to Him." (*Soorat Yoonus,* 10:72)

The Prophet ﷺ also said in this respect, "If Allah guides one man through you, this will be better for you than possessing red camels." (*Saheeh Al-Bukhaaree:* 2847; *Saheeh Muslim:* 2406) Camels were considered the most valuable property in ancient Arabia and the red variety was the most prized of all.

as the Prophet ﷺ once ordered, "Convey what you learn from me [to others], even if [what you have learnt] is one verse of the Qur'an." (*Saheeh Al-Bukhaaree:* 3274)

This was the very practice of the Prophet's companions; they would learn the principles of Islam in a few days and then they would go back to their people to call them to Islam and arouse their interest in it, especially through their high moral character.

Requirements of the Correct Manner of Inviting Others to Islam

Allah ﷻ describes the correct manner of engaging in *da'wah* work as one which is characterised by certain qualities which distinguish it from others. These qualities are as follows:

Insight and Knowledge

A caller to Islam (*daa'iyah*) must be knowledgeable about the truth to which he invites others, clearly presenting divine instructions to them, based on clear evidence: "Say: This is my Way: I invite to Allah, on the basis of a clear proof, and so do those who follow me ." (*Soorat Yusuf,* 12:108)

He does not have to know many things before he starts calling people to Islam. Whenever he learns something new, he has to teach it to others. For instance, If he learns about the necessity of not associating anyone in the worship of Allah, he ought to convey this information to others. Likewise, if he learns about some aspects of the beauty of Islam, he must convey this to them. To put it in a nutshell, he must convey anything he learns about Islam, even if what he has learned is one single verse of the Qur'an,

2 Wisdom

The Qur'an says, "Call to the way of your Lord with wisdom and fair admonition, and argue with them in the best manner possible." (*Soorat An-Nahl*, 16:125) Wisdom is the ability to make sensible decisions and give good advice at the appropriate time and place because of the experience and knowledge one has.

Given the differences between people regarding their character and level of understanding, a caller to Islam must choose the appropriate method to engage in *da'wah* work and wait for the appropriate opportunity to win them over.

He must approach them with gentleness and compassion, and engage in a calm and balanced dialogue which does not instigate ill feelings and inflame hatred. It is for this reason that Allah reminds His Messenger of the favours He bestowed upon him by making him gentle with people: "It is by Allah's grace that you deal gently with them; had you been harsh and hard-hearted, they would surely have deserted you." (*Soorat Aal-'Imraan*, 3:159)

Inviting Family Members and Relatives to Islam

A person who has been guided to Islam must do his best to call his family members and relatives to this religion, because they are the closest and dearest people to him. He ought to endure any harm he may encounter patiently whilst doing so. He should also use all possible means in order to show them the truth. As the Qur'an states, "Instruct your family to offer their prayers, and be steadfast in observing them yourself." (*Soorat Taa Haa*, 20:132)

Some callers to Islam may find that people to whom they are not related favourably respond to the invitation, whilst their closest relatives refuse to do so, which causes them a great deal of distress and disappointment. A successful caller to Islam, however, never gives up hope; he tries his best to guide them to the truth, using various methods and techniques and praying to Allah to guide their hearts, even under the bleakest of circumstances.

The Prophet did just that with his Uncle Abu Taalib. He left no stone unturned in calling him to Islam and continued doing so until the last moments of his life. When Abu Taalib was on his deathbed, the Prophet begged him, "Dear uncle, say, *laa ilaaha illallaah*, (There is no god worthy of worship except Allah) so that I may be able to intercede for you on the Day of Judgement."(*Saheeh Al-Bukhaaree:* 3671; *Saheeh Muslim:* 24) Abu Taalib, however, declined to do so, and so he died a polytheist. It was on this occasion that Allah revealed the following verse: "You cannot guide whoever you please: it is Allah who guides whom He will. He knows best those who receive guidance." (*Soorat Al-Qasas,* 28:56)

A new Muslim, as soon as he embraces Islam, must build a strong and healthy relationship with his relatives and acquaintances, Muslims and non-Muslims alike. He must also observe high moral standards when dealing with them, for Islam is not a call to isolation and withdrawal from social life.

Indeed, showing kindness to people and observing high moral standards when dealing with them is the best way to introduce them to this great religion with which Prophet Muhammad ﷺ was sent to perfect noble character.

Observance of high moral standards and good treatment must start at home, amongst family members. (See page 225)

Children's Religion

According to Islamic teachings, all human beings without exception are born Muslim, with an innate inclination to believe in Allah (*fitrah*), and that they may follow another religion following the manner in which their parents teach them and bring them up. As the Prophet ﷺ said, "Every child is born with the natural inclination to surrender to Allah (*fitrah*), (that is, to be a Muslim), but then his parents make him a Jew, a Christian or a Zoroastrian." (*Saheeh Al-Bukhaaree:* 1292; *Saheeh Muslim:* 2658)

Regarding non-Muslim parents' children, we consider them non-Muslim in this life; if they die young, Allah ﷻ, the best of judges who does not wrong anyone and who knows their secrets and yet what is more hidden, will test them on the Day of Judgement; those who obey Him will be admitted into Paradise, while those who disobey Him will be consigned to hellfire.

When Allah's Messenger ﷺ was asked about the fate of the children of the polytheists on the Day of Judgement, he replied, "Since Allah created them, He knows what sort of deeds they would have done." (*Saheeh Al-Bukhaaree:* 1317)

However, when can we consider non-Muslim parents' children Muslim in this life?

To prove this, there are different cases, including the following:

1. **If the parents,** or one of them, embrace Islam, children born to them will be considered followers of the religion of the parent that is better than the other, namely, Islam.

2. **If a child, who is able to distinguish between right and wrong but has not necessarily reached the age of puberty, embraces Islam even though his parents are not Muslim,** he will equally be considered Muslim. A Jewish boy used to serve the Prophet ﷺ. One day, the boy became ill, and the Prophet ﷺ went to visit him. He sat by his head and said, "Become a Muslim." The boy looked at his father who was also sitting by his head. His father said to him, "Obey Abul-Qaasim ﷺ ." The boy then embraced Islam. The Prophet ﷺ left saying, "Praise be to Allah who has saved him from the Fire!" (*Saheeh Al-Bukhaaree:* 1290)

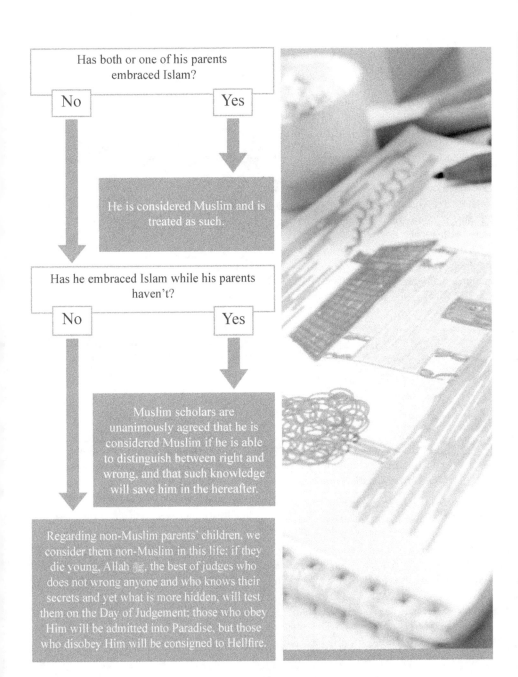

```
┌─────────────────────────────────┐
│  Has both or one of his parents │
│       embraced Islam?           │
└─────────────────────────────────┘
     │                    │
    No                   Yes
     │                    │
     ▼                    ▼
                ┌──────────────────────────────┐
                │ He is considered Muslim and is│
                │       treated as such.        │
                └──────────────────────────────┘
     │
     ▼
┌─────────────────────────────────┐
│ Has he embraced Islam while his │
│       parents haven't?          │
└─────────────────────────────────┘
     │                    │
    No                   Yes
     │                    │
     │                    ▼
     │         ┌──────────────────────────────┐
     │         │    Muslim scholars are        │
     │         │ unanimously agreed that he is │
     │         │ considered Muslim if he is able│
     │         │ to distinguish between right and│
     │         │ wrong, and that such knowledge │
     │         │  will save him in the hereafter.│
     │         └──────────────────────────────┘
     ▼
┌──────────────────────────────────────────┐
│ Regarding non-Muslim parents' children, we│
│ consider them non-Muslim in this life; if they│
│ die young, Allah ﷻ, the best of judges who│
│ does not wrong anyone and who knows their │
│ secrets and yet what is more hidden, will test│
│ them on the Day of Judgement; those who obey│
│ Him will be admitted into Paradise, but those│
│ who disobey Him will be consigned to Hellfire.│
└──────────────────────────────────────────┘
```

> Is it recommended to change one's name after embracing Islam?

The general rule is that a new Muslim can retain his name and does not have to change it at all. In fact, the changing of names was not known among the Prophet's companions, may Allah be pleased with them. Many people have embraced Islam and retained their non-Arabic names, unless the name has a bad meaning.

A name may be changed in the following cases:

1 **If it indicates servitude to other than Allah or has a meaning which contradicts Islamic beliefs:**

Names which indicate servitude to other than Allah include 'Abdul-Maseeh (slave of the Messiah), which is common amongst Arab Christians, and 'Abd-un-Nabiyy (slave of the Prophet), which is common amongst some Muslims. This also includes names which have a meaning that contradicts Islamic beliefs, suc has Shenouda (commonly used among Egyptian Christians 'the Copts' which means 'the son of God'). Glorified is He, and High Exalted above what they say!

Names which indicate one of Allah's attributes are not allowed either.

An example of this is to ascribe to someone an attribute which is completely unique to Allah, such as the title 'king of kings'.

2 **If the name implies something that is offensive or not approved of by people with sound moral values:**

Indeed, Allah ﷻ has declared all bad things without exception unlawful; therefore, it is not appropriate to retain a name which carries a bad meaning after converting to Islam, as the Qur'an states, "Evil is a bad name after faith." (*Soorat Al-Hujuraat*, 49:11)

It is recommended to change the name:

If the new Muslim name to be acquired is dear to Allah, such as 'Abdullaah (slave of Allah) and 'Abdur-Rahmaan (slave of the Most Gracious), or such names which indicate one's servitude to Allah ﷻ. These are recommended names but have nothing to do with one's acceptance of Islam.

- **A new Muslim may** change his name for no reason whatsoever, such as by changing his non-Arabic name to an Arabic name, but this is not considered recommended and has nothing to do with his acceptance of Islam.

```
                Does the meaning of the name
                contradict Islamic beliefs?
                  │                │
                 No               Yes
                  │                │
                  │                ▼
                  │      A name which carries such
                  │      a meaning must be changed.
                  ▼
       Does the name carry religious significance
           amongst followers of other religions?
                  │                │
                 No               Yes
                  │                │
                  │                ▼
                  │      It must be changed to remove
                  │      suspicions and avoid imitating
                  │                non-Muslims.
                  ▼
           Is it offensive or not approved of by people
                  with sound moral values?
                  │                │
                 No               Yes
                  │                │
                  ▼                ▼
                         It is recommended to change
                         it to a name which carries a
                              pleasant meaning.
```

If it does not carry any of the above-mentioned meanings, it does not have to be changed. In fact, many Muslims retained their non-Arabic names after their conversion in the early days of Islam.

He may change his name for no reason whatsoever; it is recommended to do so if the new name is dear to Allah, such as 'Abdur-Rahmaan (slave of the Most Gracious).

> Sunan Al-Fiṭrah (Practices dictated by Man's Pure Nature)

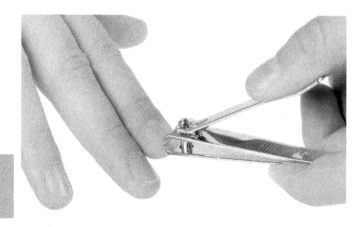

> Islam encourages Muslims to maintain the best outward appearance possible.

What Does the Phrase *Sunan Al-Fiṭrah* Mean?

Sunan Al-Fiṭrah refers to a set of hygienic or cosmetic practices enjoined by Islam that is consistent with the pure nature in which Allah has created mankind and which serves to enhance their appearance and perfect it, making Muslims combine both inward and outward perfection.

The Prophet ﷺ said, "The customs of nature (*sunan al-fiṭrah*) are five: circumcision, removing the pubic hair, trimming the moustache, clipping the nails and plucking the underarm hair." (*Saheeh Al-Bukhaaree:* 5552; *Saheeh Muslim:* 257)

Circumcision is the act of removing the foreskin (the loose tissue) covering the glans of the penis. This generally takes place in the early days after the birth of a baby boy.

It is a recommended act and one of the 'customs of nature' with regard to men. It also has numerous health benefits but is not a precondition for embracing Islam. One, however, would not be sinful if he does not get circumcised out of fear or for any other reason.

Removing the coarse hair that grows in the pubic area, the lower part of the abdomen just above the external genital organs, contributes to better hygiene and can be carried out by using any means that would serve the purpose.

Trimming the moustache: Keeping a moustache is permissible but not recommended; however, if a Muslim chooses to keep it, he must regularly trim it.

Letting the beard grow: Islam urges men to grow a beard, the hair that grows on the chin and cheeks of a man's face.

Letting the beard grow means not to shave it, in accordance with the Prophet's teachings.

Clipping the nails: A Muslim is required to clip his nails regularly in order to remove pathogenic organisms, dirt and debris that generally get underneath fingernails.

Plucking underarm hair: A Muslim is required to remove his underarm hair by plucking it or by using any other means to serve the purpose in order to keep bad odours away.

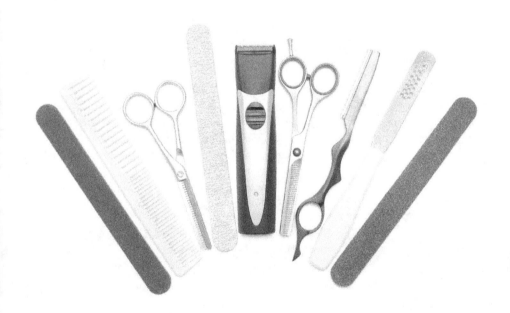

TRANSLITERATION SYSTEM USED IN THE BOOK

CONSONANTS

Arabic	Symbol Used	Approximate pronunciation/Notes
ء	'	This sound, called hamzah in Arabic, is the character which represents the glottal stop, as in Cockney "bo<u>tt</u>le".
ب	b	<u>b</u>aby
ت	t	<u>t</u>ie
ث	th	<u>th</u>in
ج	j	mea<u>s</u>ure, lei<u>s</u>ure
ح	ḥ	The sound of this letter resembles the sound of 'strong, breathy' H. The sound for <u>h</u>is produced from the proximity of the throat that the normal h is, but from an area slightly further up the throat, with more tension in the local throat muscle, with the back end of the tongue closing in against the roof of the throat immediately before the uvula.
خ	kh	The sound for this is perhaps somewhere between of that of 'h' and 'k', as far as the location of mouth where it is produced is concerned. It is generated at the back of the mouth, by pressing the back end of the tongue against the soft palate whilst forcing the air through in the outward direction, causing the uvula to vibrate. Example of the sound of kh found in English or that the English reader may be familiar with is Loch, the Scottish word for lake, where the ch in loch is pronounced as the designated kh in Arabic. Another example is the German bu<u>ch</u>, for book.
د	d	<u>d</u>id
ذ	dh	<u>then</u>
ر	r	e<u>rr</u>or (trilled)
ز	z	<u>z</u>one
س	s	<u>s</u>and
ش	sh	<u>sh</u>y

Arabic	Symbol Used	Approximate pronunciation/Notes
ص	s̲	The sound of this letter resembles the sound of 'strong' s. It is produced by involving the main trunk of the tongue, by slightly curving the centre of the front half of the tongue in the downward direction. In aid of pronouncing the sound of the 'strong' s, it would be helpful if you consider saying the normal letter 's', when the front upper and lower teeth are brought closer together reducing the airflow, thus producing the sound of the letter 's'. The opposite process is used to generate the sound of the 'strong' s, i.e. the sound is produced when slightly moving apart the upper and lower teeth, thus pronouncing the 'strong' s. An approximate pronunciation of this sound can be found in s̲on and s̲orry.
ض	d̲	The sound of this letter is somewhere near the sound of the normal d. Whereas the sound of a normal d is generated by placing the front end of the tongue at the front end of the hard palate or the roof of the mouth adjoining the top teeth, the sound of d̲ is produced by touching, to the same location, more of the front trunk of the tongue while caving in the middle part of the tongue.
ط	t̲	The sound of this letter resembles a 'strong' t. Whereas a normal t is generated by involving the front end of the tongue, the 'strong' T is generated by pressing the front end of the trunk of the tongue against the front end of the hard palate or the roof of the mouth. Also when the normal T is pronounced, the lower jaw does not move, whereas in the case of pronouncing the strong t, or t̲, the lower jaw moves outwards.
ظ	d̲h̲	The best description of this sound is that it could be the strong version of the sound of 'dh' as in the word 'there'. Whereas 'dh' is generated by placing the tip of the tongue between the upper and lower front teeth, whilst pressing against the upper front teeth, the sound for dh is generated by pressing more of the front end of the tongue between the upper and lower front teeth, whilst pressing against the upper front teeth, and the centre of the tongue is curved downwards.

Arabic	Symbol Used	Approximate pronunciation/Notes
ع	ʻ	A contraction of the throat (a pharyngealized vowel that is considered a consonant in Arabic). This symbol is used to characterize an Arabic alphabet that represents the sound of a strong 'throaty' a. Just as the sound for A is generated at the back of the throat, ʻ in the same proximity, the sound for or ʻ is also generated with the difference that the entire throat back is engaged in the process by a stroke of contraction in the muscle there. In this process more of the throat is blocked, which also involves the back end of the tongue, than when pronouncing the normal a. Just in the case of the normal a, the sound is actually generated at the time of the release of the contraction of the muscles involved.
غ	gh	The nearest sound for this is that of the French r, as in r<u>i</u>en and me<u>r</u>ci.
ف	f	<u>f</u>our
ق	q	The sound for this letter is a short and sharp version of the letter 'gh' or the French r. Whereas in the process of generating the sound 'gh' the back end of the tongue is pressed slightly against the uvula, allowing some air to flow, in the case of the sound of the Arabic alphabet represented by q, the same process takes place with the difference that the passage is completely blocked, and the sound is actually generated by the sudden release of the passage. A uvular sound produced farther back in the throat than any English k.
ك	k	<u>k</u>in
ل	l	li<u>ly</u> (pronounced dentally)
م	m	mi<u>m</u>e
ن	n	<u>n</u>o (pronounced dentally)
ه	h	<u>h</u>ave, <u>h</u>at
و	w	<u>w</u>atch (as a consonant)
ي	y	<u>y</u>et

VOWELS

Short Vowels	Approximate Pronunciation
a	b<u>u</u>t
i	p<u>i</u>f
u	p<u>u</u>t

Long Vowels	Approximate Pronunciation
aa	f<u>a</u>ther, f<u>a</u>r
ee	<u>e</u>ve, n<u>ee</u>d
oo	p<u>oo</u>l, n<u>oo</u>n

Diphthongs
aw, as in p<u>ow</u>der and sh<u>ou</u>t
ay, as in m<u>igh</u>t and k<u>i</u>te

Shaddah
The sign is transliterated by doubling the consonant. It is represented in Roman letters by doubled consonants. In actual pronunciation, the letters are merged and held briefly like the "n" sound produced in the n/kn combination in the word unknown, or the 'n' in unnerve, the 'r' in overruled and the 'd' in midday.

Symbols Used in the Book and their Meanings

Symbol Used	Meaning and Definition
ﷻ	This expression, which means, 'May He be glorified and exalted', is commonly said whenever Allah's name is mentioned.
ﷺ	This expression, which means, 'May Allah's peace and blessings be upon him', is commonly said whenever Prophet Mu<u>h</u>ammad's name is mentioned.
عليه السلام	This formula, which means 'Peace be upon him', is usually said after the name of a prophet or an angel, such as Moosaa (Moses) u or Jibreel (Gabriel)u, respectively.
رضي الله عنه	This expression, which means, 'May Allah be pleased with him', is generally used for a male companion of the Prophet e, such as Abu Hurayrah.
رضي الله عنها	This expression, which means, 'May Allah be pleased with her', is generally used for a female companion of the Prophet e, such as 'Aa'ishah.

Conclusion

What's Your Next Step?

Once you have read this book, you will have taken the first step to learn about basic matters relating to your religion. Now you need to translate what you have learnt into action and make it a reality, for knowledge without practice will be a source of great regret on the Day of Judgement.

You must also do your best to learn about other matters which you need in your daily life, but which are not covered in this this book.

A Muslim, no matter how strong his faith may be, always needs more guidance, hence the prayer, "Guide us on to the Straight Path" (*Soorat Al-Faatihah*, 1:6), which is in the greatest *soorah* in the Qur'an that a Muslim repeats daily in his prayers.

Be mindful of Allah as best as you can

Neither the present book, nor any other book, will provide you with detailed information about situations and incidents you may come across. Therefore, in addition to seeking the opinion of religious scholars, you must try your best to be mindful of Allah as much as you can regarding the daily occurrences and relationships concerning which it is not possible to refer to scholars, as evidenced by the verse, "Be mindful of Allah as best as you can." (*Soorat At-Taghaabun*, 64:16)

Try your best to stay close to Muslim community members

Try to be as close to Muslim brothers and sisters as possible, visit Islamic centres and share Muslims' joys and sorrows. Despite the Prophet's unshakable faith, Allah ﷻ commanded him to seek the company of righteous people: "Content yourself with the company of those who supplicate their Lord morning and evening, desiring His Face." (*Soorat Al-Kahf,* 18:28)

The Prophet ﷺ also warned against leaving the company of Muslims, as doing so is one of the ways that are bound to lead one astray, just as a sheep that is far from the flock becomes more vulnerable to wolf attacks.

The Prophet ﷺ said, "Stay close to one another, for the sheep that the wolf eats is the one that wanders away from the flock." (*Mustadrak Al-Haakim:* 567)

Therefore, seeking the company of Muslims is one of the ways to remain on the right path.

Doing so becomes even more necessary for new Muslims who are obviously in dire need of assistance and support.

May Allah guide you, keep you on the right path and shower His blessings upon you, both outwardly and inwardly.

Printed in the USA
CPSIA information can be obtained
at www.ICGtesting.com
LVHW020822300324
775937LV00036B/952